BUSINESS AND MANAGEMENT RESEARCH

BUSINESS AND MANAGEMENT RESEARCH

paradigms & practices

Erica Hallebone and Jan Priest

First published 2009 by
PALGRAVE MACMILLAN

Palgrave Macmillan in the UK is an imprint of Macmillan Publishers Limited,registered in England, company number 785998, of Houndmills, Basingstoke,Hampshire RG21 6XS.

Palgrave Macmillan in the US is a division of St Martin's Press LLC, 175 Fifth Avenue, New York, NY 10010.

Palgrave Macmillan is the global academic imprint of the above companies and has companies and representatives throughout the world.

Palgrave® and Macmillan® are registered trademarks in the United States,the United Kingdom, Europe and other countries

ISBN-13: 978-1-4039-9716-6
ISBN-10: 1-4039-9716-0

This book is printed on paper suitable for recycling and made from fully managed and sustained forest sources. Logging, pulping and manufacturing processes are expected to conform to the environmental regulations of the country of origin.

A catalogue record for this book is available from the British Library.

A catalog record for this book is available from the Library of Congress.

10	9	8	7	6	5	4	3	2	1
18	17	16	15	14	13	12	11	10	09

Printed and bound in China.

BRIEF CONTENTS

CONTENTS

FIGURES

TABLES

ABOUT THE AUTHORS

Dr Erica Hallebone BA(Hons), PhD, is a professorial fellow in RMIT University's Graduate School of Business. She has over 25 years experience in teaching and research supervision, covering research design and field practice, and professional development design and evaluation in areas of social policy research.

Over the past 10 years Erica has led the school's programmes in methods of management, organisation and social research methods. Erica has supervised 30 completed masters and doctoral students. She has conducted research on a number of topics which are linked by the construction of personal identity in social contexts, and more recently corporate social responsibility, sustainability and community capacity building.

Dr Jan Priest BSc, MBA, MEng, DBA, FAIM, MICD, is managing partner of InfoServ and leads InfoServ's research and consulting activities. He is also an adjunct professor in RMIT University's Graduate School of Business. He has 35 years management and consulting experience with private enterprise and government agencies specialising in better practice management of strategic and operational performance - a focus that emerged from his earlier work in technology and innovation management.

Over the past 20 years Jan has also led applied research programs into effective enterprise strategy and organisation performance with a special interest in knowledge-intensive and technology-intensive firms. This work underpins InfoServ's BOTMline® and WIKIDway® practice-diagnostic and practice-development products and services, which have been developed over two decades using the research approaches outlined in this book. (For more information, visit www.infoserv.com.au)

PREFACE

THE ORIGIN OF THIS BOOK

The book is a reaction to the fraught nature and continuing lack of coherence for doing business and management research, as demonstrated across texts that are currently available to both novice and experienced researchers.

Challenges that arise from the great majority of current business and management research texts include:

- The widespread use of different words for the same ideas, and conversely, the prevalent use of the same words for many different yet important ideas.
- Lengthy and often difficult to read and difficult to assimilate written accounts of philosophical concepts and technical principles, as well as their theoretical and practical constraints, history, interrelationships and use in research design and research practice.
- The uncritical borrowing and combining of ideas, imagery, issues and approaches from a wide range of fields such as the natural and social sciences.
- The sophistication of important but abstract concepts as well as the complexities and subtleties of practices that are distinctive to particular scientific approaches.
- The challenge of correctly or directly operationalising a wide range of scientific concepts and methods when designing and doing business and management research.
- The large and ever growing number of cookbook and methods-type research texts – very few of which even acknowledge the importance of having to deliberately select and define a form of science that offers a guiding framework for a particular business or management research problem.
- For the wide range of philosophical texts that discuss forms of science, the great majority do not make it make clear to the new researcher how to begin to evaluate and ultimately select from forms of science that initially seem appropriate to the context and the nature of a research problem.

Of the texts that directly relate to business and management research, most do not provide life cycle illustrations of the research process. By life cycle we mean the cycle from the statement of the research question and its context, through the choice of design and conduct of a particular scientific approach, to completion by reporting and using the research study's findings. Rather, most methods texts provide fragmentary illustrations of specific tasks and techniques but do not help readers to apprehend the overarching process of design and execution within a particular form of science.

ABOUT STYLE

The ideas of good business and management research are diverse and often complex. First-time readers often find it extremely challenging to initially apprehend and then assimilate a coherent and usable mental model of the big picture, comprising the various sciences, associated methodologies and their particular approaches. At the same time they must also develop a working facility with the many technical details needed to frame, design, conduct and report a rigorous and productive research study.

To help readers overcome this major challenge we have devised an overall structure together with schematics, examples, extension activities and a narrative style that make previously complex, disparate and largely inaccessible concepts more readily assimilated and usable. We expect that the book will provide most researchers, especially inexperienced ones, with a useful entry point: a set of roadmaps (that is, mental models) and conceptual definitions that help novice and other researchers to deal more effectively with the challenges of business and management research.

Three format conventions are used throughout this book for pedagogical purposes and to aid readability.

- The outer margin on each page provides space for Post-It notes to be attached without obscuring the text – or for pencil notes as reminders about passages of special note.
- In some outer margins there are two types of numbered icon as shown below. These icons point to readings, discussion exercises or conceptual emphases – each of which is explained at the end of the relevant chapter. These exercises, discussion tasks and reflections are best facilitated by an academic experienced in research.

This points to a reading and/or discussion exercise. Each exercise is designed to help the student develop a working appreciation of an important aspect of research theory and/or practice.

This highlights a focal concept that demands serious continuing critical reflection in order to develop a soundly based theoretical and practice foundation.

- Throughout many chapters various diagrams elaborate on the book's research roadmap or mental model. Shading conventions are used to highlight the overall flow of steps and the babushka-doll nature of the book's research roadmap (that is, its mental model). This can be seen in the 'topographical' format of Figure 3.3 (page 25).

THIS BOOK FILLS A GAP

We have developed this book to provide a foundation text (that is, an essential entry-level text) to help new research students (and more experienced researchers) to quickly yet reliably apprehend major elements of the research jigsaw in a way that integrates principles of good science, good research design and good research implementation and reporting. We also hope the book will serve as an aide-memoire for research project (or thesis) lecturers and tutors.

To meet this need the following features have been incorporated into this book:

- A helicopter view of three of the most distinctive and popular forms of science that are used to guide business and management research. Please note that these forms are deliberately simplified to aid their usability.

  Senior undergraduates may implement the research roadmaps as they exist in the book. Masters, PhD and professional doctorate research candidates may also need to read the philosophical and/or methodological texts to augment their work. Both levels will need to read methods texts (about for example data gathering (interviews, surveys) and data analysis (coding, statistics and so on).

- Four sections of this book are intended to help readers assimilate important principles in easy to work with modules. Within each section of the book the reader is progressively introduced to further aspects and illustrations of the similarities and differences that define three of the most common scientific paradigms and research approaches used in business and management research.

- The book has a **paradigm-centred** orientation to introducing and linking elements of the research cycle. In this way the reader is introduced to the unique structure of the research process and research life cycle, and should develop an appreciation of the importance of deliberately selecting a form of science (a paradigm) and an associated methodology (a structure of inquiry) that best suit the research context, research aims and research question.

- A one-page **research roadmap** and one-page **paradigm charts** graphically summarise otherwise hard to visualise and hard to assimilate concepts about forms of science (paradigms), types of methodologies and their associated practice issues.

- Widespread use of **graphics** to bring into a clear view a number of foundation concepts about various forms of science, a variety of research paradigms and their associated approaches and methodologies, and important keywords that help the reader to quickly and clearly understand their meanings.

- Wide-ranging **examples** (adapted from cases of strategic MIS (management of information systems) and strategic marketing) that provide practical illustrations of theoretical research issues and choices that may be expected to arise throughout a study's life cycle.

The six examples in this book are used to lead readers through the entire research process: from problem framing through design, conduct and reporting. As noted, three of the most common scientific paradigms in business and management research are illustrated, using a strategic MIS and strategic marketing example suited to each paradigm. Through the unfolding examples and the accompanying explanations of aspects of theory and practice, readers will progressively become acquainted with the differing (and sometimes similar) characteristics of each of the forms of science, and how these theoretical aspects are operationalised.

Leading on from this book there will be a set of resource links (especially a website link), which progressively offer readers structured access to linked readings, research cases, a common question–answer inquiry service, and training and learning resources for students and teachers of business and management research.

With this book design we expect readers will benefit by quickly acquiring meanings about three of the most common and important scientific approaches to business and management research; awareness of associated methodological features and technical issues that are typically linked with the three paradigms; and awareness of a wide range of issues and considerations when devising their own research studies.

WHAT THIS BOOK DOES NOT DO

This book does not present in-depth discussion of philosophical complexities and debates that have extended over the past few centuries. Also, this book does not dissect and elaborate specific research techniques and methods for dealing with data. These are covered very well by a large array of cookbooks about a wide range of research methods.

ABOUT THE EXAMPLES

The six examples in this book – three from strategic MIS and three from strategic marketing – have been adapted from actual consulting and related business and/or management practice research studies (by Jan Priest, all available at www.infoserv.com.au). In all cases, the adaptations have been approved by InfoServ Pty Ltd – an Australia-based business and management research and consulting firm.

FUTURE DEVELOPMENTS AND WEBSITE LINKS

All too often instruction in research theory and practice is seen as a necessary evil – something that is dry and tedious and to be overcome before the real work of research begins. This is reflected in the comparatively short time and effort that is devoted to learning about and critically developing research capability in undergraduate and postgraduate studies. It may also be linked to the continuing difficulty many have in generating and evaluating high-quality research.

An alternative viewpoint is that developing research know-how is best approached not as a brief and largely solitary task, but rather as an ongoing process. It should parallel rather than precede research, and be enriched by ongoing group discussions and contacts with experienced researchers and their work. A possible consequence is a research major rather than a typical semester study that precedes an undergraduate or postgraduate research project.

We intend to provide a website as an extension resource to complement this book, which will progressively include:

- cross-referenced links between other texts and cases and aspects of this book
- commentary on research cases with aspects linked to this book
- a common question–answer inquiry service which progressively builds on readers' questions about aspects of investigative theory and investigative practice
- training and additional learning resources for students and teachers of business and management research.
- a channel for feedback and suggestions to strengthen and enrich this book and its supporting resources.

ACTIVITIES AND RESOURCES

This section at the end of each chapter suggests further reading, and offers discussion and practice development activities.

EXERCISES AND QUESTIONS

1 Identify a few exemplary business or management research cases.
   (a) For each case identify their major phases and their corresponding purpose and outcome.
   (b) Does it appear that there is an underlying life cycle or does a study's structure and main steps appear to depend on the research case's aims, questions and its major theoretical and practical challenges?
2 For the research cases and their phases identified in exercise 1:
   (a) Compare and contrast the major steps between the cases, and the sorts of research questions or research challenges that each research case and its major steps address.
   (b) Discuss the underlying reasons for these similarities and differences.
3 Blaikie (1993) and Blaikie (2007) offer a comprehensive introduction to more philosophical aspects of scientific inquiry. Identify aspects of Blaikie (1993) and Blaikie (2007) that illuminate foundational underpinnings of the major theoretical and practical choices that are described in the exemplary research cases selected in exercise 1.

IN-DEPTH TOPICS

1 Review business and management research literature to find various definitions or concepts of 'paradigm'.
   (a) What fundamental features do they all share?
   (b) What implications does the concept of 'paradigm' raise for framing, answering and reporting a study about a research question or problem?

ACKNOWLEDGEMENTS

We wish to acknowledge the influence of Norman Blaikie as foundational scholar and teacher in Australia and overseas. His historically early recognition of the essential need and explored characteristics of paradigmatic pluralism in social scientific methodology was intellectually important for both of us.

As well, we wish to thank the many graduate students who have engaged with these ideas and from whom we have learned a great deal. Many have commenced their journey with some confusion and frustration but most have gone on to structure successful research projects and theses and have also made significant contributions to professional practice. It has been delightful to see so many moving from initial perceptions of dealing with demanding and apparently dry necessities of research and advanced practice development to a sense of greater intellectual power, (even enlightenment!) and professional success.

The writers also wish to thank InfoServ Pty Ltd and its clients for their interest and support as well as executives' practice reflections and suggestions that have contributed to the case illustrations and practice principles in this book.

Our students and clients have constantly emphasised the value of a 'helicopter view' to help fit designs, practices and tools to particular tasks. With this in mind we have deliberately sacrificed some depth in possible treatment of complex and fraught concepts in favour of a helicopter view of paradigms and practices. We hope this approach will help to address the urgent need to bridge the present gap between textual expositions of theoretical, philosophical and methodological concepts in the social sciences and the prolific extant 'cookbook' texts on, for instance, techniques about data (such as sampling, survey design, textual analysis, statistics and more).

The authors have enjoyed the humour and complementary experience, knowledge and talents that this book has drawn out and brought together.

Erica's thanks go to Jeff, Nicholas, Tim and Rohan Hallebone for their untiring encouragement. Jan's thanks go to Giovanna for her boundless support and advice on communicating complex ideas simply and to Michel and Sarah Priest for asking 'what, how and why' questions about consulting, research and teaching and so encouraging the reflections on which this book has drawn.

For the benefit that we have received from so many, we hope this book will help many more business and management researchers.

Erica Hallebone
Jan Priest

PART I

INTRODUCTION AND OUTLINE

KEY CONCEPTS WHEN FRAMING BUSINESS AND MANAGEMENT RESEARCH

INTRODUCTION

This book is for readers who need to understand the nature of business and management research. Normally, for such readers, there are two types of books available. One is the cookbook that deals with the theory and practice of techniques and methods. The other is the methodology book that deals with more abstract philosophical issues, about the nature of reality being studied in the actual research, research paradigms as ways of conducting research, and distinct strategies for studying these various assumed realities. Most books about methodology propose or assume a distinction between *qualitative* and *quantitative* research, as a fundamental starting point for developing a good understanding about the nature of research.

While it is common to classify research as qualitative or quantitative, there is a much more fundamental and important distinction to be made. This challenges the traditional separation between qualitative and quantitative methods.

We argue that conceiving, conducting and evaluating research according to the *paradigm* (which focuses on the philosophy of science and the logic of inquiry) and the related *design* (which focuses on the methodology and methods used to implement the paradigm) is preferable, because it is more informative and illuminating than is the quantitative/qualitative distinction. This position is developed in Chapter 2 and summarised in the concluding chapter.

Our view is that a study should not start with the choice of a methodology and associated methods. Rather, a study should start by first characterising different, and possibly competing, types of research questions or challenges, as well as different contexts for the questions. It should then recognise the worldviews implicit in the motivations, aims and corresponding literatures that fit the various types of questions. A suitable frame of reference, or research paradigm, is then chosen according to which orientation best matches the intended study's context, motivations, aims, question, constraints and likely uses. Details of the study's investigative theory and investigative practice are then developed, and executed in a way that stays mutually consistent with the chosen frame of reference or research paradigm.

In this chapter you will learn the importance and benefits of defining and implementing a consistent approach that reflects the character of the research topic and its setting. To properly and effectively combine a paradigm (that is, a particular philosophy of science and logic of inquiry) and a design (that is, a methodology and associated specific methods and techniques) can be a challenge, because choices for one often influence choices for the other. In this book we show you how to address this challenge, by explaining and illustrating how the three dimensions of philosophy, theory and practice are connected.

An important feature of this book is the use of research examples to illustrate, compare and contrast abstract concepts about the basis and practice of good research.

OVERALL STRUCTURE OF THIS BOOK

This chapter introduces the main concepts that we develop and illustrate throughout this book. The remaining chapters elaborate on the meaning and significance of these concepts, and use examples to illustrate their practical application. The outcome for readers should be a clear understanding of what is needed to help ensure that a research study is rigorous and valuable. The chapters are organised as shown in Table 1.1.

THE NEED FOR GOOD RESEARCH

As boards and executives increasingly grapple with governance issues that are more complex than the routine aspects of the firm's direction and performance, there is a growing interest in research. It is seen as one important way to

---

Table 1.1 Structure of the book

Part I Introduction and Outline
Chapter 1   Key concepts when framing business and management research
Chapter 2   Examples to illustrate a research roadmap
Chapter 3   A roadmap for research design and implementation

Part II Research Paradigms
Chapter 4   Philosophies of science: the bedrock for good research
Chapter 5   Illustrating three paradigms in action

Part III Illustrative Cases
Chapter 6   Positivist examples of investigative theory and practice
Chapter 7   Interpretivist examples of investigative theory and practice
Chapter 8   Criticalist examples of investigative theory and practice

Part IV Summary
Chapter 9   Summary of pointers for further understanding of major paradigms

Further resources: Key terms in this book, Bibliography, Index

inform directors, executives and managers about a wide range of risk and value-related matters: about legal, ethical, economic, environmental, product, marketing, technological, organisational, geopolitical, sociocultural, security and other issues.

Good business and management research should provide the information and knowledge required for well-informed and insightful governance. Reducing risks and increasing value are challenges connected with generating good management research.

Different researchers emphasise various characteristics when describing and explaining what they consider to be well-designed research, yet there is a collection of characteristics that are referred to over and over again. These constants include:

- a clear and concise statement and justification of the study's aims and objectives
- a worthy scope; one that is not just logical but also practical, achievable and important
- rigorous design and implementation to match the research's aims and objectives
- a symbiotic relationship between the theory and the practice of the research
- evidence of reflexive learning in the research process.

Good research is rigorous. Rigour is featured in both the theoretical and practical aspects of the research. It is the quality that is constructed through attention to work that is challenging, convincing, comprehensive, competent, consistent and conclusive.

In good research, theoretical and practical aspects of the research are mutually dependent; with theoretical choices about the *topical* and *investigative* aspects of research being shaped by more practical aspects of the research, and vice versa. (We use the term *topical theory* to refer to theoretical aspects of the subject matter being studied, and the term *investigative theory* to refer to theoretical aspects of the philosophy, logic, methodology and techniques of inquiry.) For instance, small budgets, limited staff and the need for findings in a short timeframe will challenge what might be an excellent theoretical design, if it requires international travel to gather comparative data through long-term case studies.

Indicators of good research include a lucid and insightful description of the research problem and its context: a clear focus, salient detail, evidence of rigorous design and conduct, and balanced and mutually consistent theoretical and practical dimensions. Good research is an interesting, carefully constructed and professionally executed investigation, and delivers a report that makes a significant and compelling contribution to knowledge.

THE SCOPE OF MANAGEMENT RESEARCH

The philosophical, theoretical and practical aspects of business and management research can be thought of as three dimensions. This idea is depicted in Figure 1.1.

In practice you will find that these three dimensions of research need to be developed together from the outset, in order to maintain their mutual consistency, rather than being developed as a sequence with little or no backtracking.

Typically the researcher starts by clarifying the research topic, which is usually summarised as a question, a problem, an assertion or a challenge. The researcher's first task is to produce a clearly defined and mutually consistent statement of the research topic's context and objectives.

The next step is to select an appropriate philosophy of science and a logic of inquiry. This choice establishes the bedrock and architectural principles on which the research project and its outcome and value are built. To do this the researcher must consider the nature of prior research on the topic area as well as the nature of the topic and its purpose.

The chosen philosophy of science and the logic of inquiry contribute to a paradigmatic choice which empowers and constrains the ongoing research effort, its reporting and subsequent use. As a topic becomes better defined, and the philosophy of science and its corresponding logic of inquiry are selected and

---

Figure 1.1

1. Research **topics**

This book uses examples from research to show the link between philosophical, theoretical and practical aspects of research.

This book's examples are drawn from:
- MIS (management of information systems)
- Marketing

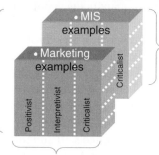

3. Research **implementation**

This book traces typical research processes in terms of four major tasks:
- Topic
- Strategy
- Design
- Reorting

2. Research **paradigm**
(Philosophy of science and logic of inquiry)

This book refers to three major perspectives in the science of doing business and management research:
- Positivist
- Interpretivist
- Criticalist

Three dimensions to research: the character of a research topic, which leads to the choice of a fitting research paradigm, which in turn prompts the study's investigative design and conduct

justified, the researcher must also devise and update the practical steps needed to conduct the study. The chosen philosophy of science, logic of inquiry and tactical plan (that is, the methodology) are the paradigmatic foundations of the study. They represent the roadmap for the researcher's journey.

A research path comprises the detailed work programme and practical execution which will satisfy the purpose of the research and remain true to the strategic requirements that the chosen philosophy of science establishes.

Figure 1.2 highlights an important relationship between the research topic, the research paradigm and the research design, which we explain and illustrate in this book. That is, the chosen research paradigm shapes the research design, but the research design does not shape the research paradigm, unless the topic is redefined to the extent that its underlying character is substantively changed. This is reflected in the common experience that research design typically remains *dynamic*, whereas the research paradigm becomes fixed early on.

Figure 1.2

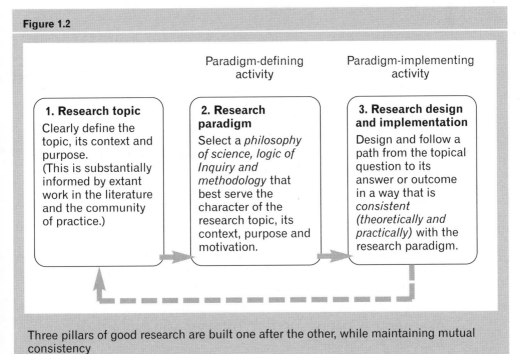

Three pillars of good research are built one after the other, while maintaining mutual consistency

As research preparation progresses, paradigm-related activity and design-related activity converge, as depicted in Figure 1.3.

Figure 1.3

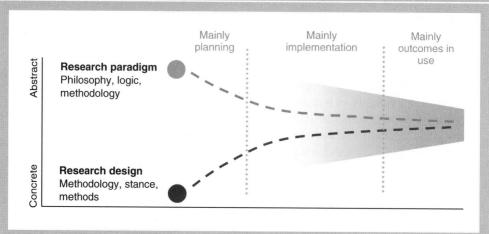

The 'research zip' is a metaphor to remind us that in good research we can see the convergence of two distinct streams of activity

Depending on the research topic and the chosen research paradigm, the procedural steps in the research path need to be refined or sometimes substantially adjusted in response to theoretical and practical constraints, problems, emerging findings, and imaginative ideas that arise but could not reasonably have been foreseen at the start of the research.

Research paths in business and management studies vary in their detail yet they share a common high-level relationship. This relationship is shown in Figure 1.4.

The research path needs focus. In business and management research, focusing the research is about developing very clear specifications for the drivers, motivations and objectives of the research project; the form and substance of the primary and supporting research questions; the strengths and weaknesses of related research; and the main arguments that underpin the chosen philosophy of science and logic of inquiry.

RESEARCH EXAMPLES HELP TO UNDERSTAND IMPORTANT RESEARCH CONCEPTS

To illustrate and draw out important dimensions of research theory and practice, we use examples throughout this book which are taken from two important areas of business and management practice. One practice area is MIS, which is concerned with management of information systems and information technology matters. The other practice area is about the management of

Figure 1.4

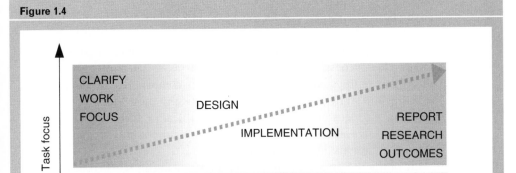

As research progresses, the emphasis shifts from design to conduct, yet each continues to inform the other

business marketing and business strategy-related activities in firms, which we refer to as strategic marketing.

We have chosen examples from MIS and strategic marketing because they have global and long-running relevance, and each offers an array of exemplary research that helps to illustrate the philosophical, theoretical and practical aspects of research and their interrelationships.

The MIS examples developed in this book (and introduced in Table 1.2) are about the effectiveness of MIS at industry and firm level; the nature of managers' knowledge and practice about MIS; and the nature of the organisational change and performance that is so often associated with the deployment and use of business information systems.

In discussing these aspects of MIS, we focus on some long-run and critical problems about MIS performance and knowledge, and use this to highlight ways in which different research approaches have influenced the state of play in MIS practice.

Throughout this book we use idiosyncratic and sometimes counterintuitive examples in order to help readers to appreciate and understand the practical and theoretical relevance, importance and consequences of particular topics and their associated research paradigm and research design. The examples below highlight this crucial relationship which is a focus of the book.

Because the nature of this relationship is so central to good research, we carefully step the reader through definitions, explanations and successive examples in order to build and reinforce a well-founded theoretical and practical understanding, and so equip the reader with a sound and practical framework that can be used to design, conduct, evaluate and use business and management research.

The strategic marketing examples (see Table 1.3) are about marketing and strategy effectiveness, mediating factors such as social and organisational culture and politics, and matters to do with competence development in marketing and strategic management. In discussing these aspects of strategic marketing, we focus on some long-run and critical problems about management knowledge and performance in order to highlight how various research approaches have influenced practice.

One of the themes we emphasise and illustrate in this book is the constant interweaving of the two different kinds of conceptual choice that a researcher must make. One kind of choice concerns decisions about static principles of

Table 1.2 MIS examples: research design fits a strategy and approach to the research topic, its context and purpose

MIS example	Question or hypothesis	Paradigm (philosophy of science and logic of inquiry)	Design (methodology, stance and methods)	Form of results
Information management practices	Are alignment-capable managers more often linked with project success than are other managers?	Objectivist and independent. Deductively generated.	Large-scale survey of managerial capabilities and project outcomes.	Statistical correlations and measures of significance between pre and post hoc data.
Managing knowledge workers	What are the distinctive characteristics of expert practice for managing knowledge workers?	Constructionist and intersubjective. Abductively generated knowledge.	Descriptive verbal and documentary data from focus groups and depth interviews.	Typifications of effective practices explained by managers and knowledge workers.
Strategic business information systems investments	Do, and how do, political and technical considerations influence executives' go/no-go decisions about investments in strategic IT-based business information systems?	Combined realist and relativist realities retroductively perceived and understood as pragmatic constructions and explanations.	A typology of practice principles associated with executives' decision making.	A model of causal links between political and other considerations on the input side and decisions and their outcomes as outputs with recommendations for enhanced practice.

Table 1.3 Strategic marketing examples: research design fits a strategy and approach to the research topic, its context and purpose

Strategic marketing example	Question or hypothesis	Paradigm (philosophy of science and the logic of inquiry)	Design (methodology, stance and methods)	Form of results
Personal electronic goods and services	Are the sales of products and services more affected by price, functionality or brand recognition?	Objectivist and independent. Deductively generated.	Statistical analyses of sales and market data from surveys and other sources.	Statistical correlations and measures of significance.
Deciding on competitive product portfolios	What characteristics of effective decision making help make (more) competitive product portfolios?	Constructionist and intersubjective. Abductively generated knowledge.	Observations, focus groups and depth interviews.	Ideal-typical decision making principles and practices associated with persistently competitive product portfolios.
The politics of choice for product portfolios	How are executive preferences and choices for the firm's product portfolio mix informed and influenced by their organisation political contexts?	Combined realist and relativist realities retroductively perceived and understood as pragmatic constructions and explanations.	A typology of practice principles associated with executives' decision making.	A model of causal links between political and other considerations on the input side and decisions and their outcomes as outputs with recommendations for enhanced practice.

inquiry, such as the choice of philosophy of science and logic of inquiry. The other kind of choice involves decisions about the research pathway. This is akin to the dynamic of selecting and using the appropriate strip map to guide the local journey, while staying true to the overall tour plan in following the research path from journey's beginning to journey's end.

Examples from MIS and strategic marketing research highlight the interweaving of the two fundamental choices about philosophy of science and logic of inquiry, and the importance of keeping their theoretical and practical levels in sync and also in sympathy with the character of the research topic and its context and purpose. The next chapters progressively elaborate, illustrate and explain choices about designing and implementing approaches to business and management research, using the research roadmap and mental models.

SUMMARY

The recurring theme in this book is that good business and management research is about the mutually consistent formulation and implementation of a research paradigm and a more detailed-level research design, which are both in sympathy with the character of the research topic, the fundamental purpose of the research and the principal research question.

This book introduces the reader to the nature of doing good research on a business or management topic by interweaving two streams:

- building and justifying a *paradigm* founded on a philosophy of science and a logic of inquiry that best fit the character and purpose of the research topic
- developing and following a *design* that is theoretically and practically sound: that is, consistent with the chosen research paradigm and sensitive to the nature of the research setting, and specific enough to address the detailed practical and theoretical challenges that must be overcome in order to justifiably satisfy the research purpose.

By discussing *examples* from MIS and strategic marketing research and management practice, we shall illustrate practical and theoretical aspects of research theory and practice.

ACTIVITIES AND RESOURCES

This section at the end of each chapter suggests further reading, and offers discussion and practice development activities.

 EXERCISES AND QUESTIONS

1 (a) Choose some examples of research projects. Judging by these, are the uses of, and meanings for, the terms quantitative and qualitative strongly associated with particular types of research questions and/or particular types of studies?

   (b) Discuss the merits and drawbacks of the distinction between quantitative and qualitative methods as a primary base for designing research.

2 Terms such as paradigm, methodology and method have multiple meanings across the research literature.

   (a) Compile a list of meanings of each term – and note the context (that is, the type of study) in which each meaning applies.

   (b) Discuss the underlying intentions of the various terms and their meanings.

    (c) What implications do your observations have for the purposes of research?

3 (a) Find references to a variety of good (in other words, frequently cited, strong, outstanding, ground breaking, seminal) studies.

    (b) Do the studies you have identified share characteristics that appear to be largely or entirely absent in weak (that is, poor or flawed) studies?

4 Maintaining coherence between a study's scientific plan of inquiry and its practical effort may result in long-running iterations and adjustments which may adversely impact on the scientific merit of the study, its budget and/or duration.

    (a) Examine cases and discuss principles and practices that appear to help manage scientific and practical tradeoffs without compromising a study's good quality and rigour.

5 (a) Find references to a reputedly outstanding business or management research study that does not exhibit a mutually consistent formulation and implementation of a research paradigm and a corresponding detailed level research design.

    (b) What implications for the design and conduct of good research arise from the results of your search?

IN-DEPTH TOPICS

1 From an examination of good versus weak studies, suggest tests to identify outstanding business or management research.

    (a) What common factors appear to be strongly represented in good research?

    (b) What factors of good research appear to be absent in weak research?

    (c) Is good research the antithesis of weak research or does the difference reflect some other type of distinction?

FURTHER READING

Blaikie, N. (1993) *Approaches to Social Enquiry*, Cambridge, Polity Press.

Blaikie, N. (2000) *Designing Social Research: The Logic of Anticipation*, Cambridge, Polity Press.

Blaikie, N. (2003) *Analyzing Quantitative Data: From Description to Explanation*, London, Sage.

Blaikie, N. (2007) *Approaches to Social Enquiry,* 2nd edn, Cambridge, Polity Press.

Burrell, G. and Morgan, G. (1979) *Sociological Paradigms and Organizational Analysis*, London, Heinemann.

Clarke, T. and Clegg, S. (2000) *Changing Paradigms: The Transformation of Management Knowledge for the 21st Century*, London, Harper Collins.

Collis, J. and Hussey, R. (2003) *Business Research Methods: A Practical Guide for Undergraduates and Postgraduates*, 2nd edn., Basingstoke, Palgrave Macmillan.

Cuff, E. C., Sharrock, W. W. and Francis, D. W. (1998) *Perspectives in Sociology,* 4th edn., London, Routledge.

Hassard, J. (1991) 'Multiple paradigms and organizational analysis: a case study', *Organization Studies*, 12 (2): 275–99.

Hassard, J. and Pym, D. (1993) *The Theory and Philosophy of Organizations,* London, Routledge.

Kuhn, T. (1970) *The Structure of Scientific Revolutions*, 2nd edn. Chicago, Chicago University Press.

Morris, T. (2006) *Social Work Research Methods: Four Alternative Paradigms,* London, Sage.

Silverman, D. (1970) *The Theory of Organizations,* London, Heinemann Educational.

Somekh, B. and Lewin, C. (eds) (2005) *Research Methods in the Social Sciences,* London, Sage.

Trigg, R. (1985) *Understanding Social Science: A Philosophical Introduction to the Social Sciences,* Oxford, Blackwell.

2

EXAMPLES TO ILLUSTRATE A RESEARCH ROADMAP

INTRODUCTION

This chapter introduces key concepts of research in five steps: characteristics of good research, exemplary cases to be used to illustrate research concepts, a mental model for structuring a research programme, illustrative case studies, and a summary of key principles. The steps are highlighted in Figure 2.1.

Figure 2.1

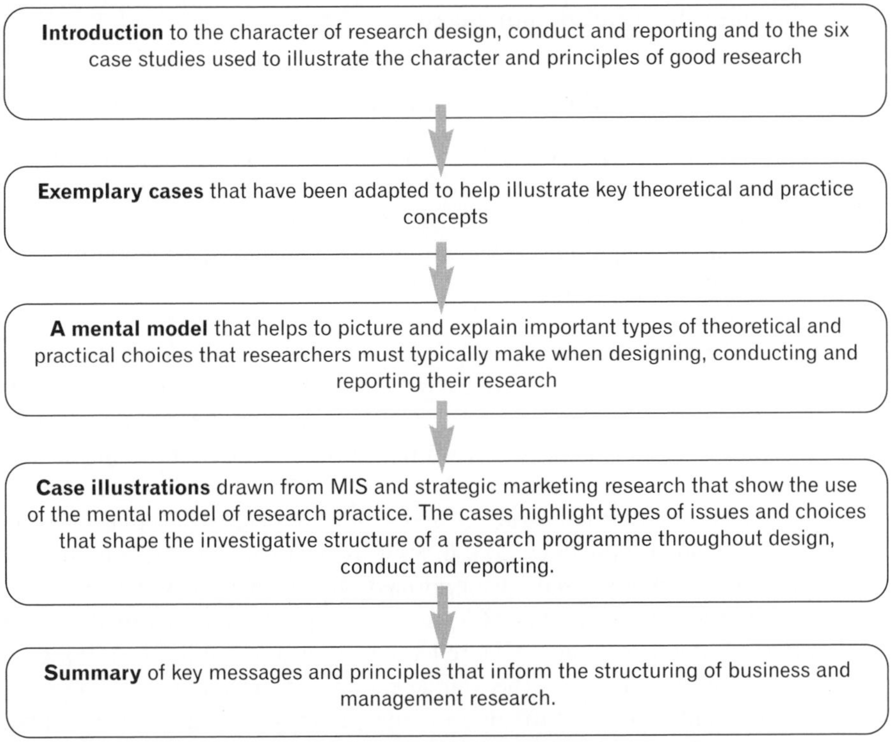

Introduction to the character of research design, conduct and reporting and to the six case studies used to illustrate the character and principles of good research

Exemplary cases that have been adapted to help illustrate key theoretical and practice concepts

A mental model that helps to picture and explain important types of theoretical and practical choices that researchers must typically make when designing, conducting and reporting their research

Case illustrations drawn from MIS and strategic marketing research that show the use of the mental model of research practice. The cases highlight types of issues and choices that shape the investigative structure of a research programme throughout design, conduct and reporting.

Summary of key messages and principles that inform the structuring of business and management research.

This chapter's outline of research practice principles is developed in five steps

INTRODUCING AND ILLUSTRATING THE CHARACTER OF GOOD RESEARCH

Chapter 1 noted several characteristics of good research, including clear rationale for a study's aims, objectives and scope, a lucid and informative review of literature, rigorous design and conduct of the study's investigative theory and the practice, and evidence of reflexive learning in the research process.

Throughout this book we refer to six examples of business and management research to illustrate important theoretical and practical aspects of research. By illustrating and reinforcing common features of research as well as important differences between research paradigms, we hope to enable you not only to choose a research approach and strategy, but also to appreciate the practice aspects of research and some important theoretical concepts.

We have selected illustrations from strategic MIS (management of information systems) and strategic marketing cases because of the ubiquitous nature of the two subject areas, the diverse practical and theoretical management and research issues that each illustration raises, and the wide relevance of these topical areas to managers throughout public administration and private enterprise. The three strategic MIS and three strategic marketing examples that are used throughout are now introduced.

Three examples of research from MIS cases

Digital information and communications technologies (ICTs) have been the cornerstone of business information systems for over half a century. From the 1950s ICT research has been almost entirely positivist, and has been directly linked with accelerating year by year improvements in the reliability, capacity, speed, utility and usability of ICT products, with corresponding reductions in their unit cost.

Parallel to this stream of remarkable improvements in long-run ICT product value has been a chronic failure to manage the delivery of sustained value from investments in the commercial use of ICTs for business processes, and for business products and services. The annual success–failure rate from managing investments in ICT (often also referred to as MIS – the management of ICT-based business information systems) remained under 20 per cent over the four decades 1960 to 2000 (Priest 2001 in www.infoserv.com.au). An examination of the types of research that have informed MIS practice show that during this period over 95 per cent of all MIS research was positivist in nature (Priest 2000 in www.infoserv.com.au). This reflects a systematic failure to do long-term exploratory research into the unique context and character of MIS practice, and to identify aspects unique to managing the long-run success of investments in ICT-based business information systems.

Positivist research has worked so well for ICTs, so why has it failed to develop theory whose use could systematically improve the MIS success rate? This is partly because of typical and fundamental differences between a majority of ICT problems and most MIS problems. These two classes of problems differ in much the same way as inanimate material behaviour differs from intelligent social behaviour.

Positivist research, which ideally seeks generalised findings from representative samples, repeatable controlled observations, transparent data and apolitical responses, is not characteristically suited to the idiosyncratic, uncontrollable, nonrepetitive, opaque, adaptive and political character of MIS practice and problems. Using the same (positivist) research approach for two important but distinctly different classes of research problems reflects a failure to match research designs and research practices to the contexts and characteristics of the research challenges.

An important message in this book is that understanding of the context and character of a substantive topic and the core research question must inform the selection of a fitting research paradigm and an effective research design. The following three MIS examples will help to illustrate this crucial message.

Example 1: Information management practices

A key challenge for information-intensive firms is to better manage investments in ICT-based business information systems. This is because failure to deliver strategically and operationally important systems usually has major adverse impacts on a firm's capital and operating budgets, as well as sustained adverse impacts on competitiveness and profitability. In 2001, groundbreaking MIS research reported on the nature of the sustained alignment between business, organisation, technology and management factors that was unique to long-run MIS success. The principles, now packaged as the BOTMline® and WIKIDway®, embody a better-practice model that has been used by managers to improve the development, delivery and value in use of key business information systems (and, more widely, a range of long-run innovation and organisation performance turnarounds and successes).

Once this new MIS model has been developed and tentatively demonstrated, an important research question is: are alignment-capable managers more often linked with (MIS) project success than are other managers?

Example 2: Managing knowledge workers

In the last half century there has been an explosion of knowledge and service work throughout the industrialised world. However, enlightened and effective human resource management of technology and service workers has not kept pace with the economic demand. One reason is because there are far too few effective knowledge-service workers for the economic demand. Another key reason is because the nature of effective knowledge-service work has remained intangible, and it has been poorly understood for much longer than was the case for work before the knowledge-service era. So an important challenge for firms is to be able to better understand how to attract, deploy and retain high-quality knowledge-service workers.

A key question for managers is, what are distinctive characteristics of expert practice for managing knowledge workers?

Example 3: Strategic business information systems investments

Industries and firms routinely look for ways to strengthen their competitiveness and performance by using information technologies to efficiently expand their market. Strategic and innovative investments in particular are undertaken in order to achieve advantages which can be an order of magnitude greater than those obtained by more routine systems investments.

Higher risks and more wide-ranging organisational impacts typically arise for firms investing in strategic or innovative ICT-based business information systems. Anecdotal accounts from chief executive officers (CEOs), chief information officers (CIOs) and other senior executives frequently refer to political and technical predispositions as well as organisation and commercial judgements as influencing the choices and actions that collectively shape the evolution and eventual outcomes of such investments.

So an important research question is, do (and how do) political and technical considerations influence executives' go/no-go decisions about investments in strategic IT-based business information systems?

Three examples of research from strategic marketing cases

When cellular mobile telephony became a reality for industrial communities across most continents in the 1980s (of course, it is now extending globally), it set the scene for creating and servicing consumer markets counted in the billions. It also changed the face of communications, and the way that government agencies as well as NGO and commercial service organisations could structure themselves.

For instance, the cell-phone markets of the first decade since 2000 are being redefined as a result of the rapid convergence of wireless broadband infrastructure with diverse retail and personal communications products and services. It is commonplace to see people with personal digital products (PDPs) that combine telephony, graphics, personal computing, internet-based trading, information services like stock market reporting, and personalised direct marketing.

The challenges and opportunities for strategic marketing include the rapid redefinition of markets as well as the development and distribution of new products and services. In this field, success may be as much a consequence of anticipating demand as it is of creating or servicing demand.

Understanding, anticipating and servicing strategic market opportunities as well as better responding to rapid innovation and diffusion of innovations by strong competitors requires a greater ability to generate knowledge and qualify hunches and choices about consumers and providers. Being able to apprehend their intentions, preferences and behaviours more quickly and incisively in order to 'stand out from the competitive and consumer crowds' is a strategic capability. It needs well-focused market and product or service research.

Effective strategic marketing requires not only a fertile commercial imagination but increasingly a well-informed understanding that crosses diverse contexts shaped by political, economic, social, technological, legal and environmental considerations. Becoming informed about markets and informing markets about products and services requires astute and disciplined approaches to research. This moves well beyond the all too common large-sample surveys with questions and assumptions grounded in understandings borrowed from foreign contexts.

Both successful and failed marketing of standout innovations reflect a key lesson: focusing, designing and conducting research must account for the context and character of the substantive research topic, as much as it must account for the purpose of the study and the core research question. The three examples of strategic marketing that are introduced below, and used as illustrations in later chapters, emphasise this important principle.

Example 4: Personal electronic goods and services (PEGS)

Traditional marketing theory suggests that price, functionality and brand awareness are three important predictive factors of a product's market share in new commodity markets. For a firm to be able to choose its marketing strategy, it is important to know the strengths of consumer preferences on for instance, price, functionality and brand.

A firm's managers who are responsible for making recommendations to the executive about the product strategy and marketing mix are generally interested in knowing patterns in customers' buying preferences for the firm's and for competitors' products and services. In particular, it is important that the firm's product managers and executives know the answer to the question: are the sales of products or services more affected by price, functionality or brand recognition?

Example 5: Deciding on competitive product portfolios

In a fast-moving PEGS environment, human expertise is reflected in the repeated ability to both integrate a variety of complex factors and produce a successful outcome. Human expertise in this environment depends on continual updating of knowledge, education, experience and exposure to well-informed alternative interpretations of market factors and market behaviour. Access to such expertise can help aspiring new market entrants to establish themselves in aggressively contested markets. It can also help established firms open new markets, as well as compete more effectively in current markets.

So an important question for a firm's strategic marketing executives is: what characteristics of effective decision making help to make (more) competitive product portfolios?

Example 6: The politics of choice for product portfolios

Various studies suggest that strategic choices about product life cycles, including product release and product withdrawal decisions, are not only based on objective rational economic considerations but are influenced by each executive's political, personal and social contexts.

The challenge that this raises is to understand how such influences operate, because this could enable more effective decision making. Consultants advising executives who are concerned with better marketing decisions will be more informed if they are able to answer the question: how are executive preferences and choices for the firm's product portfolio mix informed and influenced by their organisation-political contexts?

IMPLICATIONS

Each of the six illustrations has been chosen to highlight distinctly different practice and research perspectives. This will help the reader to clearly compare and contrast the reasoning and impacts of various investigative and practical choices in a study's design, conduct and reporting.

Notwithstanding the fact that there are, in general, many more investigative and practical research decisions than are noted and illustrated in this book, we expect that the six case illustrations will help our readers to be more aware of, and better prepared for, the challenges of characterising a research problem and its context, and designing a suitably rigorous and practical research study.

ACTIVITIES AND RESOURCES

This section at the end of each chapter suggests further reading, and offers discussion and practice development activities.

 EXERCISES AND QUESTIONS

1   Trillions of dollars are expended annually on MIS.
    (a) Identify a variety of seminal studies concerned with MIS success and failure, and classify the forms of research used.

(b) What research challenges and lessons are apparent from this brief survey?

2 (a) What are the strengths and weaknesses of natural science-based studies of MIS knowhow?

(b) How would you suggest answering the question, 'Is there MIS know how that is unique to long-run successful ICT investments?' What assumptions underpin your suggested approach?

(c) Is your approach scientific? Explain your reasons and the meaning of science that is implicit in your answer.

3 Each of the question types 'Are there ...?', 'What ...?', 'Do/how do ...?' or 'Why ...?' differ in their axiomatic assumptions and in terms of the process for answering them. Furthermore, different substantive foci for the same question type can also imply different axiomatic assumptions and different approaches to answering the question.

(a) Review a variety of studies and list the forms of primary questions that are the focus of these studies.

(b) How do research designs vary in response to the various question types identified?

4 Knowledge worker is a widely used term.

(a) Is the research literature agreed on the meaning of the term?

(b) What research implications arise from this example?

IN-DEPTH TOPICS

1 The great majority of research that has generated MIS practice knowhow is based on assumptions, approaches and methods drawn from the natural sciences.

(a) What are the characteristic assumptions of natural sciences that seem to pervade natural science-based studies of MIS?

(b) Suggest various important MIS challenges and phenomena whose context and problem character do not lend themselves to study using natural science-based assumptions, designs and methods.

FURTHER READING

Priest, J. G. (2000) *Managing Investments in Information Systems: Exploring Effective Practice,* Doctor of Business Administration thesis, Melbourne, RMIT University.

Priest, J. G. (2001) www.infoserv.com.au

3

A ROADMAP FOR RESEARCH DESIGN AND IMPLEMENTATION

A MENTAL MODEL FOR GOOD RESEARCH

As this book is about enabling researchers to choose an appropriate alternative investigative form of business or management research, a mental model will be a valuable practice and pedagogic aid if it helps to guide them in the consistent design, conduct and reporting of various investigative paradigms. The mental model shown in Figure 3.1 highlights a systematic order in which important theoretical decisions about the research approach can be made. The result is a structured approach to the research task which is mutually consistent and appropriate to the focus and context of the research.

Figure 3.1

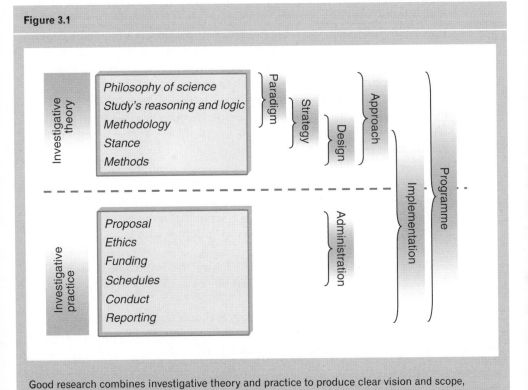

Good research combines investigative theory and practice to produce clear vision and scope, consistent assumptions, compelling and lucid reasoning, and rigorous attention to all details

The mental model sets out a preferred order in which choices about the research approach emerge. This preferred order is:

1 Choose a philosophy of science that is appropriate to the research setting and the question of interest.
2 Select the principal logical tenet(s) that best serve the form of argument about empirical evidence that will be used to develop an answer to the core research question.
3 Select the methodological premises on which the work to answer the research question will be based.
4 Choose the most appropriate stance for the researcher.
5 Select or develop specific methods to be used to generate and analyse data, and report the study.

Regardless of whether the set of choices emerges sequentially or iteratively, the principal tenet in good research is that the choices are explicit, mutually consistent and justifiably appropriate in light of the study's context and the core research question.

The mental model that follows is a guide for researchers needing to systematically identify issues and generate choices for the design and practical implementation of a quality research programme. Each key word that is shown in italics in the mental model is briefly explained, and its use is highlighted using the six examples already introduced. In later chapters the use of the mental model is elaborated for each of the three research paradigms, and there are practical illustrations using the research case studies.

The mental model combines important formal and practical elements of business and management research practice. We think its value lies in the theoretical and practical guidance offered to researchers as they construct and execute their research programme.

Figure 3.1 could be described as a research roadmap for business and management research. Its major parts comprise investigative theory (which is itself made up of five major elements) and investigative practice (which consists of six major elements). Common terms that are used to refer to various combinations of the 11 major elements are indicated with braces on the right-hand side of the figure.

Figure 3.2 highlights the scope of each of the five major elements that constitute the investigative theory that must be outlined when describing a particular approach to research.

Figure 3.3 highlights the scope of each of the six major elements that constitute the investigative practice that should generally be accounted for when properly describing a particular approach to research.

An essential starting point for readers who are relatively inexperienced in the field of business and management research is to develop an understanding and working facility with this mental model and with the language of research.

Figure 3.2

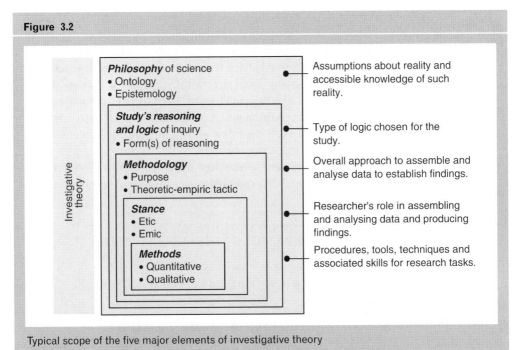

Typical scope of the five major elements of investigative theory

Figure 3.3

Proposal
- Purpose, outcomes, benefits, support
- Management and administration

This is the justification of the study and underpins support requirements.

Ethics
- Stakeholders, risks, responses
- Controls and supervision

Arrangements to minimise harm.

Funding
- Sources, conditions, reporting

Money 'in-kind' and match-support arrangements needed for the study.

Schedules
- Activity timetable
- Resources and facilities
- Financial and in-kind budget

Activity and reporting triggers to guide research tasks, administration and accountability for the study's major support arrangements.

Conduct
- Literature
- Empirical work

'In sync' research and administrative arrangements, activities and progress.

Reporting
- Papers and seminars
- Report or thesis

Technical and administrative reporting of the study's progress and eventual findings and outcomes.

Investigative practice

Typical scope of the six major elements of investigative practice

There is a common phenomenon in which different words in the literature are used with similar or the same meanings, and the same words are used with different meanings. As ambiguities these are confusing, and challenge those who need to be usefully informed about the science and craft of research. Our aim is to be clear and consistent about the meanings of words that are part of the everyday language of research, so in Figure 3.1, keywords that have a special meaning throughout this book are highlighted in bold italics. These words are briefly defined below, and their meaning and significance is explained and illustrated throughout the following chapters.

It is important that readers come to recognise and appreciate the sense in which we use these key words, rather than expect the book to provide a universally agreed meaning for each key word.

THE MEANINGS OF KEY WORDS IN THE MENTAL MODEL

The terms in italics in Figure 3.1 and supporting Figures 3.2 and 3.3 are explained in the following two sections and elaborated in Chapter 10.

Meanings for elements of investigative theory (Figure 3.2)

The mental model in Figure 3.1 helps avoid the pitfall of premature and inappropriate choice of method as the starting point rather than the end point of good science in research. To use this model effectively you need to understand clearly and use consistently its key terms. They are introduced below.

A ***philosophy*** of science refers to a set of explicit fundamental assumptions and frames of reference that underpin a way to conceive of, and know about, a particular reality being studied in a research frame of reference. These foundational assumptions are known technically as ontological and epistemological assumptions. It is good practice to state explicitly these assumptions and the rationale for their choice.

An ***ontology*** is the set of explicitly stated axiomatic assumptions (within a philosophy of science) that define the way a reality is conceived and perceived.

A *realist ontology* employs the objectivist assumptions and perspectives of a constant reality that exists. This is characteristic of the traditional natural sciences.

Methods employed in this setting commonly involve the operationalisation of concepts as variables that can typically be quantified and measured, so that relationships between the variables can be measured and compared. From this premise, the observable empirical domain of interest is considered to arise from underlying, albeit largely unobservable, cause and effect mechanisms, whose operation may be modified depending on attempts to access them. This reality may be partially obscured. Plausible theoretical knowledge of it can only be reinforced by the use of empirical tests.

A *constructionist ontology* employs the intersubjective assumptions and relativist perspectives of reality that are so distinctive in, and typical of, the social sciences. In a constructionist ontology, reality is socially constructed from individual cognitive processes informed by experience and language. This reality is commonly interpreted using linguistically negotiated constructions, which evolve into concepts that are ideal-typical abstractions of instances of manifold behavioural or observational experience.

An **epistemology** is a set of axiomatic assumptions (within a philosophy of science) that define the way knowledge about a particular view of reality (that is, an ontologically well-defined reality) is to be generated, represented, understood and used.

A *positivist epistemology* will typically seek to establish descriptive and predictive principles and rules for a reality that exists independently of an observer or participant. Knowledge is commonly generated by operationalising concepts and variables in order to test hypotheses. This method typically uses quantitative data and analytic methods.

Interpretivist epistemologies commonly seek to describe and understand socially constructed realities. They commonly aim to generate socially relative knowledge about some social phenomenon, and often proceed by interpreting experience and observation using language-based methods. This results in the production of a theoretical construct that offers a comprehensive description and insightful understanding of the phenomenon.

A *realist epistemology* is likely to be involved in both describing and explaining. A realist approach to creating knowledge about some phenomenon will often involve empirical observation of its manifestations, symptoms and consequences, and empirically validated theoretical constructions of its underlying mechanisms. We can be more confident that the right underlying mechanisms have been identified if we make counterintuitive predictions and find ways of confirming them. Similarly, the researcher needs to search assiduously for disconfirming evidence, and if this is not found it acts as a validation. The descriptive adequacy of broader and more varied patterns of regularities in observable phenomena is a confirming factor too.

The section on the study's **reasoning and logic** of inquiry argues for, and explains, the major form of reasoning to be used in answering the research question with the use of empirical data, and the particular logic(s) on which such reasoning is to be based. Particular types of logic that are later illustrated include deduction, induction, abduction and retroduction.

A study's reasoning and logic of inquiry reflects the deliberate choice of reasoning paths and associated forms of reasoning (such as deduction, induction, abduction and retroduction). Together these constitute an argument structure. A study's logic of inquiry should be consistent with the study's ontological and epistemological assumptions and choices, and may even require justification if rigour and validity are likely to be contested. Justification is more important with a study that aims to challenge conventional wisdom or apply an unusual approach to a traditional problem. When fully developed, a study's reasoning and logic reflect and tie together the choices and consequences that arise from the researcher's motives and background, the study's aims and constraints, the knowledge sought and identified in the literature, the study's overall approach and detailed procedures, the administrative aspects of the study, the study's execution, and the research report's structure and its emerging content.

Principles of reasoning such as deduction, induction, abduction or retroduction that are used in a study provide the logical basis for making claims about, and testing the integrity of, knowledge generated through the research design and empirical work. The dominant logic of inquiry shapes the process of research, just as foundations and a framework shape a building. The logic of inquiry should be a bridge between the chosen philosophy of science, and the situation-specific methodology and methods that characterise the theoretical approach to the investigation that will address the research questions.

It is not unusual for several forms of reasoning to be applied in one piece of research, although there is often an overriding logic that carries the dominant argument structure. Specific tasks within the argument structure must be addressed with the most appropriate logic for the task. This multi-phase character of logic is illustrated in our example cases later in this chapter and throughout the book.

A ***methodology*** of inquiry is a set of tactics and supporting steps that operationalise the chosen science and logic of inquiry. As a research process blueprint it highlights situation-specific arguments and choices. These involve for example sampling, assembly of data, data analysis, production and validation of findings, and eventually reporting of the study. It can be thought of as a map that describes the major phases, their primary tasks and the key steps within those tasks, which together constitute the way the research questions are to be answered. One common methodological framework is the exploratory type (as in a study intended to create a theory) and another is the experimental type (as in a study intended to test a theory).

A study's methodology operationalises the particular form of science that has been selected for the study.

A researcher's ***stance*** is an essential but too often ignored part of comprehensively rigorous research. A description of a researcher's stance must express, with supporting reasons, the relationship that the researcher will have with the process and substance of generating, assembling and analysing data, determining and validating the study's findings, and reporting the study's conduct and results. The stance must also be mutually consistent with the resulting paradigm. Deciding the researcher's stance is about acknowledging and articulating the researcher's attitude to their own knowledge and to the way they should operate in relation to the field of inquiry, and in relation to the research process overall.

For example, an *etic* (objective outsider) stance is one common position. With this stance a researcher (or research team) operates as an objective and dispassionate observer and analyst, collecting and analysing data using a theory-neutral observational and analytic language. In this orientation the researcher remains subjectively disengaged from influence on: the selection of data, the eventual meaning that is placed on the data, and its representative significance. From this perspective, validity is about: the extent to which phenomena of interest are represented. Utility or value is about the extent to which the findings are held to apply more generally, and reliability is about the extent to which successive replication of results is maintained across related population samples.

Alternatively, an *emic* (subjective insider) stance is another common position. From this orientation a researcher (or research team) operates as an engaged co-participant who deliberately and self-consciously works in the field with others, in a process that continually generates and makes sense of aggregate data. This sense-making evolves as reflexive field work. Such reflexivity is influenced by the collective meaning frames, biographical experience and world knowledge of the participants. It is also influenced by the researcher's curiosity about what the data discloses, as well as new questions it raises. From this position, validity of the findings is based on what the participants and the academy acknowledge are valuable specific and idiosyncratic descriptions, explanations and operational insights.

Methods refer to the procedures, tools, techniques and associated skills (such as sampling and interviewing) that are needed to perform the specific tasks required by the methodology. Some procedures, tools, techniques and skills may be predefined and well known, while some may be specifically devised and verified for the study. Procedures and tools tend to appear as objective artefacts (such as questionnaire construction and administration), whereas techniques and skills tend to appear as empirically and experientially grounded recitals (such as coding and reduction of qualitative data) which can be developed into repeatedly consistent performances.

To maintain a study's integrity and rigour, the choice and application of methods should be clearly described and justified. It must remain consistent with the chosen philosophy of science, the logic of inquiry and the methodology. Typical tasks for which specific methods are used include sampling, data generation (for instance, observation coding, item measurement, interviewing), statistical or text-based analysis, and presentation of findings. Choosing methods involves close attention to practical as well as theoretical (that is, investigative and substantive) requirements and constraints that must be addressed in order to maintain methodological consistency.

Particular methods and techniques are usually carefully chosen to implement particular tasks or even steps within tasks. The array of available methods and techniques is extremely large, with combinations of methods and techniques possibly being counted in the hundreds.

Examples of the wide range of tasks to which methods and techniques apply are:

- **literature reviews** (such as taxonomic analyses, citation networks, bibliometric analyses)

- **sampling** (for example purposeful sampling, random sampling, simulation)
- **data generation** (such as from forms of open interviewing and of embedded observation, event observation and measurement)
- **data reduction and analysis** (such as discourse analysis, statistical analysis, structural analysis of narrative text)
- **validation** (such as participant co-validation, peer reviews, replication)
- **presentation** of findings (for example as grounded concepts or structural equations)
- **reports** (including impersonal reports of findings as objective facts, relativist and personal accounts of the research).

The ubiquitous nature of many methods, the apparently well-defined procedures that accompany them, and the familiarity and certainty of the symbols and language that help convey their message can be appealing to the unsuspecting researcher. For the unwary researcher, the reassurance of familiar territory or common practice can encourage unjustifiable confidence and premature commitment to a method and its execution as the way to answer a research question.

As noted at the beginning of this section, the mental model in Figure 3.1 helps to avoid the pitfall of premature and inappropriate choice of method as the starting point rather than the end point of designing good science in research.

Meanings for elements of investigative practice (Figure 3.3)

Administrative and practical aspects of a research programme are called *investigative practice*, and the meanings of important aspects of such practice are introduced below.

A research **proposal** is the document that communicates the administrative aspects of a research programme, such as the main purpose and outcomes sought from the research, the expected benefits and the nature and levels of support needed to undertake the research properly. A full proposal will set out the main requirements and approach to be taken to administer and manage resources and facilities, compliance, quality, progress and stakeholder reporting. An effective research proposal clearly documents and persuades stakeholders to approve the programme's purpose, scope, approach, ethics and funding requirements. It will also alert research management to specific challenges and suggested approaches that may reasonably be expected to arise through the course of the research.

Research **ethics** is about identifying stakeholders and any corresponding ethical issues, risks, potential harm and consequent mitigation and/or response arrangements. Typically these can be expected to include policies and required procedures about empirical practices, administrative disciplines and oversight and accountability. Identifying and agreeing the way ethical issues are to be handled can often be expected to involve negotiation while accounting effectively for policy requirements. While administration and management of agreed ethical issues and treatments commences with a systematic and sensitive examination, assessment and negotiation of arrangements, it is also necessary to set out agreed-practice principles and methods for auditing and reporting implementation of agreements covering compliance and breaches. If failures in agreed ethical arrangements have serious adverse consequences for stakeholders and/or public policy interests, then principles of arrangements for treating breaches, and possible remedies, may also need to be outlined.

For most research programmes, ***funding*** is a major enabler or constraint. Suitable funds and the conditions that accompany access to funding sources, and conditions of release and accountability for their use, are inevitably an important determinant of the scope and duration of all but the most trivial research. Good research programmes include clearly specified and plausible arrangements to secure, allocate and account for funding. To this end, important elements of appropriate funding arrangements and their rationales should include a clear statement of the benefits that the study is expected to deliver. A clear statement is needed of the oversight arrangements to be employed, to ensure that funds provided are transparently and reliably linked to their effective use.

Schedules are an essential part of all well-organised and well-executed research programmes. Organising, contracting, timetabling, coordinating, controlling and reporting a study's activities, resources, facilities and funds through the unfolding course of an uncertain and changing landscape of field work (with its almost inevitable theoretical and practical problems) makes scheduling an often critical success factor in management research. Depending on the variety and complexity of the necessary schedules, expert advice may be needed to ensure their adequacy and mutual consistency.

Conduct refers to research management and administration of policies, activities, procedures and resources. It complements the hands-on work of the researcher's engagement in assembling and analysing the data as well as reporting the study. Administration and management of research helps to establish and maintain an effective balance between the research programme's evolving technical vision, scope and reports on the one hand, and its resources, support and outcomes on the other. It is an important aspect of effective research administration because issues emerging from consideration of a proposed programme's ethical, funding or scheduling requirements may be significant enough to force a rethink of some or all of a study's theoretical design.

Researchers should be alert to the changing experience and context of a research programme, and provide for practical and theoretical contingencies especially where risks are perceived to be high. For this reason there needs to be a preparatory and ongoing review of literature, covering not just new knowledge about substantive and methodological issues and the potential opportunities and threats for the study's aims and approach, but also the support arrangements that may enable continuation of the research.

Reporting refers to working papers, conference proceedings, journal papers, book chapters and books about the research as well as professional, industrial and press articles. Publication is a critical component of good research practice in much the same way as promoting innovations is as important as creating them.

Other key words used to describe aspects of a research programme

Figure 3.1 highlights several key words for various combinations of theoretical and practice aspects of research. Each of the words _paradigm, strategy, design, approach, administration, implementation_ and _programme_ has special meaning. The simple definitions apparent from Figure 3.1 are elaborated through Chapters 4 and 5, with illustrations and explanations of positivist, interpretivist and criticalist approaches to management research provided in Chapters 6, 7 and 8 respectively.

As already mentioned, since inconsistent use of terminology in the literature can sometimes confuse the reader who is in the early stages of reading research, we have paid particular attention to defining and illustrating terms in order that the reader can get behind the language and apprehend the meaning. Similarly, we strongly suggest that in documenting all aspects of research (from literature review through design and reporting) the researcher makes a point of clearly identifying key terms and their selected meanings, and making this accessible to readers.

Paradigm as we use it here embodies a combination of philosophy of science and logic of inquiry. This is rather different from the normal use of paradigm to refer to the philosophy of science alone. We use this definition because the specification of a logic of inquiry in the context of a philosophy of science is the most compact choice that determines highly distinctive and widespread, yet largely implicit, consequences for all remaining theoretical and practical aspects of a study.

Strategy refers to the distinctive combination of a logic of inquiry, methodology and stance. Because some methodologies can separately but consistently be implemented using different logics of inquiry, and because stance can vary within a combined logic of inquiry and methodology, all three must be specified and operate together before the criteria for rigour of a particular implementation can be determined. While a well-defined strategy implies only one philosophy of science, it is still appropriate to specify explicitly the chosen philosophy of science to ensure clarity and consistency in the research.

Design is the term we use when referring to the combination of methodology, researcher's stance and methods. It is this theoretical set that provides all detailed operational guidance in a study's empirical work. Design is what is often referred to when talking about a study's detailed theoretical blueprint. Design failures typically arise as failures of integrity or consistency within and between theory and practice; that is, the way in which research is designed and carried out.

Approach is the term we use to refer to all elements of investigative theory that define the study, but excluding the critically argued justification for the study's ontological and epistemological choices.

Administration refers to a study's business and contractual elements. Typically this covers the practical aspects of the research proposal, ethical and funding arrangements, and schedules of tasks, responsibilities, resources, facilities and timings that collectively describe the research activities that will be progressively undertaken. Administration typically involves the negotiation of suitable permissions and operating arrangements as well as communicating, organising support and participation, and reporting progress. Effective administration also supports the timely identification and resolution of challenges.

Implementation is the term we use when referring to all practical elements of the research that contribute to the transformation from abstract and theoretical constructs to reported finalisation. Implementation is focused on the role and activities of the researcher and other parties associated with the critical review of literature, access to and generation of data and the analysis of data, and the preparation and reporting of work, as well as emerging findings and their implications. Implementation also involves the progressive recording of a study's emerging limitations and strengths.

Programme is a term we use when referring to the whole study; that is, when referring to all the elements of the research's investigative theory and practice.

COMPARING CASES ACCORDING TO THE RESEARCH ROADMAP

Tables 3.1 and 3.2 juxtapose the three examples of the management of information systems (MIS) and the three examples of strategic marketing. The tables enable comparisons according to elements of the research approach, the consistency of which is a prerequisite of good research.

Table 3.1 highlights similarities and differences between three paradigmatically distinct modes of inquiry that correspond to three distinct types of question about a common topical issue in information management. Table 3.2 highlights similarities and differences between three paradigmatically distinct modes of inquiry that correspond to three different types of question about a common topical issue in strategic marketing. These two tables emphasize the point that it is not the topical issue that determines a particular research design but rather the form of question and its underlying purpose and context. The type of question suggests an appropriate paradigm, and as a consequence, an appropriate set of choices that are consistent with the paradigm's ontological and epistemological assumptions.

The strategic marketing examples used are about marketing and strategy effectiveness, mediating factors such as social and organisation culture and politics, and matters to do with competence development in marketing and strategic management. As with Table 3.1, Table 3.2 highlights choices using the mental model. These strategic marketing cases are further developed in later chapters.

Table 3.1 Checklist for internal consistency in three exemplary **MIS cases** representing three paradigms

MIS cases		Example 1 Information management practices	Example 2 Managing knowledge workers	Example 3 Business information systems investments
Question or hypothesis		Are alignment-capable managers more often linked with project success than are other managers?	What are distinctive characteristics of expert practice for managing knowledge workers?	Do (and how do) political and technical considerations influence executives' go/no-go decisions about investments in business information systems?
Philosophy of science	Ontology How reality is viewed	Positivist. Reality as objectively definable and independent of humans.	Constructionist. Reality as socially constructed by, and relative to, different humans.	Realist and relativist. A dual reality (e.g. as institutionalised as well as local and individualistic).
	Epistemology How knowledge is generated	Independent and objective. Positivism: Hypothetico-deductive. Linear process to generate confirmation or refutation of hypotheses derived from a theoretical position.	Relative and intersubjective. Hermeneutic interpretivism. Reflexive process to generate understanding of subjective meanings.	A composite of objective and inter-subjective data. Pragmatic critical theorising. Iterative process to generate description, explanation and the prospect of emancipation.
Argument **structure** and inquiry's main **logic**		Linear. Deductive reasoning builds and tests hypotheses. Inductive reasoning leads to generalisations.	Evolutionary (adaptive). Abductive reasoning to (re)construct typifications.	Iterative and evolutionary. Retroductive reasoning to repeatedly refine a theoretical model that is empirically grounded.

Table 3.1 continued

		Example 1 Information management practices	**Example 2** Managing knowledge workers	**Example 3** Business information systems investments
Methodology	**Purpose**	Nomothetic – qualify general findings.	Idiographic – describe specific cases.	Nomothetic – explain particular phenomena.
	Tactic	Using empirical data, test hypotheses deduced from theory.	Using participant experience, construct descriptive theory.	Using empirical data, construct explanatory transformative theory.
Researcher's stance		Etic. (The researcher is an outsider to the field of data; standing apart from the data and its source.)	Emic. (The researcher is an insider and so a participant in the generation of data.)	Etic~emic. (The researcher assumes an outsider or insider role in relation to data depending on the nature and purpose of the data.)
Main methods		Quantitative (e.g. statistical methods).	Qualitative (e.g. dialogic method).	Quantitative and qualitative (e.g. statistical and dialogic methods).
Approach and outcomes		Large-scale survey of managerial capabilities and project outcomes … *that results in* … Statistical correlations and measures of significance between pre- and post-hoc data.	Descriptive verbal and documentary data from focus groups and depth interviews. … *that generates* … Typifications of effective practices explained by managers and knowledge workers.	A typology of practice principles associated with executives' decision making. … *that results in* … A model of causal links between political and other considerations on the input side and decisions and their outcomes as outputs with recommendations for enhanced practice.

MIS cases

Table 3.2 Checklist for internal consistency in three exemplary **strategic marketing cases** representing three paradigms

Strategic marketing cases		**Example 4** Personal electronic goods and services	**Example 5** Deciding on competitive product portfolios	**Example 6** The politics of portfolio choices
Question or hypothesis		Are the sales of products or services affected more by price, functionality or brand recognition?	What characteristics of effective decision making help to make (more) competitive product portfolios?	How are executive preferences and choices for the firm's product portfolio mix informed and influenced by their organisation political contexts?
Philosophy of science	**Ontology** How reality is viewed	Positivist. Reality as objectively definable and independent of humans.	Constructionist. Reality as socially constructed by, and relative to, individuals.	Realist and relativist. A dual reality (e.g. as institutionalised as well as local and individualistic).
	Epistemology How knowledge is generated	Independent and objective. Positivism: Hypothetico-deductive. Linear process to generate confirmation or refutation of hypotheses derived from a theoretical position.	Relative and intersubjective. Hermeneutic interpretivism. Reflexive process to generate understanding of subjective meanings.	A composite of objective and inter-subjective data. Pragmatic critical theorising. Iterative process to generate description, explanation and the prospect of emancipation.
Argument structure and inquiry's main logic		Linear. Deductive reasoning builds and tests hypotheses. Inductive reasoning leads to generalisations.	Evolutionary (adaptive). Abductive reasoning to (re)construct typifications.	Iterative and evolutionary. Retroductive reasoning to repeatedly refine a theoretical model that is empirically grounded.

Table 3.2 continued

		Example 4 Personal electronic goods and services	Example 5 Deciding on competitive product portfolios	Example 6 The politics of portfolio choices
Methodology	**Purpose**	Nomothetic – create general findings.	Idiographic – describe specific cases.	Nomothetic – explain particular phenomena.
	Tactic	Using empirical data, test hypotheses deduced from theory.	Using participant experience, construct descriptive theory.	Using empirical data, construct explanatory normative theory.
Researcher's stance		Etic. (The researcher is an outsider to the field of data; standing apart from the data and its source.)	Emic. (The researcher is an insider and so a participant in the generation of data.)	Etic~emic. (The researcher assumes an outsider or insider role in relation to data depending on the nature and purpose of the data.)
Main methods		Quantitative. (e.g. statistical methods).	Qualitative (e.g. dialogic method).	Quantitative and qualitative (e.g. statistical and dialogic methods).
Approach and outcomes		Statistical analyses of sales and market data from surveys and other sources … *that results in* … Statistical correlations and measures of significance.	Observations, focus groups and depth interviews … *that generate* … Ideal-typical decision-making principles and practices associated with persistently competitive product portfolios.	A typology of practice principles associated with executives' decision making … *to produce* … A model of causal links between political and other considerations on the input side and decisions and their outcomes as outputs with recommendations for enhanced practice.

The rows above are also grouped under **Strategic marketing cases** for the example headings.

SUMMARY OF IMPORTANT PRINCIPLES

8

Good research clearly sets out and justifies the research problem, its context and its purpose with the accompanying choice of philosophy of science, the logic of inquiry, the research methodology, the stance that the researcher takes, and the study's particular methods and techniques.

Clearly stated and persuasively argued reasons for the research's purpose and its theoretical and practical scope, as well as the domains to which the research is expected to contribute, are all essential contributions to the quality of a piece of research.

Theoretical aspects of research can generally be recognised as discussion about philosophical issues that shape the identification, development and implementation of the study's overriding investigative logic, methodology and methods, as well as the critical review and treatment of topic theory from the literature that is concerned with the nature and practice of the management issues of interest.

In order to be considered as an important or even useful contribution to knowledge about management practice or management research, it is necessary, but not sufficient, for a study's investigative theory and practice to be in sync. Figure 3.4 depicts the range and type of considerations to be accounted for when balancing theoretical and practical dimensions of a research programme.

Figure 3.4

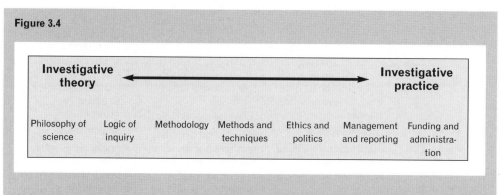

In business and management research, theoretical and practical aspects are closely connected and consistent

Good research is rigorous, with consistency between the study's assumptions and choices of ontology, epistemology, logic, methodology, stance and methods. Consistent, clear and concise statements and justifications of the study's aims and objectives are explicit; the scope is logical and practical; and implementation of the study's approach must remain mutually consistent, with the study's resources matching the focus and task of inquiry.

In conclusion, common characteristics of business and management research are reflected in rigorous attention to theoretical and practical aspects of inquiry, mutually consistent and coherent assumptions and arguments, and cogent and comprehensive development and reporting of the study. These characteristics can be generated in a systematic way using the mental model introduced in Figure 3.1.

ACTIVITIES AND RESOURCES

This section at the end of each chapter suggests further reading, and offers discussion and practice development activities.

EXERCISES AND QUESTIONS

1 (a) Discuss examples and meanings of a study's context and the core research question.
   (b) What implications arise from this for designing and conducting a study in which choices are explicit, mutually consistent and can be justified as appropriate?
2 From the literature, develop a list of definitions and meanings for each of the terms in Figure 3.1.
   (a) For each term, what common meanings are shared across the various definitions?
   (b) For each term, if there are distinct meanings, what seems to be the basis on which they are differentiated?
3 There are no universally accepted terms and meanings for aspects of research. The terms we use for elements of our research roadmap (or mental model for research, as we also call it) are working terms whose use is consistent throughout this book. They have been chosen to start the reader on the journey of understanding the science and art of research.
   (a) You are encouraged to build a glossary of terms and their various meanings – terms and meanings that vary depending on studies' substantive context, purpose and tradition.
   (b) What implications does this situation have for the way in which you record and report your research?
4 For further consideration and discussion of these forms of logical reasoning see Blaikie (2000, 2007).
5 (a) Find descriptions and illustrations of the logics of deduction, induction, abduction or retroduction.
   (b) Summarise these descriptions and illustrated meanings in your own terms, and provide examples from your own experience of everyday uses of these four logics.

6   For further discussion about methods see Blaikie (2000, 2003).

7   (a) Review some research proposals that won grant funding and some that failed to attract grant funding.

     (b) Discuss the differences that seem to separate the two groups of research proposals. What implications for research proposals arise from this comparison?

     (c) Similarly, compare research proposals for a group of successful research studies and proposals for problematic research studies. Are there any standout features that seem to separate successful studies from problematic studies?

8   Traditional reports have typically described ideas one after the other. Unfortunately this sequential presentation does not model important aspects of the research process, and especially the braiding of investigative theory and investigative practice in which analysis, planning and execution emerge more or less reflexively.

     (a) Suggest and find demonstrations of practical forms of recording and reporting 'non-linear' studies.

     (b) Review and discuss similarities and differences between the structure and style of positivist, interpretivist and criticalist studies. What lessons for reporting research arise from this comparison?

IN-DEPTH TOPICS

1   Familiarise yourself with a range of examples of outstanding business and management research studies.

     (a) Refine and/or extend the mental model we have introduced to account for common characteristics of exemplary studies which progressively become known to you.

2   Good research combines investigative theory and practice to produce clear vision and scope, consistent assumptions, compelling and lucid reasoning, and rigorous attention to theoretical and practical details. Good research also exhibits clear and persuasive evidence and argument for the importance of the central research question, and a clear rationale for the chosen form of science used to address the research question.

3   Some first-time readers may be surprised to find how different sciences produce different answers to the same question about the same substantive topic. This situation reflects a concept of knowledge and truth as being relative and idiosyncratic – that is, momentary and local as opposed to universal and permanent. This is a consequence of knowledge and truth being variously grounded in ontological and epistemological assumptions, which together form a philosophical foundation for a science.

4 (a) A logic comprises rules that are applied in order to generate a chain of consequences (propositions, constraints, possibilities and conclusions) based on foundational premises and the existence and absence of evidence.

   (b) Reasoning is the heuristic process that remains true to a chosen logic and that covers the purposeful assembly and interpretation of evidence; evidence being data in its presence and absence.

5 A methodology is an explicit and justified systematic application of a philosophy of science to a particular problem.

6 Defining and justifying a researcher's stance involves explicitly noting the relationship that a researcher has with the choice of, and rationale for, a study's methodology and the substantive data and its sources.

7 Methods are specific procedures, tools, techniques and associated skills (such as interviewing, observing, questionnaire design, statistical analysis). They are typically either established and widely understood, or purposively developed and independently confirmed for dependability before being used in specific steps or phases of a study's methodology.

8 Foundations for good research include:

   (a) The identification and pursuit of important questions.

   (b) Contextual sensitivity and fit: that is, explicit and contextually appropriate and mutually consistent scientific design and execution.

   (c) Critical appraisal of evidence and logical argument.

FURTHER READING

Blaikie, N. (2000) *Designing Social Research: The Logic of Anticipation*, Cambridge, Polity Press.

Chadwick, B. A., Bahr, H. M. and Albrecht, S. L. (1984) *Social Science Research Methods*, Englewood Cliffs, New Jersey, Prentice-Hall.

DeVaus, D. (2001) *Research Design in Social Research*, London, Sage.

Gill, J. and Johnson, P. (2002) *Research Methods for Managers,* London, Sage.

Easterby-Smith, M., Thorpe, R. and Lowe, A. (2002) *Management Research: An Introduction*, 2nd edn, London, Sage.

Jankowicz, A. D. (2005) *Business Research Projects*, 4th edn., London, Thomson Learning.

Kumar, R. (1996) *Research Methodology: A Step by Step Guide for Beginners*, Melbourne, Addison Wesley Longman Australia.

Punch, K. (2000) *Developing Effective Research Proposals*, London, Sage.

Sarantakos, S. (1998) *Social Research*, 2nd edn, Melbourne, Macmillan Education Australia.

Saunders, M., Lewis, P. and Thornhill, A. (2007) *Research Methods for Business Students*, 4th edn, Harlow, Essex, Pearson Education.

Veal, A. J. (2005) Business Research Methods: A Managerial Approach, 2nd edn, Sydney, Pearson Education Australia.

PART II

RESEARCH PARADIGMS

4

PHILOSOPHIES OF SCIENCE – THE BEDROCK OF GOOD RESEARCH

INTRODUCTION

We have discussed the importance of mutually consistent choices when developing a scientific approach that matches the purpose and character of a research task. In Chapter 3 we introduced a research roadmap (an all-important mental model) to guide the reflexive process of research design and implementation. In Chapters 6, 7 and 8 we illustrate the use of this mental model (Figure 3.1, page 23) for research approaches based on positivist, interpretivist and criticalist philosophies of science respectively. We use two examples for each of these chapters, one drawn from MIS research and one drawn from strategic marketing research. To help set the scene, a snapshot of some important similarities and differences between the three philosophical positions is presented in Tables 4.1, 4.2 and 4.3.

Table 4.1 Research aims and the form of inquiry reflect the philosophy of science

Aspect of research	Positivism	Interpretivism	Criticalist research
Purpose	Test theory or theoretical prediction.	Develop descriptive theory.	Develop theory to address real-world problems.
Using extant literature	Identify theory to test. Identify hypotheses to test the theory.	Identify need for theory. Develop sensitising concepts.	Select knowledge of structural nature. Identify approach to explain/change problem.
Form of inquiry	Develop hypotheses as posited relationships between variables.	Explore social world to develop key questions and new theory.	Empirical facts and tentative theory generate new questions and actions.
Tactic in conducting study	Hypotheses are fixed in order to test a theory. Theory is expanded, reinforced, confirmed, qualified or rejected.	Hypotheses emerge as meaning is constructed using building blocks of local integrating descriptive theory.	Combination of iterative hypothesis formation and hypothesis testing to build explanatory theory.

Table 4.1 highlights differences in the overall approach to the form of study depending on the chosen philosophy of science. Important differences are reflected in different fundamental aims of inquiry and forms of inquiry, as well as differences in the role of literature as being a primary or secondary basis for initiating or continuing inquiry.

Table 4.2 highlights differences between the way data are assembled and treated during inquiry. Important differences reflect, first, a linear, iterative or recurrent approach to assembling data; and second, a linear or threaded approach to assembling and analysing data and producing findings through the process of inquiry.

Table 4.3 highlights important differences that reflect, first, compact and objective accounts of metadata that describe the general fit between the studied phenomena and extant theory on the one hand, or elaborated and idiosyncratic exemplification of original data as structured cases or as typifying constructed local theory on the other. Second is the general and specific applicability of the findings to broader or narrower classes of phenomena.

Table 4.2 Approaches to assembling and analysing data reflect the chosen philosophy of science

Aspect of research	Positivism	Interpretivism	Criticalist research
Purpose of data	Test hypotheses. Typically answer IS~ARE (testing) questions.	Generate understanding. Typically answer WHAT (descriptive) questions.	Stimulate explanations. Answer HOW~WHY (causal) questions.
Nature of data	Collect data.	Generate data.	Combination of generation and collection.
Dealing with data	Analyse after all data collected.	Analyse concurrently with data generation.	Combination of analysis during and after data collection.
Purpose of analysis	Qualify hypotheses according to disconfirming evidence.	Produce typified meanings.	Imaginatively construct a mechanism that is validated by testing.
Process of data analysis	Statistical tests of significance.	Inductive generalisation or abductive distillation (reduction) to categories.	Iterative modelling.

Table 4.3 Similarities and differences between three philosophies of science

Aspect of research	Positivism	Interpretivism	Criticalist research
Validation	Validity as appropriate operationalisation of concepts and likely objective truth of resulting statistics.	Findings shared with participants who attribute a truth value to study's descriptions and interpretations.	Independent peer review.
Reporting	Often compact and quantitative.	Often detailed and qualitative.	Often a combination of quantitative and qualitative.
Generalisation	Produce generalisable findings and the possibility of making predictions about *general* phenomena.	Time and space specific. Deep understanding about particular or categorical phenomena.	Explanatory mechanisms to allow users to predict or explain or understand *specific* phenomena.
Representation	Nomothetic and objective statements.	Idiosyncratic and relativist statements.	Combined objective and nuanced view.

HELICOPTER VIEW OF THREE RESEARCH APPROACHES

Overwhelmingly nowadays doing empirical research requires a choice of one consistent guiding philosophical framework, and this is evident from an increasing majority of examiners who now regard the specification of the research paradigm and the justification for its choice to be mandatory in a thesis. As noted in Chapter 1, this guiding framework is usually called the research paradigm, and it reflects a fundamental choice about the philosophy of science and the scientific approach that is considered most appropriate to the purpose, context and focus of the research task.

PARADIGMS – GUIDES TO POSITIVIST, INTERPRETIVIST AND CRITICALIST APPROACHES

In this chapter we define and distinguish three alternative paradigmatic approaches for doing business and management research. Each paradigm has different characteristics. To make these paradigms more user friendly, we illustrate each as a template (see later Figure 4.8 (a template for positivist research), Figure 4.14 (a template for interpretivist research) and Figure 4.17 (a template for criticalist research)). Each template highlights important components of a research approach and the relationships between its components. We hope each template will serve as a roadmap which can help researchers to apply their chosen paradigm. Important characteristics of the three paradigms and key differences between them are also illustrated using an example about gender, education and income.

All research paradigms take a view of ontology (the assumed nature of reality being studied as realist or idealist/relativist) as a foundation step. It is the combination of a type of epistemology (a direct or indirect way of knowing – absolutist or constructionist) with the type of ontology (a view of reality) that defines and delineates the paradigm.

In this book about demonstrating how to conduct paradigmatically rigorous research, we have chosen to work with the three most cited research paradigms whose ontologies are sufficiently discrete. This enables the reader to see when important choices should be made.

In this conceptual arrangement, while some ontologies are not entirely discrete, other ontologies such as those implemented in positivism and interpretivism are widely seen as being diametrically opposed or at least distinctly different. This is shown in Collis and Hussey's (2003: 51) continuum of core ontological assumptions, in which reality is shown as:

- a concrete structure
- a concrete process
- a contextual field of information
- a realm of symbolic discourse
- a social construction
- a projection of human imagination.

The third paradigm in this book involves criticalist research, which introduces the notion that views and interpretations of reality may further be influenced by covert (unexpressed) phenomena such as power inequalities.

While there are further distinct paradigms that have been identified and applied in recent business and management research, our intention here is to introduce the three major paradigms and to illustrate their characteristics. In doing so we aim to reinforce the importance of, first, understanding the nature of all three in order to choose one at a time (the one that fits the character and purpose of a research project); and second, consistently specifying and implementing the relevant steps of the chosen paradigm.

In the philosophy of the social sciences, Blaikie (2007: 1–29) carefully distinguishes the conceptual possibility of six ontologies and six epistemologies. As this book concentrates on providing usable templates (roadmaps, or what we also refer to as mental models) for three popular paradigms for actually conducting research, the ontologies and epistemologies are typified and simplified. His ontologies for example take an overview of the various ways in which philosophers of the social sciences have handled the nature of reality, without necessarily differentiating the types of reality.

Each paradigm's template involves a series of contingent steps which must be taken by the researcher in order to complete a rigorous study. While the names of the steps are the same in each paradigm, the characteristics of the steps change subtly across each paradigm, as do the relationships between the steps. These steps are highlighted in the templates on pages 52 to 67 of this chapter.

In demonstrating the key differences between the three paradigms, it is important to be clear about types of questions that collectively demonstrate the differences between the paradigms. These are used to select, elaborate and confirm the choice and implementation of an appropriate paradigm. These types of questions and their interrelationships are depicted in Figure 4.1.

Figure 4.1

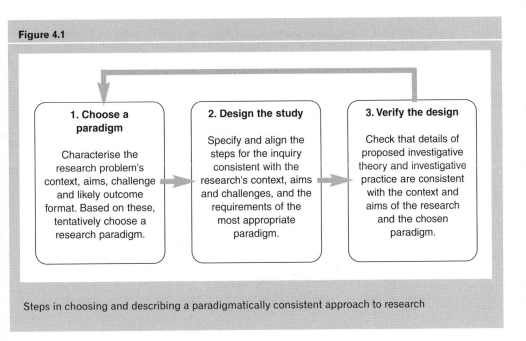

Steps in choosing and describing a paradigmatically consistent approach to research

Type 1 questions involve the derivation of a research question from a problem or a topic which specifies, or points to, a particular paradigm. For instance, if the general topic of interest is possible relationships between gender, education and income, and the aim is a study of historical or contemporary national profiles, a positivist paradigm (such as a statistical analysis from national census data) might initially appear to be appropriate.

However, if any relationship between the variables is to be explored in depth within a particular subset of the national population or within an industry, an interpretivist approach might provide more information. For instance, it could help in exploring what actually happens to men and women and how this relates to education, opportunity and income. Finally, if potential barriers to access opportunities are to be studied, a criticalist approach is indicated.

Type 2 questions are used to specify the steps needed to ensure a rigorous implementation of the research according to the chosen paradigm.

Type 3 questions are typically used to affirm, and where appropriate modify, the steps in the research design so the implementation of the chosen paradigm remains rigorous. Occasionally, a paradigm change may be needed if a fundamental change to the research question or the character of the research problem is indicated.

To help the reader to understand the three-step question-and-choice process noted in Figure 4.1, we illustrate the nature of business and management research and practice challenges that may readily be seen as positivist in nature; introduce a positivist template for conducting research into phenomena that can be viewed this way; and raise important questions that are used to identify, discriminate between and confirm the defining differences and character of the study to be conducted. The questions are: When is it appropriate to select a particular research paradigm or template? What is the relationship between extant theory and research concepts? What typical perception of reality (ontology) is assumed in the template's underlying philosophy? What sorts of questions does the paradigm's template typically address?

We need to ask what important theoretical and practical issues typically arise in relation to:

- the process of arguing from the data (for example, by induction, deduction, abduction or retroduction)
- the researcher's position (as outsider or insider)
- the nature of truth (objective or subjective, meaning realist or idealist/ relativist)
- the nature of data (text or numbers)
- the logic of inquiry (static or recursive)
- the form of the research product (for instance, documented or demonstrated)
- the use of research findings (generalizations or specific cases).

The example we use in the rest of this chapter

In this overview chapter we seek only to highlight major differences between the three paradigms or templates (depicted in Figure 4.2), and accordingly, the examples that follow (based on questions about gender, education and income) are indicative rather than exhaustive.

Example and template for a positivist approach

For the positivist example a hypothesis could be drawn up that, for similar levels of education (the independent variable), male income is significantly higher than female income (income being the dependent variable). To test this

Figure 4.2

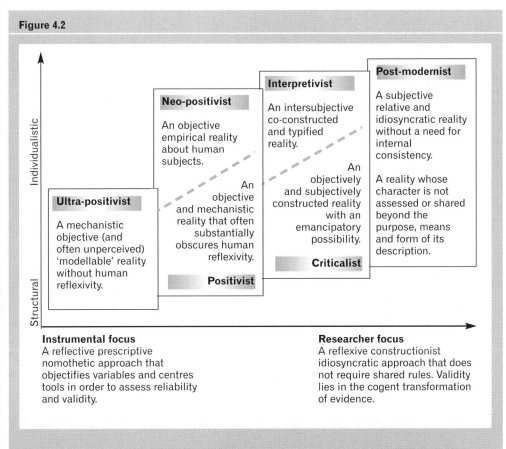

Differences between paradigms that influence fundamental choices in research design can be apprehended as differences in the way that inquiry and its context are subjectively or objectively framed

hypothesis we could choose a profession (such as law) and conduct a survey of practitioners in this profession over various appropriate geographical and practice areas in one jurisdiction (say a state, county or borough). This could be used to establish prima facie if there is a variation in income (the dependent variable) by gender for the same level of education. Statistical tests would be used to evaluate the hypothesised relationships between the dependent and independent variables.

Figures 4.3 to 4.7 illustrate elements of our template for this simple positivist example. The most obvious feature of this template is its linear format, in which each step is usually fully or substantially completed before the next. Figure 4.3 outlines the four major phases of the study, and Figure 4.4 to 4.7 show the main features of each phase.

Figure 4.3

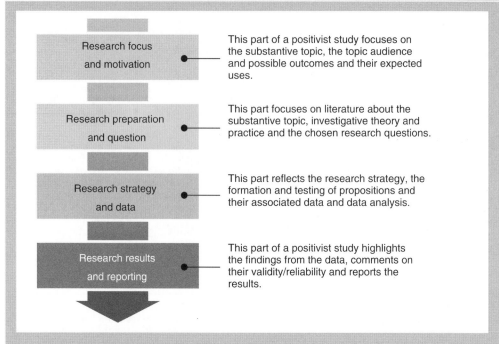

This part of a positivist study focuses on the substantive topic, the topic audience and possible outcomes and their expected uses.

This part focuses on literature about the substantive topic, investigative theory and practice and the chosen research questions.

This part reflects the research strategy, the formation and testing of propositions and their associated data and data analysis.

This part of a positivist study highlights the findings from the data, comments on their validity/reliability and reports the results.

Positivist studies typically progress through four phases in a linear step-by-step manner

Figure 4.4

Possible relationship between income and gender in the legal profession.

Legal profession in a given jurisdiction and timeframe.

Policy for professional development and remuneration.

A possible first phase (the substantive topic, topic audience and possible outcomes and use) of a positivist study of gender, education and income

Figure 4.5

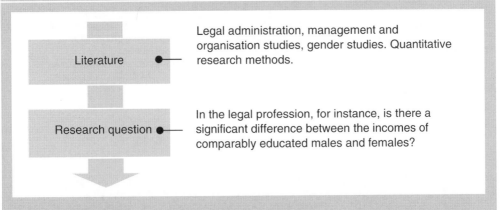

A possible second phase (literature and research question) for a positivist study of gender, education and income

Figure 4.6

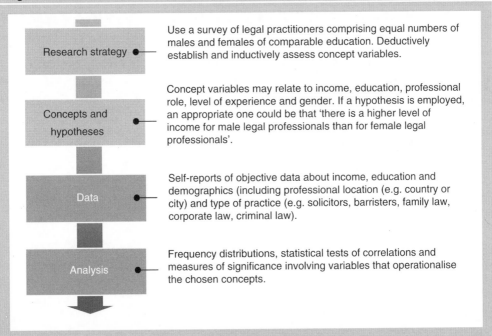

A possible third phase (research strategy and data) for a positivist study of gender, education and income

Figure 4.7

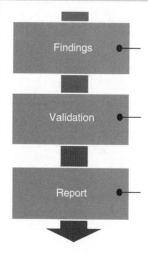

Findings — A conclusion that addresses the question based on patterns from surveys and (dis)confirming evidence about any hypotheses. Tentative answers to other questions from survey patterns and correlations between variables may be indicated.

Validation — Assessment and implications based on the scope of literature, samples used, concepts employed, choice of variables to operationalise concepts, and method and its rigour.

Report — Present the study's aims, scope, approach, findings about statistical relationships and their implications as well as reflections on the study's rigour and recommendations for further research and policy applications.

A possible fourth phase (research results and reporting) for a positivist study of gender, education and income

2   Figures 4.4 to 4.7 collectively form a template for positivist research. This template is summarised in Figure 4.8.

Figure 4.8

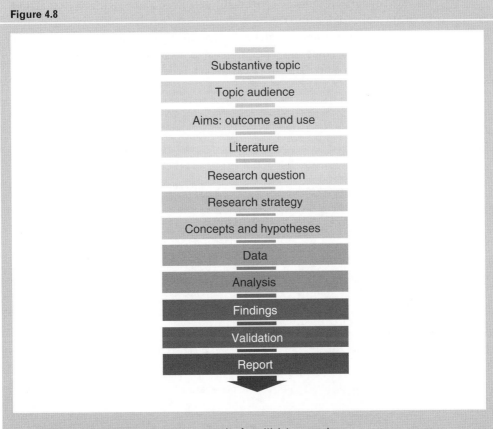

Template for the typical step-by-step approach of positivist research

Example and template for an interpretivist approach

For the interpretivist example about a research study into gender, education and income, rather than a hypothesis that aims to test theory, we would draw up questions. The study might ask male and female professionals of similar educational backgrounds whether they perceive any differences in the rewards and opportunities available to them, and if they do, what factors they think explain these. To explore and answer this question we would choose a profession (such as law) and conduct a survey of approximately equal numbers of similarly educated male and female lawyers in one jurisdiction (for instance, a state).

In-depth or focused interviews would be conducted with the respondents in order to explore concepts from the literature, and concepts that emerge from participants' reported experiences and the meanings they draw from them. In this way, qualitative data are continually generated and progressively analysed to create new insights into the topic.

These emerging findings can be checked with participants to validate their suitability as succinct but comprehensive accounts of how rewards and opportunities operate. The overall approach is depicted in Figure 4.9.

Figure 4.9

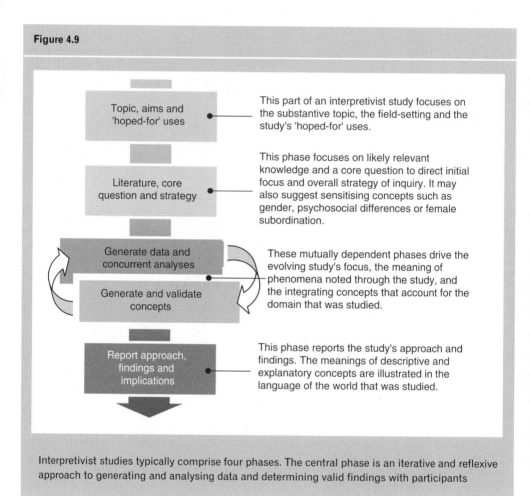

Topic, aims and 'hoped-for' uses

This part of an interpretivist study focuses on the substantive topic, the field-setting and the study's 'hoped-for' uses.

Literature, core question and strategy

This phase focuses on likely relevant knowledge and a core question to direct initial focus and overall strategy of inquiry. It may also suggest sensitising concepts such as gender, psychosocial differences or female subordination.

Generate data and concurrent analyses

Generate and validate concepts

These mutually dependent phases drive the evolving study's focus, the meaning of phenomena noted through the study, and the integrating concepts that account for the domain that was studied.

Report approach, findings and implications

This phase reports the study's approach and findings. The meanings of descriptive and explanatory concepts are illustrated in the language of the world that was studied.

Interpretivist studies typically comprise four phases. The central phase is an iterative and reflexive approach to generating and analysing data and determining valid findings with participants

The process shown in Figure 4.9 is largely linear but appears to contain two mutually dependent steps. In most cases, however, and especially in substantial and challenging interpretivist studies, it is the two mutually dependent generative steps (generate data and concurrent analyses, and generate and validate concepts) that are the major and most challenging part of the study.

The components of each of the four phases of a typical interpretivist study are shown in Figures 4.10 to 4.13. We continue to use the example of a study of gender, education and income.

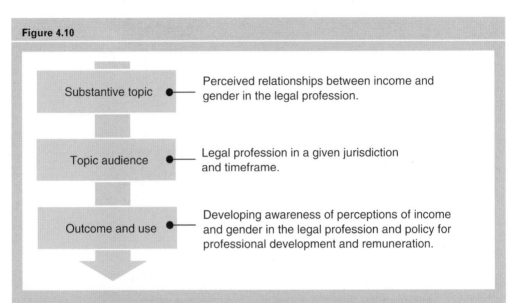

Figure 4.10

Substantive topic — Perceived relationships between income and gender in the legal profession.

Topic audience — Legal profession in a given jurisdiction and timeframe.

Outcome and use — Developing awareness of perceptions of income and gender in the legal profession and policy for professional development and remuneration.

A possible first phase (the substantive topic, client audience and possible outcomes and use) of an interpretivist study of gender, education and income

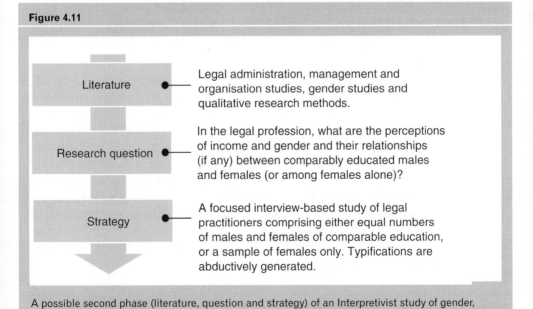

Figure 4.11

Literature — Legal administration, management and organisation studies, gender studies and qualitative research methods.

Research question — In the legal profession, what are the perceptions of income and gender and their relationships (if any) between comparably educated males and females (or among females alone)?

Strategy — A focused interview-based study of legal practitioners comprising either equal numbers of males and females of comparable education, or a sample of females only. Typifications are abductively generated.

A possible second phase (literature, question and strategy) of an Interpretivist study of gender, education and income

Figure 4.12

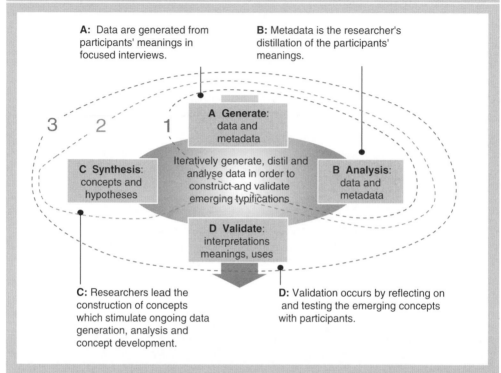

A possible third phase (generating and analysing data and deriving and validating concepts as theoretical descriptors and explanations) of an interpretivist account of gender, education and income

Important characteristics of the third phase of interpretivist study are the successive cycles (1, 2, 3 in Figure 4.12) in which data are generated and analysed in order to identify specific patterns and subtle distinctions, as might a taxonomist. This leads to integrating concepts that serve to comprehensively yet succinctly describe, and sometimes even explain, the phenomena being studied. The other distinctive activity step in this third phase is validation. Here representatives of the phenomena being studied (including but not limited to participants) test and confirm the merits of the concepts as meaningful and reliable ways of describing and accounting for the phenomena.

Together, Figures 4.10 to 4.13 provide a template for interpretivist research. This template is summarised in Figure 4.14.

Figure 4.13

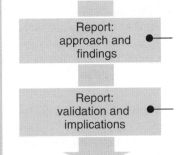

Present the study's aims, scope, approach and strategy. Present themes, typifications and implications of perceived relationships between gender and income in the legal profession.

Summarise the manner of validation of the findings and discuss the implications of the findings in terms of their possible uses and limitations.

A typical fourth phase (reporting the validated findings) in an interpretivist research project on gender, education and income

Figure 4.14

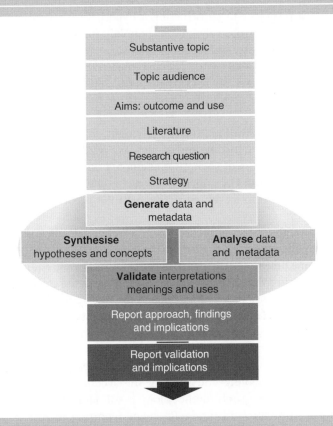

Template for the typical hybrid linear-recursive approach of interpretivist research

Example and template for a criticalist approach

In the criticalist example, a working hypothesis emerges from exploratory research which may be based on any paradigmatic approach, but quickly leads to a sense that there is some structured inequality that might be influencing reality. Using the same example as previously, the structured inequality would relate to gender differences leading to differences in professional opportunity. In order to reveal what may be deliberately or unconsciously hidden, we use a combined nomothetic and idiographic stance.

First, we develop a research question that is designed to progressively reveal confirming and disconfirming evidence for the tentative hypothesis. The aim is to judge how successful it is in challenging social constructions that are taken for granted, that might be either explicit or covert, and that might operate to systematically disadvantage some individuals or groups. Once it becomes apparent what social constructions might play this role, the researcher increasingly focuses on exploring their nuances and the mediating arrangements and resulting impacts that gender differences may have on professional opportunity and rewards.

As a precursor to constructing a hypothetical model, we use a literature search and a purposively chosen sample. The researcher combines concepts from the literature, and secondary statistical data on income and gender, with collection and analysis of primary objective survey data and in-depth or focused interviews (such as participants' reported experiences, observations and explanatory accounts). These data are then creatively synthesized into a tentative model.

Next, disconfirming evidence is sought, in the form of further secondary statistical data on income and gender. As a result of this, the initial model may be iteratively refined. Then, through more primary data generation, the model is further refined. The underlying logic in these steps is to look for disconfirming evidence. In its absence the plausibility of the hypothesised model increases.

Throughout this approach the researcher's practice skills and theoretical imagination combine to mediate the emerging focus and scope of the study. At the same time the participants' experience, power and equity interests combine to increasingly mediate the validation and use of the emerging model.

The changing proportional role of the researcher in relation to the participants is depicted in Figure 4.15, which highlights the following dynamic. First, the researcher dominates initial design work and participants are involved to the extent that their knowledge about the substantive topic is accessed together with their needs and motivations. Then participants play an increasing part in enabling and shaping the accumulation and analysis of data, although the research methodology is still largely driven by the researcher. Finally, through validation, refinement, reporting and use of findings, participants take the lead role in determining the constraints and focus for deploying

Figure 4.15

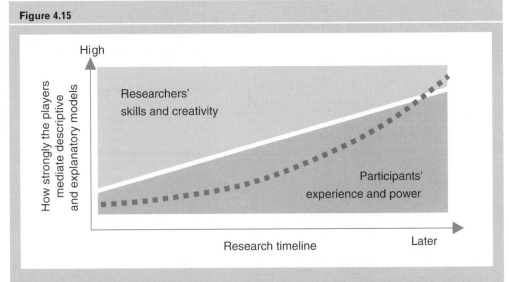

A criticalist research programme may be developed so that the initial descriptive and explanatory model proposed by the researcher evolves into a prescriptive or predictive model that is accepted and used by participants and others

practice initiatives that are informed by the research. The researcher is more likely to now be an observer and reference source who is called on to help with deployment and with the use of the research findings.

As validation of the emerging model is linked to the views of participants, the hypothesised model may be either validated or invalidated by participants. Because of the overt and covert nature of power, this validation or invalidation may be controversial. In either event the researcher must carefully design explicit processes of validation.

If different stakeholders (such as institutional power brokers and disadvantaged minorities) agree that the model reflects their reality, this will act as confirming evidence for it; if they agree that it does not, it will be disconfirming evidence of the model's merit In this way the researchers and participants will collectively present an evolving view of reality through iterative accumulation of data and its concurrent analysis and validation.

This criticalist research approach stands as a basis for informing policy as well as helping to provide guides on how policy may be implemented. Figure 4.16 depicts a typical criticalist research approach using our simple example.

A distinctive feature of this template is the overlapping nature of the various modes of research activity. This emphasises the reflexive nature of the research process, in which the very purpose of the study and its potential findings and uses may be mediated by the participants and audience as much as by the researcher(s).

Figure 4.16

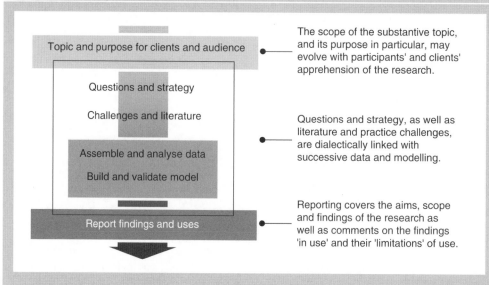

The scope of the substantive topic, and its purpose in particular, may evolve with participants' and clients' apprehension of the research.

Topic and purpose for clients and audience

Questions and strategy

Challenges and literature

Assemble and analyse data

Build and validate model

Questions and strategy, as well as literature and practice challenges, are dialectically linked with successive data and modelling.

Report findings and uses

Reporting covers the aims, scope and findings of the research as well as comments on the findings 'in use' and their 'limitations' of use.

Major modes of a criticalist research approach

Figure 4.17

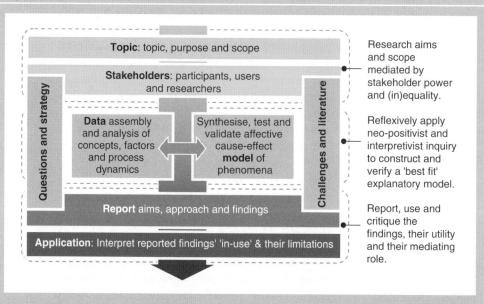

Template for typical criticalist research which develops an explanatory and predictive model from 'externally framed objective data' and 'internally framed subjective data' to account for power-equity differences between stakeholders

A slightly more expanded representation of the modes of criticalist research and their relationships is shown in Figure 4.17. This depicts the overlapping nature of all the modes, and in particular, the overarching and concurrent roles of 'Questions and strategy' and 'Challenges and literature' in informing and being informed by the assembly and analysis of data and the synthesising and testing of successive explanatory models.

Typically, criticalist research reflexively combines interpretivist and neo-positivist forms of inquiry into different but related aspects of the phenomenon of interest. Reflexivity is often in the form of a dialectic between, first, the evolving high-level purpose, scope and approach to inquiry, and second, a detailed-level synthetic and analytic process that produces progressively better explanatory models to account for, and predict, the phenomenon of interest. Figure 4.17 tries to show this.

The research modes shown in Figure 4.17 are linked through a process that aims to successively generate increasingly more informative and revealing explanations that account for comprehensive retrospective data, and predictions designed to disconfirm the best explanatory model constructed so far. Central to this process is the researcher's theoretical imagination, which is best supported by their familiarity with the field of inquiry and a wide survey of literature. It is also essential to develop a disciplined way to retroductively affirm or modify tentative theoretical models using primary and secondary empirical data.

The process of creating more comprehensive and rugged models ceases when, despite diligent effort, disconfirming evidence can no longer be generated or located, and when the best explanatory model meets acceptable descriptive and explanatory criteria that are set by researcher(s) and by representative participants from the field of inquiry.

To provide an example of the sorts of choices that this research approach suggests, we shall again use research about remuneration and gender in the legal profession.

The components of each of the three phases of a typical criticalist study (as shown depicted in Figure 4.17) are outlined below and summarised in Figures 4.18 to 4.21.

Figure 4.18 shows how the *focus* may be, for instance, on objective and subjective relationships between gender, qualifications and income in the legal profession, with the aim of establishing an explanatory and prescriptive (or predictive) model to inform policy and facilitate change. A core group of *stakeholders* could be considered as the cohort of male and female legal practitioners, legal practice industry bodies and academic institutions who train practitioners and also research in the field.

Figure 4.18 also introduces the criticalist agenda of seeking to construct explanatory and prescriptive *models* that account for power and differences between stakeholders. This political dimension may become apparent through many, if not all, of the steps of a criticalist study. For instance, the study's *focus*

Figure 4.18

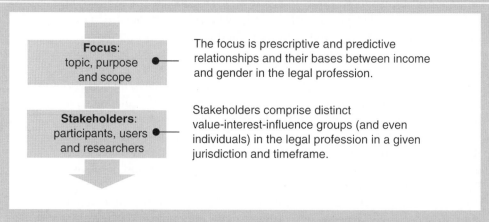

In criticalist research, the research focus and stakeholders are mutually dependent and may continue to shape the research

may be subject to the perceptions and positions of employees, managers, policy makers and related industry groups, and each of these groups may have separate interests in focusing and bounding the study, its findings and possible uses. These perceptions and positions may reflect diverse social structures and beliefs, corporate motives, professional concerns and personal intentions as far as income levels, qualifications and gender are concerned.

In terms of our salary-gender-qualifications example, Figure 4.19 shows how *strategy* may be the progressive construction of a working hypothesis from stakeholders and from literature. This would evolve as nomothetic and idiographic stances are combined through deductive, inductive and abductive logic to construct a model of patterned inequalities which is then retroductively validated.

Literature could be expected to span professional, industry and academic publications and exhibitions that underpin both statistical and idiographic insights about regularities, trends and diverse perspectives on historic and current arrangements. This will then inform the construction and testing of an initial model linking income and gender.

Questions might focus on two areas of interest: first, patterns and explanations, partly structured by elements of inequality, that may account for linkages between remuneration and gender arrangements in the legal profession; and second, whether there are groups within the legal profession who wish to alter the status quo.

Challenges may be expected to include matters to do with how we recognise, illuminate and deal with covert differences in realities (including opportunities), and the nature of the researcher's role in political studies in

Figure 4.19

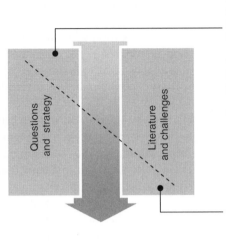

Question: in the legal profession is there a significant difference between the incomes of comparably educated and experienced males and females?

Strategy: construct a tentative model from literature, statistics and participants' perceptions and experiences and iteratively refine it for explanatory and predictive strength.

Literature: about legal administration, management and organisation studies, gender studies and quantitative~qualitative research.

Challenges: are political and technical and so must recognise and deal with multifaceted aspects of power, knowledge and disclosure at individual, interpersonal, group and institutional levels.

Four modes of a typical criticalist research approach

which stakeholders' positions about reality or change may be unclear and/or contested.

These are illustrations of the nature of strategy, literature, questions and challenges, but there are some more general aspects that are also worth noting at this introductory stage.

Criticalist research typically formulates and deals with two classes of questions: first, questions about variables and their interrelationships, and second, questions about power and (in)equality between stakeholders. In Figure 4.19 the core question about salary, qualifications and gender variables may be elaborated with sub-questions about substantive and mediating variables (such as employee status). The researcher helps to reveal and illuminate the way in which power and differences between stakeholders influence the study's variables and their interrelationships with questions like 'Is there a structure of (in)equality that is differentially perceived by stakeholders?' and 'Is political influence present/absent in the study's scope or conduct?'

The research strategy sequences the research questions and indicates how they will be answered; typically combining statistical data-oriented inquiry with (inter)subjective inquiry about stakeholders' perceptions and accounts of what happens and why.

Literature refers not only to publications about studies and practice in the substantive field, but also to publications about modes and methods of inquiry and their contextual efficacy.

Methodological and substantive challenges of a conceptual and practical nature inevitably limit a study. For this reason an important early design task is to negotiate the study's scope and likely deliverables so as to best balance the requirements for disciplined research with the need for informative and helpful outcomes.

Formulation and clarity about questions, strategy, literature and challenges more or less evolve as a criticalist study progresses. It is mutual consistency between these four aspects that helps to ensure informative and useful progress with the twin detailed tasks of assembling and analysing data, and constructing and testing a satisfactory explanatory and predictive model. The result is a succession of models that are refined and tested so as to eventually offer the most comprehensive and reliable explanatory, predictive and prescriptive model. This model can then be used to enhance representation and equity rather than amplify the disenfranchising use of power.

Assembling and analysing data, and then synthesising and testing or validating an acceptable explanatory and prescriptive or predictive model, may be expected to include the concurrent generation and analysis of primary

Figure 4.20

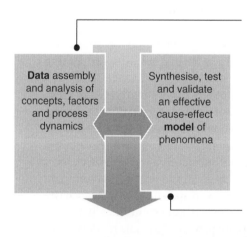

Data typically comprises statistical data about employees' salary, gender and qualification as well as participants' own specific comments about practices, experiences and their explanations about the nature of, and motivations for, perceived practices.

Data assembly and analysis of concepts, factors and process dynamics

Synthesise, test and validate an effective cause-effect **model** of phenomena

Tentative models that attempt to explain the what, how and why of qualification, gender and salary outcomes are constructed and tested to best fit objective/structural data and personal accounts of actual practice and its perceived rationale.

In a criticalist study, data and modelling activities co-evolve objective survey data and in-depth subjective data from focused interviews. The purpose is to establish mutually consistent typified concepts from regularities in the data. Progressive synthesis of emerging hypotheses and analytic constructs is expected to evolve and refine a model which is constantly tested against an active search for disconfirming evidence. Validation is expected to involve a deliberate and ongoing process in which different stakeholders react to the model's basis and utility.

Figure 4.21

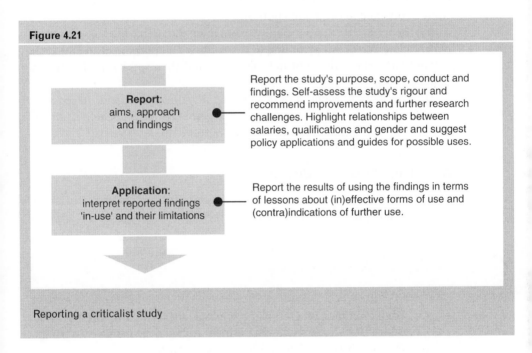

Reporting a criticalist study

Finally, there are two major aspects to reporting a criticalist study. The first aspect is about the study's aims, scope, approach, strategy, findings and their implications, as well as reflections on the study's rigour and recommendations for further work. Describing the findings requires a description of the model that illuminates previously covert realities and also provides policy options. The second aspect presents reflective comments about the study's design and conduct, and suggestions about issues for further study and how this might be carried out. The second aspect would follow findings in practice in the event that such experience exists. Reports of such experience would comment on insights from use of the findings and the results that arose from such use, as well as suggestions about aspects of the findings that were affirmed or challenged and tips for targeting further application.

CONCLUSION

Our explanation in this chapter of the three paradigms we have focused on, and the details of how they could be put into practice using the example about income and gender in the legal profession, should show that we can expect dramatic variations in the research design, consequent revelatory power and knowledge that is likely to arise from a study conducted within different research paradigms, even when the topic is the same. So, it follows that the choice of paradigm must reflect a prudent judgement about the fit between the study's context and the study's purpose.

It is the researcher's responsibility to weigh up the strengths and weaknesses of candidate paradigms according to the context and purpose of the research before finally choosing a research paradigm and then specifying the study's design details.

The templates introduced in this chapter are offered as a guide to research according to each of the three paradigms. Together with the research roadmap in Figure 3.1, the templates serve heuristic purposes for researchers.

ACTIVITIES AND RESOURCES

This section at the end of each chapter suggests further reading, and offers discussion and practice development activities.

 EXERCISES AND QUESTIONS

1   (a) Find examples of exemplary seminal positivist, interpretivist and criticalist research studies in business and management research.
    (b) On what basis are they considered exemplary?
    (c) What systematic ways are there of finding (reputedly) exemplary research studies?

2   (a) Construct a comparative table (the same as, or an alternative to Tables 4.1, 4.2 and 4.3) that highlights important differences and similarities between the exemplary studies identified in Exercise 1. (Note: this exercise can usefully be extended to cover other forms of scientific study in business and management research, and not just positivist, interpretivist and criticalist forms of research.)

3   (a) Identify some of the debates that persist in relation to the concept of scientific paradigms and scientific traditions.
    (b) Note the implications for choosing, justifying and applying a particular scientific paradigm to a business or management research problem of interest to you, or to one that you know is of major importance.

4   (a) From your readings in the philosophy of science, develop your own

meanings and illustrations for the following terms: objective, subjective, intersubjective, meaning, truth, realist, idealist, relativist.

(b) When meanings in the literature differ, consider the contexts in which these different meanings apply, and note the implications that arise for developing a working concept of science.

IN-DEPTH TOPICS

1   Construct, in your own terms, and with illustrations that you have directly experienced, descriptions and examples of the meaning of ontology and epistemology.

2   (a) Examine the structure of a variety of exemplary or seminal positivist research studies.

   (b) To what extent do they broadly fit the template shown, and do they share a structural pattern that is distinctly different from that shown in the template (Figure 4.8)?

3   (a) Examine the structure of a variety of exemplary or seminal interpretivist research studies.

   (b) To what extent do they broadly fit the template shown, and do they share a structural pattern that is distinctly different from that shown in the template (Figures 4.9 to 4.13 and combined in Figure 4.14)?

4   (a) Examine the structure of a variety of exemplary or seminal criticalist research studies.

   (b) To what extent do they broadly fit the template shown, and do they share a structural pattern that is distinctly different from that shown in the template (Figure 4.17)?

N.B.: As the basis for designing and conducting a rigorous research study, the choice of a scientific paradigm must consider, and justify (through evidence and logical argument), the fit between the study's context (for example, the characteristics of the substantive phenomenon of interest) and the study's specific purpose, focus and core research question.

FURTHER READING

Anderson, R. J., Hughes, J. A. and Sharrock, W. W. (1987) *Classic Disputes in Sociology*, London, Allen & Unwin.

Babbie, E. (2008) *The Basics of Social Research: Issues, Methods and Process*, 2nd edn, Ballmoor, Buckingham, Open University Press.

Blaikie, N. (2007) *Aproaches to Social Enquiry*, 2nd edn, Cambridge, Polity Press.

Bulmer, M. (1982) *The Uses of Social Research: Social Investigation in Public Policy-Making*, Contemporary Social Research Series, London, George Allen & Unwin.

Bulmer, M. (ed.) (1982) *Social Research Ethics: An Examination of the Merits of Covert Participant Observation*, London, Macmillan Press.

Chalmers, A. E. (1976) *What is this Thing called Science?* St. Lucia, University of Queensland Press.

Hughes, J. (1976) *Sociological Analysis: Methods of Discovery*, Walton-on-Thames, Surrey, Nelson.

Hughes, J. (1980) *The Philosophy of Social Research*, New York, Longman.

Lewins, F. (1992) *Social Science Methodology: A Brief but Critical Introduction*, South Melbourne, Macmillan Education Australia.

May, T. (1997) *Social Research: Issues, Methods and Process*, 2nd edn, Ballmoor, Buckingham, Open University Press.

Outhwaite, W. (1987) *New Philosophies of Social Science: Realism, Hermeneutics and Critical Theory*, London, Macmillan Education.

Sayer, A. (1984) *Method in Social Science: A Realist Approach*, London, Hutchinson.

5

ILLUSTRATING THREE PARADIGMS IN ACTION: A GUIDE TO THE NEXT THREE CHAPTERS

Following on from the six research examples outlined in Chapter 2, the next three chapters illustrate in more detail key elements of the three paradigms in action. Chapter 6 discusses the positivist paradigm, Chapter 7 the interpretivist paradigm and Chapter 8 elaborates the paradigm of criticalist research. Each of these chapters highlights, then details, specific features of important components of each paradigm so you can gain an overall appreciation of typical essential characteristics and differences between the paradigms. This approach emphasises the importance of fitting investigative theory and investigative practice to the context and purpose of each research problem.

Each of the following three chapters is presented in three sections. The first section reminds the reader of major elements of investigative *theory* and investigative *practice* that typify the research paradigm being illustrated. *Theory* spans the research question, the philosophy of science, principal logic of inquiry, research methodology, researcher's stance and research methods. *Practice* spans the proposal, ethics, funding, scheduling, conduct and reporting.

The second section summarises, in a tabular format, important principles of research theory and practice that apply to two examples provided in the chapter. This helps the reader to apprehend at a glance important aspects of investigative theory and practice to consider when formulating a research approach.

The third section of each chapter presents two examples of research planning choices and their rationale, which span investigative theory and investigative practice for the research paradigm on which the chapter focuses. Each chapter provides one information management and one strategic marketing example.

RESEARCH DESIGN AND IMPLEMENTATION CHOICES

The choices that researchers make reflect awareness of philosophical, epistemological and practical issues and possible responses. When taken together, these more or less reflect the power, suitability and rigour of a research-based approach to addressing a challenging inquiry.

Principles of what constitutes good research usually reflect at least two things: general principles that apply to many paradigms, and specific principles that only hold for specific paradigms. Taken together, patterned evidence of the general and specific principles is a basis for doing and also assessing research.

Important decisions that collectively help to typify a paradigm in action are informed by a combination of the nature and context of the substantive research topic, the research roadmap and the character of the selected paradigm. This is shown in Figure 5.1.

Each of Chapters 6, 7 and 8 uses an information management and a strategic marketing example to highlight considerations that reflect the paradigm choice and research roadmap in action. Tables 5.1 to 5.6 summarise these six examples.

Figure 5.1

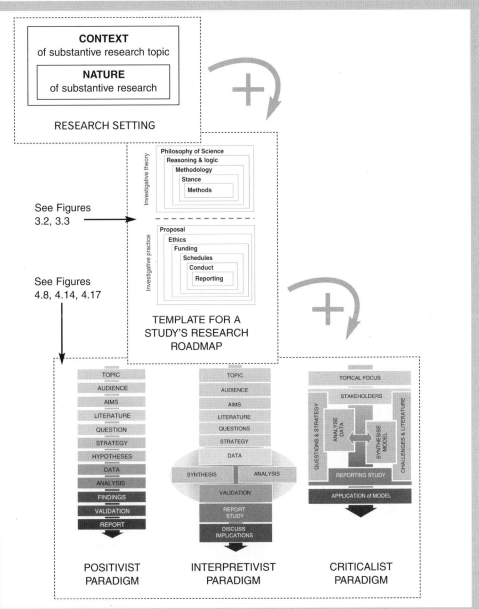

Research design and implementation choices are successively informed by three perspectives

Table 5.1 Illustrative elements of investigative theory when proposing, scoping, resourcing and managing a **positivist study**

Investigative theory			
Positivist research		**Example 1** Information management	**Example 4** Electronic service goods
Question or hypothesis		Are alignment-capable managers more often linked with project success than other managers?	Are the sales of products and services more affected by price, functionality or brand recognition?
Philosophy of science	**Ontology** How reality is viewed	**Positivist** Reality is assumed to be objectively definable and exists independently of humans.	
	Epistemology How knowledge is generated	**Independent and objective** A hypothetico-deductive structure which follows a linear process to generate confirmation or refutation of hypotheses derived from a theoretical position.	
Argument **structure** Inquiry's main **logic**		**Linear** **Deductive** reasoning builds and tests hypotheses. **Inductive** reasoning leads to tentative generalisations.	
Methodology	Purpose	**Nomothetic** – create and qualify general findings.	
	Tactic	Using empirical data, test hypotheses deduced from theory.	
Researcher's **stance**		**Etic** – the researcher operates as a dispassionate outsider.	
Main **methods**		**Quantitative** (e.g. statistical methods).	
Approach and outcomes		Large-scale survey of managerial capabilities and project outcomes *… that results in …* statistical correlations and measures of significance.	Statistical analysis of sales and market data from surveys and other sources *… that results in …* statistical correlations and measures of significance.

Table 5.2 Illustrative elements of investigative practice when proposing, scoping, resourcing and managing a **positivist study**

Investigative practice		
Positivist research	**Example 1** Information management	**Example 4** Electronic service goods
Proposal focus to highlight …	The importance of alignment scores as indicators of alignment capability and its importance in reducing the high failure rate of investments in IT systems.	The importance of knowing the comparative significance of price, functionality and brand on buying decisions.
Indicative **ethical** issues	Institutional discrimination that may constrain the study, taint the data and limit or result in misuse of findings.	Biasing the sample or the data and using results to manipulate unwitting customers.
Likely **funding** sources	Prospective value of the study invites government, industry and firm funding and in-kind support.	Funding to be sought from individual firms that might benefit from results.
Significant **scheduling** considerations	Operationalise the concept of alignment and administer the survey instruments to the sample.	Sampling, administration and analysis of questionnaire.
Key **conduct** factors	Organisationally and socially sensitive research administration and management as well as sound technical supervision of the research.	
Reporting	(a) Importance of the study for improved firm and industry practice (b) Ethical expression and use of findings (c) Further research challenges.	

Among other commonalities, both positivist examples feature:

- an objective nature of the reality studied
- standardisation of research instrument
- measurable variables
- direct apprehension of reality (positivist epistemology).

Table 5.3 Illustrative elements of investigative theory when proposing, scoping, resourcing and managing an **interpretivist study**

Investigative theory			
Interpretivist research		**Example 2** Managing knowledge workers	**Example 5** Deciding on competitive product portfolios
Question or hypothesis		What are the distinctive characteristics of expert practice for managing knowledge workers?	What characteristics of effective decision making help make (more) competitive product portfolios?
Philosophy of science	**Ontology** How reality is viewed	**Constructionist** Reality as perceived relative to a participant's explicit and enacted experience and consequently being socially constructed by, and relative to, different humans.	
	Epistemology How knowledge is generated	**Relativist and intersubjective.** A process of reflexive hermeneutic interpretation of intersubjective experience generates and validates meanings and associated theory.	
Argument **structure** Inquiry's main **logic**		**Adaptive** (evolutionary) . **Abductively** create and verify theoretical concepts from abstracted significations. **Inductively** reason and test creatively founded themes and theoretical concepts that are grounded in data about experience.	
Methodology	Purpose	**Idiographic** – describe the nuances of specific instances and their distinctively idiosyncratic meanings and, from this, form an integrating set of descriptive and/or explanatory concepts and principles.	
	Tactic	Iteratively generate intersubjective data with participants and, in parallel with data generation, construct descriptive/explanatory theory.	
Researcher's **stance**		**Emic**: the researcher explicitly operates as a (quasi) insider with the research sample.	
Main **methods**		**Qualitative** (e.g. hermeneutic analysis of language within a dialogic method).	
Approach and outcomes		Focus groups and depth interviews . . . *that result in* . . . typifications of effective practices explained by managers and knowledge workers.	Observations, focus groups and depth interviews . . . *that result in* . . . ideal typical decision making principles and practices associated with persistently competitive product portfolios.

Table 5.4 Illustrative elements of investigative practice when proposing, scoping, resourcing and managing an **interpretivist study**

	Investigative practice	
Interpretivist research	**Example 2** Managing knowledge workers	**Example 5** Deciding on competitive product portfolios
Proposal focus to highlight …	(a) The importance of knowing distinctive features of expert management practice as well as improved ways to know this. (b) The value of a tentative theory of expert practice to help manage knowledge workers.	(a) The value of better understanding effective decision practices and the study scope needed for this outcome. (b) The value of alternative marketing strategies to better match consumer preferences.
Indicative **ethical** issues	Protect weak participants and employees from adverse impact of disclosures in the study, and avoid preferential treatment of stronger interested parties.	Manipulation of data and support by stakeholders with competing values, interests and influence with resulting possible discrimination between customer segments.
Likely **funding** sources	Government funding support as well as industry and specific firm support.	Funding from individual firms and industry associations interested in the benefits of such a study.
Significant **scheduling** considerations	Access to busy senior managers and informative and experienced knowledge workers as well as technical support for data analysis.	Negotiate budget and timetable. Interim reports to maintain support. Get good focus groups and access to diverse consumer views.
Key **conduct** factors	Locate appropriate experts, analyse data and interpret findings.	Sensitising concepts, sampling, data interpretation and theorising.
Reporting	Methodological improvements and uses for education and marketing.	

Among other commonalities, both interpretivist examples feature:

- the social construction of reality (ontology)
- hermeneutic epistemology
- narrative and discursive data (such as text)
- generation of typologies from data.

Table 5.5 Illustrative elements of investigative theory when proposing, scoping, resourcing and managing a **criticalist study**

Investigative theory			
Criticalist research		**Example 3** Business information systems investments	**Example 6** Politics of portfolio choices
Question or hypothesis		Do (and how do) political and technical considerations influence executives' go/no-go decisions about investments in strategic IT business information systems?	How are executives' preferences and choices for the firm's product portfolio mix informed and influenced by their organisation-political contexts?
Philosophy of science	**Ontology** How reality is viewed	**Realist and relativist.** Dual reality: objective realities exist as institutional arrangements concurrent with local and individualistically relied on subjective realities.	
	Epistemology How knowledge is generated	**Pragmatic constructionist** – a composite of objective and inter-subjective data from which knowledge of reality is negotiated. An iterative process of pragmatic critical theorising generates a descriptive and explanatory model which is further used in a prescriptive or predictive way for the purpose of emancipation.	
Argument **structure**		**Iterative** and evolutionary development of plausibility that increases with more diverse evidence and the absence of contradiction.	
Inquiry's main **logic**		**Retroductive** reasoning iteratively refines an analogic model that is grounded in diverse objective and subjective data.	
Methodology	Purpose	**Nomothetic** – explain particular phenomena.	
	Tactic	Using empirical data, construct explanatory theory to inform change.	
Researcher's **stance**		**Etic/emic.**	
Main **methods**		**Quantitative and qualitative** (thread statistical and dialogic methods).	
Approach and outcomes		A typology of practice principles *... that results in ...* a model of causal links and actions between funding decisions and funding outcomes for investment cases.	Classify and test elements of case-specific decision making *... to produce ...* a model of causal links between characteristics of social context and new product choices.

Table 5.6 Illustrative elements of investigative practice when proposing, scoping, resourcing and managing a **criticalist study**

	Investigative practice	
Criticalist research	**Example 3** Business information systems investments	**Example 6** Politics of portfolio choices
Proposal focus to highlight ...	The importance of knowing more about decisions that enhance the life time value of a firm's portfolio of strategic IT-based business information systems.	The importance of knowing about, and being able to better mediate, the impact of organisational-political influences on decisions that affect the overall strengths of a firm's product portfolio.
Indicative **ethical** issues	Manipulation of data and findings to advantage or disadvantage executives as well as particular institutional views.	Discrimination and misuse of resources with differential advantage to different areas of the firm and its customers.
Likely **funding** sources	The potential value of the study implies that industry and government support should be sought plus support from firms.	Funding from individual firms that see benefit in the types of results that may emerge from such a study.
Significant **scheduling** considerations	Obtaining comparable objective life-time data for each business information system in the sample. Identify and access executives' and stakeholders' relevant first-hand experiences with sample cases.	Obtaining comparable product portfolio data. Identifying and accessing executives with first-hand experience of decisions, their contexts and their consequences.
Key **conduct** factors	Good technical supervision and strong samples with rich and comparable data. Wise political counsel about how to deal with political influence as well as ensure good participation and access to busy executives.	
Reporting	Industry and practice uses of the new model and accounts of, and reflections on, its explicit/implicit practice and ethical implications as well as advice about further research.	

See Chapter 8 for a comprehensive illustration of these elements of a typical criticalist study using Example 3 (business information systems investments) and Example 6 (politics of portfolio choices).

Among other commonalities, both criticalist examples include:

- dealing with or accepting dual realities (ontologies)
- higher research reflexivity (for example researcher, participants, other stakeholders)
- integration of structural/institutional/patterned data with discursive data.

In the case of a criticalist epistemology, it is important to recognise that power and systemic inequities (subtle or blatant) may manifest as a pragmatic influence on the selection and comparative interpretation of objective and subjective data, and in this way power can be expected to mediate socially constructed meanings. In turn, the consequent generated meanings and experience of constructing these meanings may be expected to mediate the ongoing nature of power. This likely dynamic in criticalist research must be accounted for in design, conduct and reporting. In particular it is prudent to treat, as somewhat prescient and transient, the generation, verification and use of knowledge in the form of a model of causal links between political and other considerations on the input side and decisions and their outcomes as outputs.

ACTIVITIES AND RESOURCES

This section at the end of each chapter suggests further reading, and offers discussion and practice development activities.

EXERCISES AND QUESTIONS

1 Examine a variety of seminal or exemplary business and management studies.
   (a) Do they all exhibit explicit, justified and mutually consistent ontological, epistemological and practical positions and treatments?
   (b) If they do not, does there appear to be a distinguishing feature that separates those studies that do from those that do not?
   (c) What implications do the above findings have for your intended research?
2 Select a topical area of interest and review a variety of leading positivist, interpretivist and criticalist studies on the topic.
   (a) What general principles (that is, principles that are independent of the particular paradigms expressed or implied) appear to be exhibited across these different studies?
   (b) What implications do your observations have for designing and developing chains and patterns of evidence to answer a research question convincingly?
3 Examine a range of exemplary positivist studies in business and management research and in behavioural fields beyond business and management studies.
   (a) Do the four characteristics noted at the bottom of Table 5.2 apply to all these studies?
   (b) Are there other characteristic assumptions that also apply to all these studies?

4 Examine a range of exemplary interpretivist studies in business and management research and in behavioural fields beyond business and management studies.
  (a) Do the four characteristics noted at the bottom of Table 5.4 apply to all these studies?
  (b) Are there other characteristic assumptions that also apply to all these studies?
  (c) What implications do your findings suggest for designing and conducting exemplary interpretivist business and management studies?
5 Examine a range of exemplary criticalist studies in business and management research and in behavioural fields beyond business and management studies.
  (a) Do the three characteristics noted immediately after Table 5.6 apply to all these studies?
  (b) Are there other characteristic assumptions that also apply to all these studies?
  (c) What implications do your findings suggest for designing and conducting exemplary criticalist business and management studies?
6 (a) From your own experience and using first-hand accounts from experienced organisation researchers, list examples of subtle, and also blatant, forms of power that have influenced the selection and/or interpretation of data.
  (b) From your examination of a variety of reputedly exemplary criticalist management studies: (i) Are forms and influences of power/inequalities on the development and interpretation of data explicitly acknowledged and discussed? (ii) What implications do your tentative findings have for designing, conducting and reporting a criticalist study?

FURTHER READING

Blaikie, N. (2000) *Designing Social Research: The Logic of Anticipation*, Cambridge, Polity Press.

PART III

ILLUSTRATIVE CASES

POSITIVIST EXAMPLES OF INVESTIGATIVE THEORY AND PRACTICE

6

INTRODUCTION

In this chapter about examples of two positivist studies, the illustrations and reasoning address elements shown in the Question or hypothesis row of Table 5.1. These elements are the scientific **approach and outcomes** and the research **strategy** including the chosen methods (such as techniques of data generation, data reduction and analysis).

The chapter does not include detailed discussion of the philosophy of science, strategy, methodology, stance or methods already covered in earlier chapters and shown in the rows that highlight aspects of investigative theory in Table 5.1.

We deliberately avoid specific and detailed discussion of technical aspects of positivist methods and techniques (as there is already a vast literature on this). Rather, our purpose here is to emphasise and illustrate the importance of contingent choices that help to establish the overall integrity within and between a positivist study's investigative theory and investigative practice.

KEY ELEMENTS IN POSITIVIST STUDIES

Positivist studies can be thought of as comprising two distinctive but mutually dependent parts. Investigative theory accounts for and describes design choices and their justification based on principles appropriate to the paradigm. Investigative practice accounts for constraints and practical possibilities.

Investigative theory and investigative practice each apply to distinctive steps of positivist research. Positivist research is characterised by its typical linear structure, which is indicated in Figure 6.1 and was discussed in Chapter 4.

Investigative theory

Investigative theory comprises the following elements.

Positivist studies assume that an objective reality (ontology) exists and that neutral observation by researchers is possible. Key elements of such studies typically include the following elements.

Figure 6.1

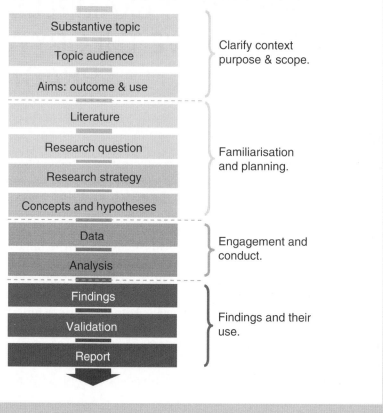

Typical structure of positivist studies

Linear reasoning

The logic for addressing the question in a positivist study typically depends on a linear chain of deductive and/or inductive reasoning. Linear reasoning typically involves collecting evidence and assessing it against the question or hypothesis in a predetermined way. The general orientation in this process is that steps already done do not get redone or altered as a result of later steps.

Choice of central concepts and their operationalisation as variables

The development of concepts is a common early step in attempting to form or confirm descriptive and explanatory theory for a phenomenon or a class of phenomena, whether they are complex or straightforward. A variable is a measurable proxy for a key aspect of a concept, and its typical form is nominal, ordinal or interval.

Selecting aspects of a concept to be measured usually reflects a judgement about theoretical and practical elements of the study. Theoretical considerations include assessments about the study's validity and reliability inasmuch as it depends on the chosen variables (proxies) as authentic representatives of the phenomenon of interest, as well as depending on the forms and methods of their measurement.

Practical considerations include assessments of the actual ease or difficulty with which corresponding measurements of selected variables can be achieved, the sensitivity of the measures and the ways in which they are later able to be analysed, compared and contrasted.

Measurement of variables

Variables are the result of abstracting and operationalising concepts as objective and measurable. There are typically three types of variables: independent, dependent and intervening. Variables may be either discrete (such as units or categories) or continuous (such as height or income); in the case of continuous variables, we must distinguish clearly between the nature of the variable, and the instrument and unit of measure that are used to record instances of the variable). Magnitudes of the independent variable are measured in order to assess its assumed relationship with the dependent variable, with best efforts made to identify and control for intervening variables which may affect assumed relationships between the other two types of variable.

When it comes to measuring variables, important considerations in positivist studies usually include:

- The structure of the positivist study. For instance, is it an experimental study, survey or an observational study? In experimental studies, the independent and known intervening variables may be deliberately set, whereas in observational studies these input variables are simply measured and recorded as they occur – independently of the researcher.
- The form of the study. For instance, is it a snapshot study, a modelling study or a longitudinal study. In each of these three cases, protocols and their associated disciplines are needed to ensure commensurability between all instances of a variable as well as clarity about the contexts in which instances of variable's measures are recorded – so that interpretation of patterns, anomalies and other tests of posited relationships can be incisively interpreted.

Considering intervening factors

It is important to attempt to recognise and account for likely intervening variables. This typically occurs through:

- sample design and specification of demographic data to be collected
- data analysis that considers the sample's demographic characteristics

when analysing associations between dependent and independent variables
- reporting and interpreting findings.

Consideration must also be given to other factors such as:

- vigilance about the assumption and nature of causality
- strong correlations not necessarily implying causality between the variables
- incomplete knowledge about substantively important concepts and the possibility of further intervening variables.

Population and sampling

2

A technically and purposively appropriate representative sample needs to be chosen to reflect the relevant population of the research and the intended use of the findings.

Generally, there are two important aspects to be considered when designing a positivist study:

- a clear description (and rationale) for the nature of the population and its defining characteristics (for the representativeness and breadth of sampling)
- the purpose of a sample – which might be for investigating the wider merits of a particular theoretical proposition, testing the merits of a methodological improvement associated with an existing and accepted theoretical proposition, or challenging a theoretical proposition and hence some underlying theory.

Depending on the purpose of sampling, the nature of the relevant population and the choice of its sample may be best assessed together with the merits and limitations of the consequent study.

Once the rationale and characteristics of the population and sample have been determined, it remains to describe the protocols and note the specific methods needed to select the samples and collect associated data instances.

Measurement of relationships between variables and tests of significance

2

This is about the reduction of datasets into metadata as metrics and other procedurally determined representations that typically characterise patterns, regularities, clusters, relationships and their associated conditions that may be derived from the dataset(s). The result is a concise and informative set of findings which are crucial in answering the research question or testing a hypothesis. Typically these metadata are descriptive statistics (such as frequency distributions or (co)variance) and/or inferential statistics (such as measures of significance of relationships between variables in appropriate population samples).

Interpreting findings

This reflects a disciplined and craft-based set of activities that translate the findings into usable knowledge within explicitly stated limitations. Skilful interpretations can help avoid the misuse of statistics and statistical relationships. In this part of positivist research it is important to identify and assess limitations on the meaning of patterns, irregularities and derived metameasures in samples appropriately drawn from relevant populations.

Results as inferences from findings

These arise from the skilful application of extant and traditionally accepted knowledge as well as a creative theoretical imagination. This may produce interpretations which, after further analytic and empirical testing, can be used to produce inferences and conclusions about the meaning of statistics and other metadata. It is also the case that in situations beyond the circumstances in which the knowledge was generated, inferences, implications and tentative conclusions may be drawn. In such cases further testing is needed to warrant increasing the truth value of such out-of-bounds inferences and tentative theory.

Critique of validity and reliability

It is commonly valuable to reflect on the study's conduct with reference to the extent to which the operationalised variables are adequate proxies for the theorised concepts they represent. With respect to reliability it is also important that the conduct of the study be adequately described so that other researchers can confidently and cogently affirm the study's merits, and also build on its approach and findings.

Investigative practice

Investigative practice comprises the following elements.

Proposal

This typically identifies the motivation, importance of and purpose for the study as they relate to methodology, substantive theory and empirical practice. It is not uncommon to expect there to be competition for access to research resources, including but not limited to funds. So, it is often the case that a political and/or commercial aspect of a research case must be apprehended and addressed. This goes to consideration of the processes, timings and participants in review and approval processes as well as a focus on both academic merit and practicalities.

Ethics

This typically relates to institutionalised positions on substantive and philosophical theory, research practice and reporting, and differential impacts on researchers and other living and material things that may arise during the conduct of, or as a result of, the research and its findings.

An important and often useful orientation when developing an ethics proposal for a research study is to consider the various stakeholders – those with influence and also those with little or no influence – and identify:

- prospects for harm to stakeholders arising directly from the motives, scope, design, conduct and expected uses of the study's findings
- proposed policies, design choices and supervisory and implementation practices that specifically avoid or mitigate harm to the extent that this is acceptable to impacted stakeholders .

Funding

The means and permissions needed to resource the research design and its implementation are essential to allowing for effective research progress and outcomes. It is not unusual to expect that funding a study will depend on rhetoric and persuasion as well as reasoned evidence about the purpose, conduct and expected benefits of the study.

Successfully accessing established as well as new funding schemes frequently depends on the specific characteristics of a proposed study. There are particular requirements and constraints that must be fulfilled if a grant application or funding proposal is to succeed. For this reason, it is essential to find and work with those who have substantial successful experience in funding applications if a research proposal is to succeed. Finally, in-kind support and access to facilities can affect the capacity of a research project to meet its aims as much as winning access to direct funding.

Schedules

These typically span important theoretical and practical blocks of work including

- establishing the study and its operational resources
- literature reviews
- theoretical and practice design
- assembling and analysing data
- assessing the merits and limitations of the findings and their use
- formally reporting and more broadly promulgating the study and its findings.

Conduct

This typically covers implementation of the research design through to and including the generation and verification of the study's findings. Important aspects of conduct that often need to be planned for, described and supervised, or even formally reviewed and reported, include:

- administration and stakeholder communication throughout a study
- development and training in specific tools and techniques;
- supervising or auditing proposed ethical policy and practice
- overseeing the preservation of confidentiality and data integrity as well as related security issues
- technical supervision to ensure rigour meets the standards required by the study's aims and commitment.

Reporting

This usually spans the study's purpose, scope and constraints, highlights of the study's conduct, presentation of the study's findings, discussion of likely practical uses of the findings, and a critique of the study with recommendations regarding substantive and research theory.

Tables 6.1 and 6.2 highlight aspects of investigative theory and investigative practice respectively that are associated with positivist investigations of MIS practice (Example 1) and strategic marketing of personal electronic service goods (Example 4). Following the two tables, each aspect of investigative theory and then investigative practice is illustrated and discussed; first for Example 1 and then for Example 4.

Table 6.1 Highlights of investigative theory for two **positivist** examples

Investigative theory			
Positivist research		**Example 1** Information management	**Example 4** Electronic service goods
Question or hypothesis		Are alignment-capable managers more often linked with project success than other managers?	Are the sales of products and services more affected by price, functionality or brand recognition?
Philosophy of science	**Ontology** How reality is viewed	**Positivist** Reality is assumed to be objectively definable and exists independently of humans.	
	Epistemology How knowledge is generated	**Independent and objective** A hypothetico-deductive structure which follows a linear process to generate confirmation or refutation of hypotheses derived from a theoretical position.	
Argument **structure** Inquiry's main **logic**		**Linear** **Deductive** reasoning builds and tests hypotheses. **Inductive** reasoning leads to tentative generalisations.	
Methodology	Purpose	**Nomothetic** – create and qualify general findings.	
	Tactic	Using empirical data, test hypotheses deduced from theory.	
Researcher's **stance**		**Etic** – the researcher operates as a dispassionate outsider.	
Main **methods**		**Quantitative** (e.g. statistical methods).	
Approach and outcomes		Large-scale survey of managerial capabilities and project outcomes *… that results in …* statistical correlations and measures of significance.	Statistical analysis of sales and market data from surveys and other sources *… that results in …* statistical correlations and measures of significance.

Table 6.2 Highlights of investigative practice for two **positivist** examples

Investigative practice		
Positivist research	**Example 1** Information management	**Example 4** Electronic service goods
Proposal focus to highlight …	The importance of alignment scores as indicators of alignment capability and its importance in reducing the high failure rate of investments in IT systems.	The importance of knowing the comparative significance of price, functionality and brand on buying decisions.
Indicative **ethical** issues	Institutional discrimination that may constrain the study, taint the data and limit or result in misuse of findings.	Biasing the sample or the data and using results to manipulate unwitting customers.
Likely **funding** sources	Prospective value of the study invites government, industry and firm funding and in-kind support.	Funding to be sought from individual firms that might benefit from results.
Significant **scheduling** considerations	Operationalise the concept of alignment and administer the survey instruments to the sample.	Sampling, administration and analysis of questionnaire.
Key **conduct** factors	Organisationally and socially sensitive research administration and management as well as sound technical supervision of the research.	
Reporting	(a) Importance of the study for improved firm and industry practice (b) Ethical expression and use of findings (c) Further research challenges.	

EXAMPLE 1: INFORMATION MANAGEMENT PRACTICES

Investigative theory

Investigative theory for this positivist study is discussed below.

Question

Are alignment-capable managers more often linked with project success than are other managers?

Nature of linear reasoning

To address this question an inductive logic is used to argue from cumulative evidence in the data. This involves gathering observed corresponding instances of the variables of interest in order to test the posited relationship between the variables. From these observed instances a statistically based estimate is made of the strength or weakness of an association between variables.

Induction involves moving from a collection of single (idiosyncratic) data instances to conclude whether a general (nomothetic) relationship exists.

Choice of central concepts and their operationalisation as variables

The independent variable is 'alignment-capable manager'. This is a scalar value between 0 and 10 which is determined from questions about three independent dimensions – awareness, practice and focus. The three dimensions are:

- awareness of business, organisation, technology and management factors
- practice competencies that are typical in managerial and leadership activity
- focus that reflects the decision and action bias across business, organisation, technology and management factors.

The dependent variable is 'project success'. This is a scalar value between 0 and 10 which is determined from questions about two independent dimensions – value and risk. The two dimensions are:

- value arising from stakeholders' project linked capabilities and expectations
- risks arising from stakeholder's project linked experiences and expectations.

Assessment of the scalar value of both variables is typically determined either from answers to questionnaires administered as a survey, or as a result of structured evaluation by a certified consultant using a standardised data collection instrument.

A likely intervening variable is 'manager's duration in a project'. In this example it is commonly the case that several (project) managers may be linked with a project's evolution and outcomes, and that the duration of a manager's involvement with a project can be expected to influence more or less the project's outcome.

Another possible intervening variable is 'project novelty'. For projects that are much larger than, and/or significantly different from, a firm's common experience, it is possible that alignment-capable managers will not be sufficient to ensure project success.

Awareness of these intervening variables may be reflected in the duration of the study as much as the definition of the population and the selection of the population's sample.

Measurement of variables

In this example values for alignment-capable manager and project success are assessed by constructing two questionnaires that will be administered together via a large scale and population representative survey. The resulting data will be reduced into statistical correlations with measures of significance between the variables which constitute the evidence in the data that is sought by the study's logic of inquiry.

In this example it is commonly the case that several (project) managers are linked with a project's evolution and outcomes. The duration of a manager's involvement with a project can also be expected to influence more or less the project's outcome.

Considering confounding factors

While intervening variables help to account for known factors that may mediate findings and interpretations of statistical associations between independent and dependent variables, other (sometimes unknown factors) may also influence descriptions about and/or explanations of the behaviour of dependent variables. In this example we might expect firms' IT maturity, strategic stability and governance practices to be associated with project outcomes in immeasurable or unanticipated ways.

Tactics to help consider confounding factors such as the above commonly include redefining definitions of populations and/or samples, as well as more finely grained initiatives spanning data generation, data reduction and statistical analysis, and even the interpretation of findings.

Population and sampling

The purpose of this study is to help inform the better management of technology projects across a range of industries and types of projects. Designing a strata sample (at least 120 respondents and at least 30 projects) comprising a wide variety of project types and sizes, industry types, and firm sizes and maturity can be expected to help ensure informative representation. A variety of demographic characteristics such as age, educational background, professional experience and gender would also be included.

Measurement of relationships between variables and tests of significance

From the survey responses the scalar values of the independent and dependent variables are subjected to descriptive analysis (such as statistical measures of association, like correlation and measures of significance) and inferential analysis (such as generalisability from the sample to the study's population).

Interpreting findings

There are usually two ways in which findings about statistics are technically reported and interpreted; first, the factual aspects of the findings, and second, a plain speaking statement that conveys the practical meaning and limitations of these facts.

Inferences from results

The implications and consequences of the findings are discussed with particular reference to possible conditions under which extrapolation is appropriate and wider use of the findings may be considered reasonable.

Critique of validity and reliability

A conventional and important aspect of reporting positivist research covers consideration about the related concepts of validity and reliability. *Validity* is concerned with the extent to which operationalisation of theoretical concepts is appropriate and dependable. A proper discussion of validity must include the identification of intervening variables which may change the hypothesised relationship between the independent and dependent variables, and the extent to which the chosen sample truly represents the population from which it is drawn in order to test the relationship.

Reliability is concerned with the repeatability and replicability of the approach and findings by the same and/or other researchers operating in the same paradigm and in a similar context. This depends on a comprehensive and accurate description of the setting, steps and contingent choices that collectively constitute the intended and actual research approach.

Investigative practice

Investigative practice for this positivist study comprises the following elements.

Proposal

The motivation is to generate useful knowledge about alignment-capable managers and project success, and in doing so, to qualify a theory about factors associated with the long-run success of IT-based business information systems projects.

Ethics

The substantive theory to be tested challenges widely assumed knowledge that is relied on by commercial and academic institutions, and this may influence support for, and critique of, the study and its findings. Executive participants have reputations and careers to protect, while also disclosing data and supporting research that could be used to affect their and others' reputations and careers.

Funding

Because of the immediate and ongoing importance of findings that affirm associations between alignment-capable managers and long-run IT business systems success, funding from three sources is likely:

- from firms (such as IT-intensive corporations needing to significantly reduce the cost of IT systems failures)
- information industry bodies (such as professional computer societies and commercial associations of technology services providers)

- governments wishing to strengthen relevant management education and IT-reliant industries.

Schedules

Important scheduling considerations include access to sufficient data, and verification of findings.

Conduct

Important elements of conduct cover implementation of the research design through to and including the generation and verification of the study's findings. Sourcing and collecting data on projects and data about executives' and managers' profiles is a challenging aspect of this study, and can be expected to require political and social sensitivities as well as methodological rigour and competence.

Reporting

Highlights of the reporting process can be expected to cover:

- the aim of the study, to help address the chronically bad failure rate of investments in IT-based business information systems
- findings that can be used to help improve the long-run outcomes of IT-based business information systems
- contributions to methodology and substantive theory that may usefully inform further research.

EXAMPLE 4: PERSONAL ELECTRONIC SERVICE GOODS

Investigative theory

Investigative theory for this positivist study is discussed below.

Question

Are the sales of products and services more affected by price, functionality or brand recognition?

Nature of linear reasoning

To address this question we first use a deductive logic to generate three hypothesised relationships:

- between sales (a dependent variable) and price (the independent variable)
- between sales (the dependent variable) and functionality (an independent variable)
- between sales (the dependent variable) and brand-recognition (an independent variable).

There might be three alternative hypotheses to be tested, that:

- sales success is most affected by price competitiveness
- sales success is most affected by functionality of the product
- sales-success is most affected by brand recognition.

Once the hypotheses have been established, inductive logic is used to argue from data instances (which could be generated from a questionnaire-based survey, for instance) that general relationships do or do not hold, and therefore that the corresponding hypotheses are supported (for now) or disconfirmed. From these instances a statistically based estimate is made of the strength or weakness of any associations between the dependent and some or all of the independent variables.

Choice of central concepts and their operationalisation as variables

The independent variables are 'price', 'functionality' and 'brand association'. Price is any positive scalar value. Functionality is a set of nominal categories that are prioritised by respondents; these categories describe the product's capabilities (including new or unique features) compared with other products for the same market. Brand association is a composite of nominal categories: familiarity with the brand or brand novelty, and attribution of trust in the brand compared with others.

The dependent variable is 'sales success'. This is a compound value comprising total revenue and total quantity sold over a specified period.

Some possible intervening variable(s) may confound relationships between the variables. In this example, which is concerned with consumer choices about new forms and updated versions of personal electronic goods and services (sometimes colloquially referred to as techno-gadgets), confounding factors such as peer sensitivity, economic climate, consumers' discretionary income levels, age and level of education may affect sales success.

Awareness of these intervening variables may be accounted for through redefining the study's population and/or sample structure, as well as through collection of demographic data and the subsequent reduction and analysis of data and its reporting and interpretation.

Measurement of variables

In this example corresponding data instances of 'price', 'functionality', 'brand association' and 'sales success' are collected through a questionnaire administered as a survey of the sample of consumers. To test the hypotheses, the resulting data will be reduced into statistical correlations with measures of significance calculated between the variables. Together, these constitute the evidence in the data that is sought by the study's logic.

Considering confounding factors

Judging from extant theory about buying behaviour, it can be expected that in this example, confounding factors such as economic and social pressures will also mediate consumer choices. Factor and cluster analyses based on sample characteristics can be expected to highlight likely mediating effects of these intervening factors.

The reporting and interpretation of the findings can also be expected to help users of the research account for the possible role of these exogenous factors on top of any statistical associations that the study may find.

Population and sampling

This study aims to better inform product and marketing managers who are responsible for anticipating and delivering products that successfully capture and retain a significant and profitable share of particular markets or market segments. Designing a strata sample of several hundred sources that reflects a wide variety of consumer types (differing by, for example, age, education, discretionary income levels, economic climate and peer sensitivity), brand and product offers, and buying choices can be expected to help ensure broad representation.

Measurement of relationships between variables and tests of significance

From the survey responses the values of the independent and dependent variables are subjected to descriptive analysis (such as statistical measures of association and measures of significance) and inferential analysis (such as generalisability from the sample to the study's population).

Interpreting findings

There are usually two ways in which findings about statistics are technically reported and interpreted, first, the factual aspects of the findings, and second, a plain-speaking statement that conveys the practical meaning and limitations of these facts. In this case it is expected that the findings will show the extent to which a statistically significant relationship between the dependent variable (sales success) and each of the independent variables (price, functionality, brand association) exists (if at all). The study would also be likely to report the extent to which any demonstrated associations are mediated by the intervening variables (age, education, discretionary income levels, economic climate and peer sensitivity).

Inferences from results

In this form of study, the implications and consequences of the findings are discussed with particular reference to possible conditions under which extrapolation is appropriate and wider use of the findings may be considered reasonable.

The aim of this study is to assist with product and marketing choices. It can be expected that characteristics of future target populations and product characteristics will increasingly differ from those concepts and salient features on which the study was exemplified. For this reason, users of these types of studies need to be critically aware of the inherent limitations of such studies, and the declining relevance that increasingly occurs as study findings are applied to divergent settings.

Critique of validity and reliability

A conventional and important aspect of reporting positivist research covers consideration about the related concepts of validity and reliability. *Validity* is concerned with the extent to which operationalisation of theoretical concepts is appropriate and dependable. A proper discussion of validity must include the identification of intervening variables which may change the hypothesised relationship between the independent and dependent variables, and the extent to which the chosen sample truly represents the population from which it is drawn in order to test the relationship.

Reliability is concerned with the repeatability and replicability of the approach and findings by the same and/or other researchers operating in the same paradigm and in a similar context. This depends on a comprehensive and accurate description of the setting, steps and contingent choices that collectively constitute the intended and actual research approach.

Investigative practice

Investigative practice for this positivist study comprises the following elements.

Proposal

The motivation is to generate useful knowledge about factors that affect consumers' buying decisions about electronic consumer goods.

Ethics

The substantive theory to be tested can be used to manipulate consumers' buying decisions, so there is an ethical consideration involving the use of the knowledge generated in this study. If data gathering and/or the validation of research findings involves consumers disclosing their preferences and choices, then such participation must consider the level of understanding and disclosure that is informed and voluntary.

Funding

The immediate benefit of the knowledge generated in this study can be expected to at least inform, if not result in, improved marketing and sales outcomes. So funding by the firm that is expected to benefit is the most likely source of money and in-kind support for such a study. A further possible prospect for support may be from an industry body, but only if that body sees that the study may help to inform its members about benefits that may arise from changes in marketing and sales practices for personal electronic consumer goods.

Schedules

Important scheduling considerations include

- access to sufficient data
- access to consumers
- patterns of sales before and after changed marketing initiatives.

Conduct

This typically covers implementation of the research design through to and including the generation and verification of the study's findings. Sourcing and collecting data about techno-gadget sales and a sample of consumers' disclosures about their buying considerations and buying choices are also key aspects of the study. Analysis of data and interpretation of associations and relationships between variables are the remaining challenging tasks of such a study.

Reporting

In the reporting process highlights can be expected to cover:

- extant knowledge about consumers' buying considerations and choices
- new knowledge about consumers' consideration of brand, price and features for a particular class of techno-gadgets
- a critique of a positivist-based market research methodology.

ACTIVITIES AND RESOURCES

This section at the end of each chapter suggests further reading, and offers discussion and practice development activities.

EXERCISES AND QUESTIONS

1 The ideal-typical reasoning in classic positivist studies is a linear chain of deductive and/or inductive reasoning in which steps already done do not get redone or altered as a result of later steps.

(a) Examine classic positivist studies for variations of this ideal-typical format, and critique the strength of the variations in light of their context, purpose and challenges.

(b) Do your findings cancel the typified assertion made in this book or merely offer a qualified tradeoff?

2   In positivist studies, findings that pertain to a population's sample often appear as statistics or formulae. Both formats typically propose some regularity: that is, within specified constraints and with specified likelihood, findings are applicable to the population as a whole. What other forms of positivist findings are there, and how is confidence in their generalisability (to the sample's population) expressed?

3   Identify as wide as possible a set of rules, styles and explicit limitations associated with interpreting the metadata (such as statistics and formulae) that positivist studies generate from empirical data and hypothesis testing. What implications does this have for concepts of rigour, truth and utility in positivist research?

4   (a) Review the literature on interpreting descriptive and inferential statistics.

(b) What principles can you identify for interpreting statistical metadata?

5   Prepare nuanced definitions and illustrations of the concepts of validity and reliability together with illustrations that clearly highlight the subtleties and differences within and between these two concepts.

6   Morals may be thought of as positions on what are considered to be good or bad states, with ethics being about the process of reaching and enacting a decision on what is moral.

(a) Discuss the relevance and practicalities of having to take a moral position, and design and conduct ethical research.

(b) What is the relevance of morality in a positivist science that is taken to be impartial and objective?

Review the literature on ethics associated with positivist business and management studies.

(c) Note important moral and ethical dilemmas that the ontological and epistemological assumptions of positivist science raise when human subjects and diverse cultural contexts are involved.

(d) Suggest processes and tests that can be used to ensure that research design and practice is ethical.

7   (a) Identify institutional sources of funding for research of the type in which you are interested.

(b) Identify patterns and paradoxes in the way public and private (industry and corporate) funding for positivist research appears to be allocated.

(c) What questions are raised by your initial scan of funding sources and allocations?

8   There are many types of schedules that are associated with well-administered and well-managed research programmes. Obvious ones include resource, activity, funding, reporting, and compliance schedules.

(a) Examine a variety of positivist studies of relevance to your field of interest.
(b) What sorts of schedule were involved other than timetables and funding/expenditure schedules?
(c) What types of schedule are most common, and what implications does this have for your planned research project?
(d) Discuss the sorts of practical requirements and constraints that may typically affect planning, implementation and progress reporting.

IN-DEPTH TOPICS

1 (a) What possibilities and corresponding difficulties arise when proposing a proxy (variable) for an aspect of a non-trivial business and management phenomenon?
   (b) What criteria do you propose for devising or selecting a (proxy) variable or a set of variables for a positivist study of some business or management phenomenon?

2 On what basis should common and distinct features of a population composition be described and understood for the purpose of:
   (a) defining a sample of the population?
   (b) asserting that a finding about a population's sample is of relevance to the population?

FURTHER READING

Anderson, J. and Poole, M. (1998) *Assignment and Thesis Writing*, 3rd edn, Milton, Queensland, Jacaranda Wiley.

Blaikie, N. (2003) *Analyzing Quantitative Data: From Description to Explanation*, London, Sage.

Blaxter, L., Hughes, C. and Tight, M. (2001) *How to Research*, 2nd edn, Ballmoor, Buckingham, Open University Press.

Booth, W. C., Colomb, G. G. and Williams, J. M. (1995) *The Craft of Research*, Chicago, University of Chicago Press.

Bryman, A. (1992) *Research Methods and Organisational Studies*, London, Routledge.

Cresswell, J. W. (2003) *Research Design: Qualitative, Quantitative and Mixed Methods Approaches*, 2nd edn, Thousand Oaks, California, Sage.

De Vaus, D. A. (1995) *Surveys in Social Research*, 4th edn, St. Leonards, New South Wales, Australia, Allen & Unwin.

Evans, D. (1995) *How to Write a Better Thesis or Report*, Melbourne, Melbourne University Press.

Frankfurt-Nachmias, C. (1997) *Social Statistics for a Diverse Society*, Thousand Oaks, California, Pine Forge Press.

Germov, J. and Williams, L. (1999) *Get Great Information Fast*, St. Leonards, Australia, Allen & Unwin.

Kent, R. (2001) *Data Construction and Data Analysis for Survey Research*, Basingstoke, Hampshire, Palgrave.

Kranzler, G. D. and Moursund, J. (1999) *Statistics for the Terrified*, 2nd edn, Upper Saddle River, New Jersey, Prentice-Hall.

Polonsky, M. J. and Waller, D. S. (2005) *Designing and Managing a Research Project: A Business Student's Guide*, Thousand Oaks, California, Sage.

Rose, D. and Sullivan, O. (1996) *Introducing Data Analysis for Social Scientists,* 2nd edn, Buckingham, Philadelphia, Open University Press.

Saunders, M., Lewis, P. and Thornhill, A. (2007) *Research Methods for Business Students*, 4th edn, Harlow, Essex, FT Prentice-Hall/Pearson Education.

Stacey, M. (1969) *Methods of Social Research*, Oxford, Pergamon.

7

INTERPRETIVIST EXAMPLES OF INVESTIGATIVE THEORY AND PRACTICE

INTRODUCTION

Interpretivist studies span a wide, diverse and sometimes misunderstood range of methodologies and logics of inquiry, including ethnography, grounded theory, social phenomenology and structuration theory. Rigorous interpretivist studies share an explicit and recognised ontology and epistemology, which are idealist/relativist, constructionist and intersubjective. This excludes post-modernism, as a research orientation which dispenses with an objective ontology and favours researcher-based subjectivities independent of respondents' realities (extreme subjective relativism) and therefore cannot be included in this book. Interpretivism also obviously excludes positivism whose ontology and epistemology is characteristically realist/objectivist and observer neutral.

Figure 7.1 (which is based on the discussion in Chapter 4) is indicative of the structure of interpretivist studies.

In this chapter, which discusses two sample interpretivist studies, the illustrations and explanations address elements shown in the Question or hypothesis row of Table 5.3. These elements are the scientific **approach and outcomes** and the research **strategy** including the chosen methods (such as techniques of data generation, data reduction and analysis). This chapter does not include detailed discussion of the philosophy of science, strategy, methodology, stance or methods already covered in earlier chapters and shown in the rows that highlight aspects of investigative theory in Table 5.3. We deliberately avoid specific and detailed discussion of technical aspects of interpretivist methods and techniques (as there is already an extensive literature on this).

Our purpose here is to emphasise the nature of, and illustrate the importance of, contingent choices that help to establish the overall integrity within and between an interpretivist study's investigative theory and investigative practice.

KEY ELEMENTS IN INTERPRETIVIST STUDIES

Interpretivist studies can be thought of as comprising two distinctive but mutually dependent parts: investigative theory, which accounts for and describes design choices and their justification based on principles appropriate to the

Figure 7.1

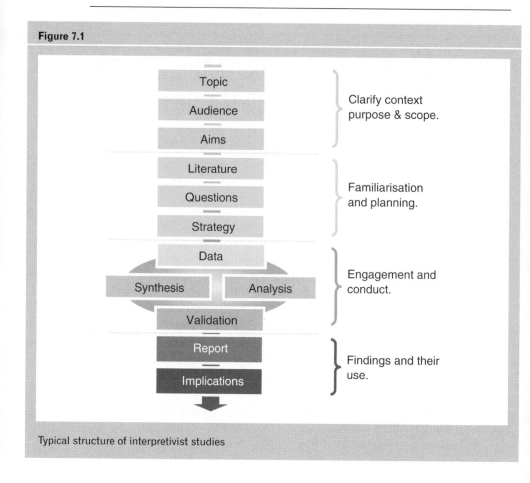

Typical structure of interpretivist studies

paradigm, and investigative practice, which accounts for practically available possibilities as well as constraints.

Investigative theory underpins the study's approach and methodology, while investigative practice develops methods and working arrangements through which methodology is implemented.

Investigative theory

The logic of inquiry in interpretivist studies involves two parallel streams of activity: one, the formation and refinement of the research question, and two, the formation and refinement of descriptive and/or explanatory knowledge through data reduction and analysis. The definition and evolution of the question can proceed deductively, inductively and/or abductively. Also, the creation and modification of concepts may proceed inductively and/or abductively. It is this duality that also differentiates interpretivist epistemologies from those in positivist studies. The nature of these key elements is made manifest in the following way.

Nature of linear-recursive reasoning in interpretivist studies

Data is generated and interpreted, and the research question is adjusted, through the use of sensitising concepts from the literature and the researcher's theoretical imagination. In this way good questions co-evolve as data is continuously generated, reduced and analysed via themes into typifications. The result is the emerging production of insightful, subtle, diverse and sometimes surprising concepts and convincing new knowledge.

Interpretivist studies assume subjective and intersubjective realities (ontology) and knowledge production (epistemology) by researchers in consultation with the research participants.

Interpretivist studies typically identify and interact face to face at an individual and small group participant level, and may involve participants' disclosures about other people, for instance. Consequently, ethical care must be taken to obtain informed consent and maintain agreements about confidentiality, publication and future use of these studies' findings.

As indicated in Figures 4.9 and 4.14, the key activities in interpretivist studies generally do not proceed in a linear fashion, but rather occur in a reflexive and co-evolutionary manner. Notwithstanding this distinctive difference from the positivist approach, important elements of interpretivist studies typically focus on:

- *sensitising concepts and familiarisation*
- the choice and nature of *nominal and ordinal variables*
- *question formation and evolution*
- consideration of *confounding factors*
- *population sampling and data generation*
- *data distillation, concept confirmation and analysis*
- *reporting of the study's findings* in a way that incorporates language from the field as well as theoretical language
- a *critique of the research* design and conduct.

Sensitising concepts and familiarisation

This spans familiarisation with literatures in related academic disciplines and substantive or related substantive fields. It also involves entering the field in order to form a tentative question as well as establish a starting awareness of relevant or possibly relevant concepts, as ideas which both enable and limit the researcher's orientation and sensitivity about the topic, and their initial approach to inquiry.

Nominal and ordinal variables

Within this paradigm the use of the term *variable* is used, not in the sense associated with positivist studies, but rather to identify an aspect of a concept or a relationship between concepts. It is best to set up categories as mutually exclusively and exhaustively as possible. The word *nominal* simply indicates that a variable can only be known through its description (for instance, as a set of attributes) but not by further classifying (as a member of a category) that would enable it to be ranked. *Ordinal* variables are those that are able to be ranked.

To move from a sensitising or other starting concept it is usual to select concepts as variables (often nominal), as tentative representations of these starting concepts. This helps to delineate a clearer starting point, from either the literature and/or exploratory research. This process of delineation and resulting focus creates an attendant risk that some later useful avenue of inquiry or intrinsic aspect of interest may be ignored, so the task for the researcher is to repeat the sensitising process from time to time.

Question formation and evolution

Throughout the study, a prime task of the researcher is to ask and refine the best question to elicit the most valuable knowledge.

Considering confounding factors

In interpretivist studies confounding factors may change depending on the stage of the study. Recognition of apparent confounding factors may of itself represent valuable knowledge rather than something to be controlled for or even excluded. So the crucial tasks for the researcher are to incorporate this awareness into the latest question as well as astutely interpret the data.

Population, sampling and data generation

A technically and purposively appropriate representative sample needs to be chosen to reflect the relevant population of the research and the intended use of the findings. Data generation is a task that grows from four key steps:

- sensitising concepts drawn from the literature and the researcher's ideas of research concepts that are appropriate to the context
- successive refinement of questions
- discursive verbal and/or text and/or nominal or even ordinal categorical data (which may be defined as part of the development of sensitising concepts or which may emerge in data analysis)
- generating typical forms of data from, for instance, interviews, content analysis of documentary material, focus groups and observations.

In an interpretivist study, concepts are rarely drawn directly from the literature without some sensitising modification in the first instance. Sensitising concepts are usually developed from theoretical and/or empirical ideas in the substantive (that is, the topical) literature as well as the researcher's ideas and other sources.

While the study is guided by a core question, sub-questions and even sample participants may be redefined as inquiry proceeds. This process occurs as deeper and wider understanding of the phenomenon of interest emerges from tentative theorising about the accumulating data. Such theorising may produce progressively richer concepts or occasionally an impasse that demands a new approach.

The various forms of data are typically textual, and generated from people's verbal accounts, written observations and documentary sources. Verbal accounts normally arise from interviews which take three main forms: the structured interview which resembles a questionnaire, the focused interview covering a range of topics rather than specific questions, and the unstructured interview which resembles a conversation. Focus groups take place with multiple respondents at the same time. In focus groups, participants are usually selected for their ability to express and hear a range of views, and therefore either identify with and elaborate on those views, or similarly, articulate nuanced or contrary views.

Content analysis is an iterative process in which themes and resultant typifications are distilled from systematic and imaginative macro reviews of all the data, and micro-level reviews of subsets of the data that express or refer to some distinctively common quality or phenomenon.

When eliciting and interpreting participants' data and subsequently reducing and analysing it, it is imperative for the researcher and the participant to know and be able to describe the context from which the data is drawn, because the meaning of data is influenced by its context.

Data distillation, concept confirmation and analysis

This step of interpretivist research distils all the data into compact theoretical notions, which together interpret the phenomenon that the data represents in a comprehensive and insightful way. The step involves a dialectic process of condensation and integration. In condensation, many specific themes (such as age) and forms within themes (such as child, adolescent, adult) are constructed from the data while preserving the overall variety and completeness of the data.

In integration, typifications are constructed, each of which represents a new idea about some quality or characteristic unique to a subset of themes and/or their individual forms. From these typifications, a compact set of theoretical concepts is formed which subsumes these typifications, and best accounts for them by offering comprehensive and insightful meaning about the phenomenon that has been studied. Some principles that help interpretivist researchers conduct this stage of their research relate to reduction, condensation and integration.

Reduction is about an initial categorisation of data according to themes. For instance, age may be represented in all instances of data (such as five-year-old, young person, child, baby boomer, senior citizen, teenager, adolescent) that explicitly refer to instances or different forms of the same characteristic. For efficient reduction we generally convert all instances into a uniform mode of coding (such as particular decades or young, middle aged, elderly).

Condensation is about identifying and describing typifications. A typification sometimes resembles a stereotype but is entirely original, being grounded in the data, and richer in subtle meaning. It refers to the combination of qualities or characteristics of a set of themes, each of which shares a common thread within the theme while still preserving nuanced variety. A simple example which also reflects various world views (and coincidentally resembles stereotypical views) is radical youth and conservative middle age.

Integration is an activity that systematically and imaginatively develops concepts and theory from abstractions of typifications and their interrelationships. The results are a small set of concepts that account for most, if not all, of the identified typifications, plus a new and helpful interpretive framework with meanings to help apprehend how the concepts operate and are interrelated. When used together the concepts and theory enable a comprehensive and insightful understanding of the phenomenon studied.

Reporting the study's findings

This should be an interesting account in the everyday language and style that participants used to recount their worlds and the meanings they attribute to their experiences and their sense of them.

Critique of research

It is important to reflect on the study's conduct with particular reference to both the researcher's and participants' roles in data generation, data interpretation and validation of eventual concepts and associated interpretive theory. In particular, in interpretivist studies, researchers are not objective dispassionate observers but rather collaborators – especially in the interpretation of data. Furthermore, as interpretivist studies usually seek to explore and describe particular phenomena rather than uncover generalisations, interpretivist critiques must expose the idiosyncratic nature of the study, notwithstanding its aim to inspire and generate concepts and theory.

Investigative practice

Investigative practice comprises the following elements.

Proposal

The research proposal typically identifies the substantive context of the proposed study, the researcher's motivation, the importance of and purpose for the study, highlights of the anticipated methodology, and expected impacts on and benefits for stakeholders.

Ethics

Ethics relates to institutional positions on substantive theory, philosophical theory, research practice and reporting, and differential impacts and possible harm to researchers and others during the conduct of, or as a result of, the research and its findings.

Funding

This concerns the monetary and other resources and facilities that are needed for the research study. The scope and success of funding requests can be expected to depend not just on reasoned evidence about the purpose, approach to and expected benefits of the study, but also on rhetoric and persuasion to evoke the prospect of value.

Schedules

Schedules typically span important theoretical and practical blocks of work, including:

- establishing the study and its operational resources
- literature reviews
- theoretical and practice design
- assembling and analysing data
- assessing the merits and limitations of the findings and their use
- formally reporting and more broadly promulgating the study and its findings.

Conduct

Conduct usually refers to implementation of the research design, through to and including the generation and verification of the study's findings.

Reporting

This usually spans the study's purpose, scope and constraints, highlights of the study's conduct (through data generation, analysis and validation), presentation of the study's findings, discussion of likely practical uses of the findings, and a critique of the study, with recommendations regarding substantive and research theory.

The rest of the chapter illustrates a typical approach to interpretivist study using Examples 2 and 5. The illustration starts with two tables. Table 7.1 notes typical features of investigative theory for these examples: that is, an interpretivist study about the management of knowledge workers, and an interpretivist study about decision making for competitive product portfolios. Table 7.2 notes typical features of investigative practice for these two examples. Illustrative choices for each of these two examples are then discussed.

EXAMPLE 2: MANAGING KNOWLEDGE WORKERS

Investigative theory

Major elements of investigative theory that apply in this case are illustrated below.

Question

What are distinctive characteristics of expert practice for managing knowledge workers?

Motivation for the study

To generate a typology of managerial principles and practices that are characteristic of persistently effective knowledge worker management, and so help inform more effective managerial development.

Nature of linear-recursive reasoning in interpretivist studies

This question is addressed in two phases. The first is linear and the major and subsequent phase is recursive. Sensitising concepts about expert practice in the management of knowledge work are first developed from the literature. These are subsequently possibly modified according to the researcher's experience (rather than as result of operationalised variables) and as a consequence of the abductive logic used, in which data is recursively generated, used and analysed.

Sensitising concepts and familiarisation

As well as elaborating and refining initially established sensitising concepts from the substantive literature, other sources of inspiration and clarification may arise from participants' own stock of knowledge and interpreted experience. In this way the researcher's interpretive framework is adjusted and expanded throughout the research process in order to better encapsulate participants' meanings while also facilitating use of the researcher's understandings. This leads to the necessary rich and shared intersubjective meanings on which the paradigm depends.

In this example there are three initial sensitising concepts: that of expert practice, manager and knowledge worker.

Nominal and ordinal variables

In the study there are three initial nominal variables: expert practice, managing and knowledge workers. As the purpose of the study is to create a

Table 7.1 Highlights of investigative theory for two **interpretivist** examples

Investigative theory			
Interpretivist research		**Example 2** Managing knowledge workers	**Example 5** Deciding on competitive product portfolios
Question or hypothesis		What are the distinctive characteristics of expert practice for managing knowledge workers?	What characteristics of effective decision making help make (more) competitive product portfolios?
Philosophy of science	**Ontology** How reality is viewed	Reality is **constructionist.** Reality as perceived relative to a participant's explicit and enacted experience and consequently as socially constructed by, and relative to, different humans.	
	Epistemology How knowledge is generated	Knowledge is **intersubjectively** generated and verified. A process of reflexive hermeneutic interpretation of intersubjective experience generates and validates meanings and associated theory.	
Argument **structure** Inquiry's main **logic**		**Iterative** and **dialogical.** **Abductively** create and verify theoretical concepts from abstracted typifications. **Inductively** reason and test creatively founded themes and theoretical concepts that are grounded in data about experience.	
Methodology	Purpose	**Idiographic**: describe the nuances of specific instances and their distinctively idiosyncratic meanings and, from this, form an integrating set of descriptive and/or explanatory concepts and principles.	
	Tactic	Iteratively generate intersubjective data with participants and, in parallel with data generation, construct descriptive/explanatory theory.	
Researcher's **stance**		**Emic:** the researcher explicitly operates as a (quasi) insider with the research sample.	
Main **methods**		**Qualitative** (e.g. hermeneutic analysis of language within a dialogic method).	
Approach and outcomes		Focus groups and depth interviews *... that result in ...* typifications of effective practices explained by managers and knowledge workers.	Observations, focus groups and depth interviews *... that result in ...* ideal-typical decision making principles and practices associated with persistently competitive product portfolios.

Table 7.2 Highlights of investigative practice for two **interpretivist** examples

<table>
<tr><th colspan="3">Investigative practice</th></tr>
<tr>
<td>Interpretivist research</td>
<td>**Example 2**
Managing knowledge workers</td>
<td>**Example 5**
Deciding on competitive product portfolios</td>
</tr>
<tr>
<td>**Proposal** focus to highlight ...</td>
<td>(a) The importance of knowing distinctive features of expert management practice as well as improved ways to know this.
(b) The value of a tentative theory of expert practice to help manage knowledge workers.</td>
<td>(a) The value of better understanding effective decision practices and the study scope needed for this outcome.
(b) The value of alternative marketing strategies to better match consumer preferences.</td>
</tr>
<tr>
<td>Indicative **ethical** issues</td>
<td>Protect weak participants and employees from adverse impact of disclosures in the study, and avoid preferential treatment of stronger interested parties.</td>
<td>Manipulation of data and support by stakeholders with competing values, interests and influence with resulting possible discrimination between customer segments.</td>
</tr>
<tr>
<td>Likely **funding** sources</td>
<td>Government funding support as well as industry and specific firm support.</td>
<td>Funding from individual firms and industry associations interested in the benefits of such a study.</td>
</tr>
<tr>
<td>Significant **scheduling** considerations</td>
<td>Access to busy senior managers and informative and experienced knowledge workers as well as technical support for data analysis.</td>
<td>Negotiate budget and timetable. Interim reports to maintain support. Get good focus groups and access to diverse consumer views.</td>
</tr>
<tr>
<td>Key **conduct** factors</td>
<td>Locate appropriate experts, analyse data and interpret findings.</td>
<td>Sensitising concepts, sampling, data interpretation and theorising.</td>
</tr>
<tr>
<td>**Reporting**</td>
<td colspan="2">Methodological improvements and uses for education and marketing.</td>
</tr>
</table>

tentative (descriptive) model of expert practice to help manage knowledge workers, it is important to explore the nature and meanings of expert practice, managing, knowledge workers as experienced and as understood in the field, and then to integrate these insights into a model of concepts and their theoretical integration.

As the study proceeds, the tentative model may indicate that some of its components are ordinal as well as nominal. For instance the types and levels of practice, managerial competence, and the workers' knowledge may all be considered as ordinal variables.

Two likely considerations (which may operate like intervening variables) are industry type and practice specialty. In this example it is commonly the case that different industries and different specialist fields of practice peculiar to an industry strongly influence characteristics that uniquely identify demonstrable and typical notions of expertise, managing, knowledge work and knowledge worker. For instance, notions of expertise, managing and knowledge worker can be expected to vary significantly across different industries such as legal practice, health care, data communications, shipping and education. And within each of these industries, notions of expertise, managing and knowledge worker can further be expected to vary with practice specialties such as legal administration, diagnostics, data security, container handling and internet-based interactive courseware.

Awareness of these possible intervening factors and other likely considerations may be accounted for as changes to the duration of the study. They may also result in the amplification and qualification of questions, and may be reflected in the way data is reduced and analysed. Also, it may be necessary to refine the population and/or sample.

Question formation and evolution

The major research question is: are there distinctive characteristics of expert practice for managing knowledge workers? Therefore the key sensitising concepts are about expert practice, managing and knowledge workers.

Generation of data for the three concepts

Two key starting choices in forming an approach to generate data concern, in order of the choice to be made, are first, the relative importance of the *concepts* within the research question, and second, the manner of *data generation* (such as observation, interview or focus group).

Regarding the first of these, in starting and sequencing the research process the three concepts in the question as noted above (expert practice, managing and knowledge workers) should be prioritised. This logically reflects the purpose of the study and the order in which participants may most readily start to recognise and offer good data. This logical and pragmatic choice reflects not only the researcher's interest and substantive knowledge but the industry represented by the chosen sample. In this example we choose to start with an inquiry focused on knowledge workers because they are most readily identified in the chosen industry. And, much less will be known about expert practice, which is the purpose of the study.

The next step of choosing the research technique will need to generate data about the key concept of expert practice by focusing on knowledge workers in the sample industry or industries. We choose to start inquiry by interview rather than observation as language is the mode that knowledge workers commonly use to construct, express and coordinate their work. If an interview is chosen, the next choice concerns the mode of interview (that is, structured, focused or in-depth exploratory). In this example, given a starting choice of inquiring about knowledge workers using focus group interviews, the researcher could extend the scene using themes identified from the literature to stimulate more examples about the nature and characteristics of knowledge work in their industry and the way in which they are managed or influenced by management practice and climate.

From the beginnings in these early explorations, subsequent interviews (possibly complemented by an observational study and revised sample) would seek to identify and describe the widest possible range of elements of expert practice and relevant management that serve the study's objectives.

Two common dilemmas arise in interpretivist studies. The first concerns how to deal with an impasse that arises when new data confounds the emerging themes and resulting typifications that have been constructed by the researcher. The second is when to cease data generation and theorising: in other words, judge that theoretical saturation has occurred. The first dilemma may require a complete change of research question or approach, and occasionally a study may have no alternative but to be stopped. The second is a normal and inevitable decision that reflects a mix of pragmatic considerations (for instance, the findings are sufficient for the purpose) and theoretical factors (for example, the findings are widely valid and represent insightful new knowledge).

Considering confounding factors

Types of confounding factors that may occur typically include context factors, modal factors and diversity factors.

Examples of possible confounding context factors are politically inhibiting elements within some sectors of the sample, limitations on disclosure as a result of commercial in confidence or related arrangements, participants' inclination to exaggerate or colour accounts, and inequality-mediated (such as culturally or demographically grounded) differences which affect participants' disclosures and/or interpretations.

Examples of possible modal factors in this case are misunderstandings in the use of language between the researcher and participants, and participants' reluctance and/or inability to express their tacit knowledge.

Examples of possible diversity factors in this case are the exclusion of informative descriptive instances of relevant concepts (such as contemporary expert practice in the industry being studied), and outlying but potentially perceptive views.

Population, sampling and data generation

The purpose of this study is to identify distinctive characteristics of expert practice in the management of knowledge workers, and so help to improve both expert practice and the management of knowledge workers.

Initially a purposeful sample which targets a wide range of participant experiences can be expected to help broaden the initial sensitising concepts developed by the researcher. The initial purposeful sample may lead to the further identification of focus group participants to reflect suitably broad demographics as well as richer substantive experience. From these adjusted samples the researcher expects to generate deeper and more comprehensive theoretical knowledge grounded in participants' data. This emerging yet deliberate sampling method is typical of an interpretivist study.

Data distillation, concept confirmation and analysis

As noted earlier, this step of interpretivist research distils all the data into compact theoretical notions which, together, interpret the phenomena that the data represents in a comprehensive and insightful way. This distillation process involves three important activities: reduction, condensation and integration.

Reduction involves categorising data according to common or similar aspects of a common attribute called themes. Some of the themes will emerge as principal themes, as they are more enlightening with regard to illuminating the research question.

Condensation of principal and other themes generates a few broad typifications (which sometimes resemble stereotypes but are entirely original – being grounded in the data, and being richer in subtle meaning). Broad typifications reveal interrelationships between themes and also highlight patterned differences between respondents' meanings. In the case of condensation it is important to recognise that interrelationship and patterned differences arise not just as the result of a purely mechanical procedure, but also as a result of a creative, imaginative and reflexive activity that the researcher constructs from the data. (Typifications can be thought of as referring to combinations of qualities or characteristics of a set of themes each of which shares a common thread within the theme while still preserving nuanced variety. A simple example which also reflects various world views (and coincidentally resembles stereotypical views) is radical youth and conservative middle age.)

Integration of all typifications is done to form a tentative theory, which is a compact way of accounting for most, if not all, of the data and answering the research question in terms of a set of concepts and their interrelationships. The resulting interpretive framework and meanings help to apprehend how the concepts operate and are interrelated. When used together, the concepts and theory enable a comprehensive and insightful understanding of the phenomena studied.

The first step of *reduction* often starts with some form of coding to help locate a theme that is implied by many instances of participants' data which appear to refer to the same notion. In this example about knowledge workers, a theme of searching[A] can be expected to be identified from participants' transcripts, with sub-themes such as classifying[A.1] (to make up a search string) and sourcing[A.2] (to select a database). For instance several participants may each provide many examples of an activity of 'Googling' on the internet to find website references that are related their questions or interests. What all such instances share is the task of turning an inquiry into a procedure that uses a common tool and conventions to provide further leads, and sometimes even answer the original questions. Three further examples of themes that plausibly emerge as principal themes can be expected from managers' and knowledge workers' accounts relating to problem-solving^B, and discriminating^C and social-perceptiveness^D by managers who are reputedly expert.

The theme of problem-solving^B has sub-themes such as efficiency$^{B.1}$ (good use of time and resources), success$^{B.2}$ (the proportion of problems successfully resolved), difficulty$^{B.3}$ (reflecting the complexity, ambiguity and equivocality in situations), and experience$^{B.4}$ (reflecting a variety of challenges and effective learnings).

The theme of discriminating^C has sub-themes such as selecting$^{C.1}$ (choosing what to deliberately include), rejecting$^{C.2}$ (consciously choosing what to set aside), and evaluating$^{C.3}$ (making informed judgements about relative merits of the selected items).

The theme of social-perceptiveness^D has sub-themes such as self-awareness$^{D.1}$, empathy$^{D.2}$ and insight$^{D.3}$.

The next step is *condensation*, in which some sub-themes are combined from across the various identified themes to construct a comparatively small number of typifications of aspects of expert managerial practice. Drawing on the illustrative themes above, one plausible typification is that of INFORMED-GUIDE, which combines sub-themes (from the problem-solving theme) about successful$^{B.2}$ problem solving in difficult$^{B.3}$ situations, with the sub-theme of evaluating$^{C.3}$ (drawn from the discriminating theme) and high insight$^{D.3}$ (which is a sub-theme of social perceptiveness).

A second possible typification is that of COMPLIANT-PROBLEM-SOLVER, which comprises sub-themes of difficulty$^{B.3}$ and experience$^{B.4}$, which are components of the problem-solving theme, together with the sub-themes of enlightened rejecting$^{C.2}$ (from the discriminating theme), and empathy$^{D.2}$ and insight$^{D.3}$ (from the social perceptiveness theme).

A third likely typification is that of POLITICALLY-ASTUTE-ADMINISTRATOR, which combines sub themes of efficiency$^{B.1}$ (from the problem-solving theme), evaluating$^{C.3}$ (from the discriminating theme) and self-awareness$^{D.1}$ and insight$^{D.3}$ (from the social perceptiveness theme).

For the purpose of illustration the fourth typification that we refer to is that of LEADER, which combines the sub-themes of success$^{B.2}$, experience$^{B.4}$, selecting$^{C.1}$, rejecting$^{C.2}$, self-awareness$^{D.1}$ and empathy$^{D.2}$. These examples of condensation reinforce the point that typifying is a process in which the researcher creatively uses participants' meanings to look beyond surface themes in order to discern more fundamental patterns and differences across all the data.

The step of *integration* systematically and imaginatively develops concepts and their mutual dependence from distillations of typifications and their interdependencies. The researcher's task in integration is to imaginatively and systematically develop an increasingly more compact yet comprehensive theoretical understanding of reported and observed phenomena. Drawing on the four typifications exemplified in the condensation activity above, here is a plausible theoretical construction that is consistent with the themes and typifications:

> Expert management reflects a balanced orientation to LEADING and INFORMED-GUIDE, and these two practices are usually given greater precedence over POLITICALLY-ASTUTE-ADMINISTRATION and COMPLIANT-PROBLEM-SOLVING.
>
> Where the latter two compete for attention, then the choice is context-dependent; for instance, in highly competitive aggressive organisations COMPLIANT-PROBLEM-SOLVING is a more acceptable orientation than POLITICALLY-ASTUTE-ADMINISTRATION, whereas in traditional bureaucratic organisations POLITICALLY-ASTUTE-ADMINISTRATION is usually more effective than COMPLIANT-PROBLEM-SOLVING.

The logic of inquiry

The logic of inquiry in this section predominantly reflects abduction in action. Within this overriding logic are task-specific logics such as deduction (in which implications and associations are drawn from related facts) and induction (in which general assertions are generated from many instances of a class of data or relationships).

It is also important to recognise that in this section we have highlighted what an interpretivist research approach must aim for. It remains for the researcher to select and use appropriate methods within this overall logic.

Reporting the study

In interpretivist studies the meanings, implications and consequences of tentative theoretical assertions are illustrated in the language of the field, and then discussed with particular reference to application as well as to provide sensitising concepts for further research. In doing this, it is important to clearly identify the time frames, locations and social context of the study to ensure that all use of the findings is well considered.

In addition, substantive and formal theoretical implications and limitations are discussed with a view to informing further topical research as well as further development in the theory and practice of management and/or business, and in the development of the philosophy and methodology of interpretivist study.

Critique of research

Critical review includes the technical aspects and practical tradeoffs in relation to research approach (such as sampling and design), ethical questions, data generation methods, representativeness of data, data conversion; and validity.

Sampling frequently raises the need to balance representation, adequate variety and accessibility. Design inevitably requires choices between ideal and practicable strategies and logics of inquiry that fit with the sample and the paradigmatic assumptions. Ethical challenges readily arise in relation to freedom to disclose and retain anonymity, the interpretation of data, and the implicit or explicit support or harm that may arise from the use or withholding of research findings. The data generation methods may be questioned on the grounds that other methods may elicit more valid and/or valuable data.

Representativeness of data is usually rated as less important in an interpretivist study. However it is extremely important to include a sufficiently diverse range of informants in order to explore the research topic and construct useful or illuminating substantive theory.

Data conversion, which involves reduction, condensation and integration, inevitably involves the first-order and second-order constructs. First-order constructs involve accurate apprehension of the participants' meanings, which demands the researcher's sensitivity and understanding of their language and contexts. On the other hand, the development of second-order constructs (in the process described above) requires some disciplined creativity and insight on the part of the researcher, which reflects an ability to alternately be immersed in and removed from the researcher's and the participants' worlds. Crucially, it is necessary to describe how this process proceeds in order that the rigour, scope and limitations of the study can be judged.

In interpretivist studies, validity refers to a sub-sample of participants' recognition of the themes in the findings and possibly (even preferably) the typifications. The sub-sample is defined by the researcher and participants together as the study unfolds, and participants' recognition affirms that essential meanings have been identified.

Investigative practice

Investigative practice for this interpretivist study comprises the following elements. They are not exhaustive but can reasonably be considered as appropriate to this example.

Proposal

If, for instance, the researcher's motivation is to identify principles unique to expert management practice as well as to develop research theory appropriate to the investigation of expert human practice, then the proposal needs to present intended scope, practice supervision, required permissions and necessary support requirements that are in line with these motives.

In addition to succinctly incorporating motivational implications, there are obvious requirements to be presented including the importance of the study, anticipated methodological highlights, and resource and facility requirements.

Ethics

Knowledge workers, managers of knowledge workers, the study's researchers, and organisations providing funds and facilities as well as participant access are examples of stakeholders who may have competing interests. It is necessary to identify ethical risks within and between each stakeholder group, and get agreement to ethical principles that the design and its implementation must account for.

For instance, ethical risks that may arise in this type of study may be associated with identification or exclusion of some managers as expert; providing resources, facilities and participant access subject to linking the study's scope with specific types of management or worker practices; or using the findings to (de)select and/or (re)evaluate the performance of managers and knowledge workers.

Funding

This type of study can be expected to generate findings that benefit industry-level management research and management education, and also inform the orderly review and improvement of practices within firms. For this reason, it can be expected that government, industry and firm-specific funding and provision of in-kind resources and facilities be sought for this type of study.

Schedules

It is often difficult to conduct quality interpretivist studies according to a fixed-duration (or even fixed-budget) project schedule. This is because key steps such as data generation and interpretation evolve, with ongoing work directed as a result of emerging issues, leads and dead ends.

Incorporating contingency elements into schedules and budgets is one practical approach. It may also be appropriate to structure the research so that interim findings and parallel or even largely independent streams of work can be undertaken, so that the effect of changes to time and money schedules, as much as to the scope of the study, can be accommodated with less wide-ranging impact.

Other nontrivial scheduling considerations that are often linked with interpretivist studies include negotiating and sustaining access to appropriate firms and their managers and knowledge workers; generating data using depth interviews and focus groups; iteratively interpreting emerging data in order to develop validated meanings and descriptive concepts about expert managerial practice; and verifying the substantive theory that the study constructs from the data.

Conduct

This covers implementation of the research design through to and including the generation and verification of the study's findings. Constructing a sample that includes readily accessible participants who voluntarily offer candid and rich accounts as managers and knowledge workers is as much a matter of the way the study is presented and marketed, as it is a matter of the way researchers connect with, and develop, an engaging, stimulating and professional relationship with participants through data generation, interpretation and validation.

The logistical and organisational challenges of handling large volumes of spoken and written language-based data, and the substantial workload needed to concurrently and iteratively (re)interpret the growing body of data, are also a major practical consideration for interpretivist studies. In this example this would involve reviews with cohorts of participant managers and participant knowledge workers in the first instance, and eventually a possible wider sample of managers and knowledge workers chosen from beyond the participating firms in order to strengthen the validation of the findings.

Reporting

Highlights can be expected to cover the aim of the study (to help develop principles for competent management of knowledge workers); findings that can be used to help improve the development of relevant managerial practice; and contributions to methodology and substantive theory that may usefully inform further research.

EXAMPLE 5: DECIDING ON COMPETITIVE PRODUCT PORTFOLIOS

Investigative theory

Major elements of investigative theory that apply in this interpretivist study are illustrated below.

Question

What characteristics of effective decision making help to make (more) competitive product portfolios?

Motivation for the study

The aim is to generate a typology of decision principles and decision practices associated with persistently effective product portfolio management, and so help inform the promulgation of better managerial decision practices.

Linear-recursive reasoning, sensitising concepts and familiarisation in interpretivist studies

This question is addressed in two phases. The first is linear, and the major and subsequent phase is recursive and is guided according to an abductive style of reasoning.

In the linear phase the researcher progressively selects sensitising concepts about the management of product portfolios. These are developed from the literature and, in particular, include concepts about the anticipation and assessment of changing product needs and the various stages of products' life cycles. In the second phase the initial sensitising concepts may be modified, not as a result of operationalised variables, but rather as a consequence of: abductively generating and analysing data related to the anticipation and assessment of choices about product portfolios' component mixes and their subsequent outcomes; and at the same time incorporating the researcher's relevant experience.

As well as the researcher's own stock of relevant experience, other sources of inspiration and clarification may arise from participants' stock of knowledge and interpreted experience. In this way the researcher's interpretive framework is adjusted and expanded throughout the research process in order to better encapsulate participants' meanings while also facilitating use of the researcher's understandings. This leads to the necessary rich and shared intersubjective meanings on which the paradigm depends.

In this example there are three initial sensitising concepts, which concern strategic competitive choices about the future of each product in a portfolio, anticipation of each product's strategic factors as precedents to strategic decisions about each product's future, and assessment of the consequences of the strategic choices for the products in the portfolio.

Nominal and ordinal variables

In the study there are three initial nominal variables: strategic choice, anticipation and assessment. The purpose of the study is to create a tentative (descriptive) model for making and validating strategic decisions about a product portfolio. With this purpose, it is important to explore the nature and meanings of product portfolio, strategic decisions, decision making, and assessment of decisions according to the way experienced executives and managers understand and work with these concepts in the field. The resulting theoretical concepts may then be integrated into a practice model that describes expert strategic decision making for product portfolios in fast-changing markets for personal electronic goods and services.

As the study proceeds, the tentative model may indicate that some of its components are ordinal as well as nominal. For instance, the types of products and their levels of market acceptance, the purposes and forms of decision making and associated levels of decision competence, and the modes and degrees of relevant and competent anticipation and assessment may all be considered as ordinal variables.

Three likely considerations (which may operate like intervening variables) are industry type, which may refer to the class of personal electronic goods and services that are typically provided; market type, which may reflect the sophistication of typical buyers; and a firm's market position, which can be taken to reflect its share relative to competitors. In this example it is commonly the case that different industries, different market types and different levels of market position may strongly influence characteristics of demonstrably effective anticipation, strategic decision making and outcomes of decisions affecting the product portfolio.

Notions of effective anticipation, decision making and subsequent assessment of decisions about products within a firm's product portfolio can all be expected to vary significantly between industries (such as gaming based entertainment versus personal investments) and the forms of products or services (such as personal electronic goods and services) that each industry sells to its markets. This is partly at least as a result of differences between product-linked factors like development lead-time, development cost, run-out time, sunk cost, switching price, market demand, customer contract terms, inertial demand, enabling technologies and evolving tastes. For instance, in personal investments, strategic portfolio decisions are likely to depend heavily on good demand and capacity research, and on knowledge about possible enabling technologies, whereas for gaming-based entertainment, effective portfolio decisions can be expected to depend much more on innovation research, product and market scanning, and exploration of improved branding, production and distribution solutions.

Awareness of possible intervening factors and other likely considerations may be accounted for as changes to the scope and duration of the study. They may also result in refinement of the defined population and/or sample, amplification and qualification of questions, and adjustments to the way data are reduced and analysed.

Question formation and evolution

The major research question is, what are the characteristics of effective decision making for (the composition of) a firm's competitive product portfolio? As already noted, the key sensitising concepts are about strategic competitive choices about the future of each product in a portfolio, anticipation of each product's strategic factors as precedents to strategic decisions about each product's future, and assessment of the consequences of the strategic choices for the products in the portfolio.

Generation of data for the three concepts

In order to develop an approach to generating data, choices must be made about, first, the relative importance of the concepts within the research question, and second, the manner of data generation (for instance observation, interview or focus group).

To decide on the relative *importance of the concepts* within the research question, the researcher must account for the motivation and purpose of the research. These considerations must then be reflected in the order and extent to which the various concepts are consequently explored with participants. For instance, in this example, if the primary concept were considered to be about decision making followed by anticipation, then questions and invitations to participants to offer data (instances, experiences and reflections) on the nature and meaning of decision making might be delayed. Instead the exploration could start by focusing on decision outcomes and their assessment, and then anticipation, as precursors that set the scene in participants' terms. Only when context has been established in the language, experience and instances of relevance to participants is the central concept of decision making explored. The order and impact of these choices satisfies the exploratory and dialogic nature of interpretivist inquiry, as well as the practical need for a clear and grounded focus within which participants offer and elaborate on relevant data.

Decisions about the mode(s) of *data generation* to be used depend, at least, on the type of data sought and on the degree to which rich data, revealing nuances and insightful sources about experiences and their interpretations are needed to fulfil the study's aims and scope. Practical considerations (such as time, money and logistical aspects of field work) also influence choices of modes of data generation.

In this example, early-stage exploration that seeks to establish, in participants' language, starting concepts about strategic choices, anticipatory factors and decision assessments may involve document reviews and interviews with key players nominated by participants. Later on, the researcher will expand, refine and eventually verify theoretical concepts whose meanings are illustrated with rich and nuanced instances and relationships, using data that are generated using practice observations, focus groups and extensive in-depth interviews.

With this type of approach there always remains the possibility that no settling concepts emerge to comprehensively account for the data generated. In this case the options are to either reframe the study's questions and approach, based on the data and emergent findings, or to judge that the study's aims and scope cannot be met, and the study should be stopped. The first option is common. The second option is indicated if practical resources (for instance, time or money) are insufficient for further useful research and/or if reframing has failed to, or is unlikely to, produce useful substantive or theoretical outcomes.

Considering confounding factors

Types of confounding factors typically include context factors, modal factors and diversity factors. In this case possible confounding context factors are commercial in-confidence constraints that limit disclosure or interpretation of data, participants' psychologically grounded inclination to colour their accounts, and politically, culturally or demographically mediated influences on sample selection, as well as on the disclosure or interpretation of data.

Examples of possible modal factors in this case are misunderstandings in the use of language between the researcher and participants, and participants' reluctance and/or inability to express their tacit knowledge.

Examples of possible diversity factors are the exclusion of informative descriptive instances of relevant concepts (for instance of anticipation, decision making and assessment of decision outcomes), and outlying but potentially perceptive views.

Population, sampling and data generation

The aim of this study is to identify characteristics of effective decisions associated with the mix of a firm's product portfolio. A consequence of such knowledge is improved decision making for product portfolios in general.

Initial sensitising concepts developed by the researcher from the literature are modified by using data about decision-making practices and experiences, which are drawn from a purposeful sample of respected decision makers and respected observers of portfolio decisions and their outcomes. This evolution-ary process is likely to help identify other participants and related data, which eventually reflect a broad demographic with rich substantive experience of effective and ineffective decision making. The substantive knowledge that is produced in this way can be expected to help systematically generate more comprehensive substantive theoretical knowledge of decision-making practice and outcomes. This deliberately evolutionary method of sampling, data generation and theory formation is typical in many interpretivist studies.

Data distillation, concept confirmation and analysis

As noted at the start of this chapter, this step of interpretivist research distils all the data into compact theoretical notions, which together interpret the phenomena that the data represents in a comprehensive and insightful way. This process includes three important activities: reduction, condensation and integration.

Reduction sorts the data into themes according to common or similar aspects of a common attribute. Some of these constructions will emerge as principal themes, as they are more enlightening with regard to illuminating the research question. They frequently start with some form of coding to help discern a theme that is implied by many instances of participants' data which appear to refer to the same, but implicit, notion.

Condensation of principal and other themes forms a few broad typifications which are collectively comprehensive, and each of which is entirely original, grounded in data, rich in subtle meaning and revealing of interrelationships and patterned differences between constituent themes. A typification highlights common aspects of constituent themes whilst preserving and highlighting nuanced variety between constituent themes.

Integration of all typifications directly generates a tentative theory, which is a compact way of accounting for all the data and answering the research question in terms of a set of concepts and their interrelationships. The resulting interpretive framework and associated meanings help to show how generated substantive concepts operate and are interrelated. When used together the concepts and theory enable a comprehensive and insightful understanding of the phenomena studied.

The first step is *reduction*. In this example about decision making for product portfolios, a theme of clarity^A can be expected to be identified from participants' transcripts, with sub-themes such as relevance$^{A.1}$ (to decision purpose), reliability$^{A.2}$ (involving the confidence in the truth value of different sources of data) and confidence$^{A.3}$ (concerning the tangibility and equivocality of data). Other themes and their sub-themes that can be expected to be identified are:

- urgency^B (with sub-themes of importance$^{B.1}$ for the overall portfolio and the opportunity cost$^{B.2}$ of delaying a decision)
- risk^C (with sub-themes of scope$^{C.1}$, which relates to economic political and technical factors, impact$^{C.2}$ on a firm's reputation as well as its market and financial position, and likelihood$^{C.3}$ of an impact being realised)
- complexity^D (with sub-themes of novelty$^{D.1}$ of decision criteria, product-synergy$^{D.2}$, meaning impacts on related products on the portfolio, and uncertainty$^{D.3}$, associated with decision participants, decision process, timing and decision data)
- wisdom^E (with sub-themes of insight$^{E.1}$, about reframing traditional perspectives, worldviews$^{E.2}$, being the tacit and alternative institutionalised assumptions about the purpose, participants, processes and criteria for decision making; and permission$^{E.3}$, about the psychological and sociopolitical mediation of the content and practice of communicating as part of decision making).

The next step is *condensation*. In this step some sub-themes may be combined from across various identified themes to construct a relatively small number of typifications of features of decision-making practice and effectiveness. Drawing on the illustrative themes above, one plausible typification is CENTRALITY, which combines the sub-themes of importance$^{B.1}$ (from the urgency theme), impact$^{C.2}$ and likelihood$^{C.3}$ (from the risk them) and product synergy$^{D.2}$ (from the complexity theme). A second possible typification is PRUDENCE, which comprises the sub-themes of: opportunity cost$^{B.2}$ (from the urgency theme), scope$^{C.1}$ and impact$^{C.2}$ (the from the risk theme), novelty$^{D.1}$ and uncertainty$^{D.2}$ (from the complexity theme), and insight$^{E.1}$ and worldviews$^{E.2}$ (from the wisdom theme). A third likely typification is POLITICAL-NOUS, which combines the sub-themes of importance$^{B.1}$ (from the urgency theme), scope$^{C.1}$ (from the risk theme), and worldviews[E.2] and permission[E.3] (from the wisdom theme).

These examples of condensation reinforce the point that typifying is a process in which the researcher creatively uses participants' meanings to look beyond surface themes in order to discern more fundamental patterns and differences across all the data.

The last step is *integration*. Integration systematically and imaginatively develops concepts and their mutual dependence from distillations of typifications and their interdependencies. The researcher's task in integration is to imaginatively and systematically develop increasingly more compact yet comprehensive theoretical understanding of reported and observed phenomena. Drawing on the four typifications exemplified in the condensation activity above, here is a plausible theoretical construction that is consistent with the themes and typifications:

> Making effective decisions about a product portfolio's mix reflects a clear focus and separation of CENTRAL considerations from more marginal ones together with PRUDENT attention to strategic contingencies. However the process is not entirely objective because astute considerations that reflect POLITICAL-NOUS also mediate decision making.
>
> It is the politically astute balance of concern for a relatively small number of core factors and strategic risks as opposed to more wide ranging considerations and predominantly economic assessment that can set the most effective decisions apart from others.

Major logic of inquiry

The major logic of inquiry in this example reflects abduction in action, whereby case studies of strategic choices are explored using semi-structured or unstructured interviews with executives in order to generate tentative abstracted typifications grounded in emerging participant data. The process stops when the concepts generated offer comprehensive and stable descriptive and explanatory insight despite continuing data generation.

Within this overriding logic are task-specific logics such as deduction (in which implications and associations are drawn from related facts) and induction (in which general assertions are generated from many instances of a class of data or relationships). It is also important to recognise that in this section we have highlighted what an interpretivist research approach must aim for. It remains for the researcher to select and use appropriate methods within this overall logic.

Reporting the study

In interpretivist studies the language of the field is used to communicate meanings, implications and consequences of tentative theoretical assertions. This enables the theoretical constructions developed through interpretivism to be explained and illustrated in terms that are meaningful to, and verifiable by, participants, as well as enabling outsiders such as other researchers and colleagues in related fields of substantive practice to draw on the research.

The tentative theoretical concepts also provide sensitising concepts for further research. In doing this, it is important to clearly identify the time frames, locations and social context of the study to ensure that there is only well-considered use of the findings. In addition, substantive and formal theoretical implications and limitations are discussed with a view to informing further topical research as well as further development in the theory and practice of management and/or business, and in the development of the philosophy and methodology of interpretivist study.

Critique of research

Critical review includes the technical aspects and practical tradeoffs in relation to research approach (sampling, design and so on), ethical questions, data generation methods and the representativeness of data, data conversion and veracity. The merits of the research approach depend on the nature of the sample as well as technical design and the like. Sampling considerations involve the need to balance representation, adequate variety and accessibility. Design inevitably requires choices between ideal and practicable strategies and logics of inquiry that fit with the sample and the paradigmatic assumptions.

Ethical challenges readily arise in relation to freedom to disclose and retain anonymity, the interpretation of data, and the implicit or explicit support or harm that may arise from the use or withholding of research findings.

The data generation methods may be questioned on the grounds that other methods might have elicited more valid and/or valuable data. Representativeness of data is usually rated as less important in an interpretivist study. However it is extremely important to include a sufficiently diverse range of informants to make it possible to explore the research topic and construct useful or illuminating substantive theory.

Data conversion, which involves reduction, condensation and integration, inevitably involves the development of first-order and second-order constructs (Schütz 1963 a, b). First-order constructs involve accurate apprehension of the participants' meanings, which demands the researcher's sensitivity and understanding of their language and contexts. On the other hand, the development of second-order constructs (in the process described above) requires some disciplined creativity and insight on the part of the researcher, which reflects an ability to alternately be immersed in, and removed from, the researcher's and the participants' worlds. Crucially, it is necessary to describe how this process proceeds in order that the rigour, scope and limitations of the study may be properly judged.

In interpretivist studies, validity refers to a sub-sample of participants' recognition of the themes in the findings and possibly (even preferably) the typifications. The sub-sample is defined by the researcher and participants together as the study unfolds, and participants' recognition affirms that essential meanings have been identified.

Investigative practice

Investigative practice for this interpretivist study comprises the following elements. They are not exhaustive but can reasonably be considered as appropriate to this example.

Proposal

If, for instance, the researcher's motivation is to identify principles unique to effective portfolio decisions and to develop research theory appropriate to the investigation of effective decision making, the proposal needs to present intended scope, practice supervision, required permissions and necessary support requirements that are in line with these motives.

In addition to succinctly incorporating motivational implications, there are obvious requirements to be presented including the importance of the study, anticipated methodological highlights, and resource and facility requirements.

Ethics

Executives, product and portfolio-related specialists, the study's researchers, and organisations providing funds and facilities as well as participant access are examples of stakeholders who may have competing interests. It is necessary to identify ethical risks within and between each stakeholder group, and get agreement to ethical principles that the design and its implementation must account for. For instance, ethical risks that may arise in this type of study may be associated with identification or exclusion of some executives, managers and specialists as expert; providing resources, facilities and participant access subject to linking the study's scope with specific types of product portfolios and decision practices; and using the findings to (de)select and/or (re)evaluate the performance of decision makers and decision outcomes.

Funding

This type of study can be expected to generate findings that benefit industry-level management research and management education, as well as informing the orderly review and improvement of practices within firms. For this reason, it can be expected that industry and firm-specific funding and provision of in-kind resources and facilities be sought for this type of study.

Schedules

It is often difficult to conduct quality interpretivist studies according to a fixed-duration (or even fixed-budget) project schedule. This is because key steps such as data generation and interpretation evolve, often unpredictably, with ongoing work directed as a result of emerging issues, leads and dead ends. Incorporating contingency elements into schedules and budgets is one practical approach. It may also be appropriate to structure the research so that interim findings and parallel or even largely independent streams of work can be undertaken, so that the effect of changes to time and money schedules as much as to the scope of the study can be accommodated with less wide-ranging impact.

Other nontrivial scheduling considerations that are often linked with interpretivist studies include negotiating and sustaining access to appropriate firms and key decision makers as well as portfolio managers and customers, generating data using in-depth interviews and focus groups, iteratively interpreting emerging data in order to develop validated meanings and descriptive concepts about effective decision making, and verifying the substantive theory that the study constructs from the data.

Conduct

This covers implementation of the research design through to and including the generation and verification of the study's findings. Constructing a sample that includes readily accessible participants who voluntarily offer candid and rich accounts as decision advisers, decision makers and portfolio managers is as much a matter of the way the study is presented and marketed as it is a matter of the way researchers connect with, and develop, an engaging, stimulating and professional relationship with participants through data generation, interpretation and validation.

The logistical and organisational challenges of handling potentially large amounts of spoken and written language-based data, and the substantial workload needed to concurrently and iteratively (re)interpret the growing body of data, are also major practical considerations for interpretivist studies. In this example this would involve reviews with cohorts of decision makers in the first instance, and eventually a possibly wider sample of related managers, specialist advisers and portfolio customers chosen from beyond the participating firms in order to strengthen the validation of the findings.

Reporting

Highlights can be expected to cover the aim of the study to help develop principles for competent portfolio decision making, findings that can be used to help improve the development of relevant managerial decision practices, and contributions to methodology and substantive theory that may usefully inform further research.

ACTIVITIES AND RESOURCES

This section at the end of each chapter suggests further reading, and offers discussion and practice development activities.

 EXERCISES AND QUESTIONS

1 Using bibliometric studies, locate exemplary texts and journal articles on interpretivist methods and techniques for generating and analysing data and reporting interpretivist studies.

2 In interpretivist studies we refer to the generation of data, whereas in positivist studies we refer to the collection of data. Discuss the different meanings and their implications for research design, conduct and reporting.

3 (a) Review a diverse range of interpretivist studies and prepare a list of the variety of ethical challenges and corresponding arrangements involved.
   (b) Discuss the list and its implications for focusing, designing, conducting, reporting and using interpretivist research.

4 (a) Use bibliometric studies to select a small number of exemplary interpretivist studies on a topic that you are interested in, and review others' critiques of these studies.
   (b) What sorts of strengths and weaknesses arise, and what are the implications of this for designing, conducting and reporting a model interpretivist study on this topic?

5 Questions bring with them implicit assumptions about what exists, as well as what form of inquiry and what product of inquiry will form a basis for answering the question.
   (a) Review a variety of seminal interpretivist studies, and if possible talk to the researchers who conducted the studies. Note their primary and subsidiary research questions, and the process through which these questions arose.
   (b) What assumptions, what forms of inquiry and what products of inquiry were associated with each of these questions?
   (c) Discuss the implications for interpretivist research that arise from your brief review and discussion.

6 From a review of interpretivist research literature, identify forms of data and corresponding technical problems and solutions associated with generating and making sense of them.

IN-DEPTH TOPICS

1   The term 'linear-recursive' sounds like a contradiction in terms. Discuss its meaning and its research implications at both a theoretical and practical level.
2   Key words such as theme, typification, subtext, abstraction, distillation, ideal-typical have various meanings throughout interpretivist research. Scan interpretivist literature and develop a compact set of definitions and illustrations that clearly express the concepts associated with these key words.

FURTHER READING

Arksey, H. and Knight, P. (1999) *Interviewing for Social Scientists: An Introductory Resource with Examples*, London, Sage.

Bauman, Z. (1978) *Hermeneutics and Social Science: Approaches to Understanding*, London, Hutchinson.

Blaikie, N. (2007) *Approaches to Social Enquiry: Advancing Knowledge*, 2nd edn, Cambridge, Polity Press.

Blumer, H. (1969) *Symbolic Interactionism: Perspective and Method*, Englewood Cliffs, New Jersey, Prentice Hall.

Bryman, A. (1988) *Quantity and Quality in Social Research*, London, Unwin Hyman.

Collis, J. and Hussey, R. (2003) *Business Research Methods: A Practical Guide for Undergraduates and Postgraduates*, 2nd edn, Basingstoke, Palgrave Macmillan.

Craib, I. (1992) *Anthony Giddens*, London, Routledge.

Denzin, N. K. and Lincoln, Y. S. (eds) (2000) *Handbook of Qualitative Research*, 2nd edn, Thousand Oaks, California, Sage.

Flick, U. (2002) *An Introduction to Qualitative Research*, 2nd edn, London, Sage.

Giddens, A. (1971) *Capitalism and Modern Social Theory: An Analysis of the Writings of Marx, Durkheim and Max Weber,* Cambridge, Cambridge University Press.

Giddens, A. (1976) *New Rules of Sociological Method*, London, Hutchinson.

Giddens, A. (1979) *Central Problems in Social Theory: Action, Structure and Contradiction in Social Analysis,* London, Macmillan.

Giddens, A. (1984) *The Constitution of Society: Outline of the Theory of Structuration*, Cambridge, Polity Press.

Gubrium, J. F. and Holstein, J. A. (1997) *The New Language of Qualitative Method*, New York, Oxford University Press.

Gummerson, E. (2000) *Qualitative Methods in Management Research*, 2nd edn, Thousand Oaks, California, Sage.

Hallebone, E. L. (2001) 'Phenomenological Constructions of Pyschosocial Identities' in R. Barnacle (ed.), *Phenomenology: Qualitative Research Methods*, Melbourne, RMIT University Press.

Hammersley, M. (1992) *What's Wrong with Ethnography?* London, Routledge.

Hammersley, M. and Atkinson, P. (1983) *Ethnography Principles in Practice*, London, Tavistock.

Kvale, S. (1996) *InterViews: An Introduction to Qualitative Research Interviewing*, Thousand Oaks, California, Sage.

Laing, R. D. (1967) *The Politics of Experience and the Bird of Paradise*, Harmondsworth, Penguin.

Mason, J. (1996) *Qualitative Researching*, London, Sage.

Morse, J. M. and Richards. L. (2002) *Readme First for a User's Guide to Qualitative Methods*, Thousand Oaks, California, Sage.

Rubin, H. J. and Rubin, I. (1995) *Qualitative Interviewing: The Art of Hearing Data*, London, Sage.

Schütz, A. (1963a) 'Concept and theory formation in the social sciences', in M. A. Natanson (ed.), *Philosophy of the Social Sciences*, New York, Random House.

Schütz. A. (1963b) 'Common-sense and scientific interpretation of human action', in M. A. Natanson (ed.), *Philosophy of the Social Sciences*, New York, Random House.

Schütz, A. (1970) 'Interpretive sociology', in H. R. Wagner (ed.), *Alfred Schutz on Phenomenology and Social Relations*, Chicago University of Chicago Press , pp. 265–93.

Schütz, A. (1976) *The Phenomenology of the Social World*, London, Heinemann.

Schütz, A. and Luckmann, T. (1973) *The Structures of the Life World*, trans. R. M. Zaner and H. T. Engelhardt, Chicago, Northwestern University Press.

Seale, C. (1999) *The Quality of Qualitative Research*, London, Sage.

Shaw, I. (1999) *Qualitative Evaluation: Introducing Qualitative Methods*, London, Sage.

Silverman, D. (1985) *Qualitative Methodology and Sociology*, Aldershot, Hampshire, Gower.

Silverman, D. (2000) *Doing Qualitative Research: A Practical Handbook*, London, Sage

8

CRITICALIST EXAMPLES OF INVESTIGATIVE THEORY AND PRACTICE

CONTEXT

Of the three research paradigms featured in this book, the criticalist perspective is the most recent, and as a research methodology is relatively undeveloped. While considerable work has been done on the theoretical need for this perspective (e.g. Alvesson and Wilmott 1988, 1992; Alvesson and Deetz 1996), clear methodological guidelines are yet to be developed.

If this need for a criticalist perspective is acknowledged, then an implementation path is suggested by Johnson and Duberley (2000: 177–92), who provided a basis to articulate theoretical principles of a pragmatic critical realism. This orientation helps to bridge the gap between a perceived need for a criticalist perspective on research about issues of inequalities (which manifest as power differences) within business and management, and the need for guidance in how to conduct such research.

In a four-cell matrix which features various ontologies and epistemologies in research paradigms, Johnson and Duberley (2000: 180) located four quadrants, one of which (the southwest quadrant) is an objectivist ontology with subjectivist epistemology. With this, the objective ontology combined with a constructionist epistemology comprises what they call *pragmatic-critical realist research*. This is the inspiration for the research approach illustrated by the two examples featured in this chapter. (From now on, and for brevity, we refer to pragmatic critical realist research as *criticalist research*.)

INTRODUCTION

Following from the above, rigorous criticalist studies will share an explicit realist ontology and a constructionist and subjective, and sometimes intersubjective, epistemology. Figure 8.1 highlights the major steps and the way they combine to guide the research process.

To explain and illustrate the nature of research in this paradigm it is useful to refer to theoretically coherent practice guides. This chapter presents a possible set of such guides which are exemplified using two cases; one in MIS and one in strategic marketing. The guides offered here are founded on explicit and internally consistent ontological, epistemological and methodological assumptions. In this introduction we highlight key ontological assumptions,

Figure 8.1

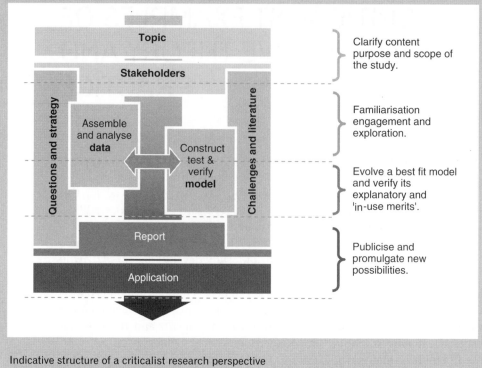

Indicative structure of a criticalist research perspective

typical epistemological positions, and important elements of methodological strategy. This is done in order to set the scene for a possible set of practice guides that criticalist researchers may refer to in order to establish and assert the integrity of their research, as much as to develop useful actionable knowledge.

Foundational assumptions of a critical researcher's view of reality (ontology) are referred to in Johnson and Duberley (2000: 131–2). Also following on from Morrow and Brown (1994) and Kincheloe and McLaren (1998), Johnson and Duberley (2000) reminded us of the following:

- All thought is mediated by socially and historically grounded power relations.
- Human subjectivity is mediated by conscious and unconscious language.
- Concepts and facts about institutional phenomena are dynamic and mediated by the social context in which they arise and are experienced.
- Societies are characterised by both privilege and oppression, which are exacerbated by acceptance of such differences as natural.

- Mainstream research practices often unwittingly contribute to the continuation of the reproduction of class, race, gender and other inequalities.

In order to access and/or generate knowledge within this paradigm, assumptions (and resulting questions) that reflect a criticalist epistemology include:

- There is no theory-neutral observational language or process by which reality may be accessed.

- Ideally the truth value of collected subjectivities increases when more consistencies and fewer inconsistencies are discovered with objective data.
- The truth value of subjective consciousness being constructionist/relativist may also include a false consciousness. Such consciousness manifests as patterns within and between language, actions and consequences that are inconsistent and incoherent with others' patterns of language, actions and consequences (such as institutional differences).
- Unwitting interpretations often mediate interrelationships between ideologies and subjective realities.

- Fundamentally, from the above, it follows that a crucial role for researchers is to be reflexively aware of their own presuppositions and values.
- Also, advisedly, the purpose of criticalist research is for the researcher to help the researched to develop reflexivity that supports the empowerment needed to mitigate inequality and initiate, for instance, organisational change with practical and/or political consequences.

In dealing with all of the above, a key epistemological dilemma concerns what Bhaskar (1989) referred to as transitive and intransitive realities. Transitive realities refer to people's varying interpretations, and intransitive realities refer to researchers' systematic constructions in the form of causal mechanisms. The dilemma is that given the assumption of no theory-neutral observational and interpretive language, a choice must be made about the true merit of the researcher's postulated causal mechanism compared with people's varying interpretations. At the same time, these players' power differences are part of the phenomena they are jointly trying to understand.

From these positions, a criticalist research approach employs a strategy of inquiry which uses a retroductive logic (Bhaskar 1989: 16). Using this logic we can identify regularities in data about individual meanings (transitive realities) and regularities in objective data about observed phenomena, and then postulate and test explanatory (cause–effect) mechanism(s) which can stand as a metaphor, analogy or model of some underlying, but inaccessible reality. These mechanisms represent presently hidden and assumed underlying realities (or intransitive concepts). In this strategy, increasing tangible evidence and consistent explanations reinforce the assertion that the postulated underlying cause–effect reality plausibly exists. In this process it can be argued that, despite the unavoidable flaw of self-referential verification and ethical study, truth is increasingly asserted as the weight of subjective and objective evidence increases independently of diverse interests. Consequently participants and researchers are led to a new synthesis of reality, and the possibility of ethical egalitarian change informed by the knowledge generated.

Some difficulties which should be addressed when designing and conducting criticalist research include:

- Is there a best order in which to mix exploratory research and literature search in order to postulate tentative deep structures or even causal models?
- Is there a best order in which to generate sufficient data so as to postulate tentative deep structures or even causal models?
- How do we gather empirical evidence, and what constitute sufficient regularities in data?
- How is a comprehensive and plausible model constructed?
- How is a choice to be made between simple but less well-supported postulates and more complex and better-supported postulates?
- How is a model tested, and what constitutes sufficient evidence for verification?
- When have we sufficient weight of evidence to outgun the self-referential flaw mentioned above?

Retroduction cycles through developing a description of phenomena, generating and collecting data about the phenomena, identifying regularities across the data, postulating an underlying deep structure and a causal mechanism for the observed phenomena (or as a condition for the observed phenomena), and testing the postulated causal mechanism or causal condition. The cycle of retroductive inquiry stops when the weight of comprehensively consistent evidence for a plausible causal mechanism and associated deep reality is accepted by diverse interests as being more stable, more informative and more enabling than any other known and well-tested alternative.

KEY ELEMENTS IN CRITICALIST STUDIES

Recently, the number and urgency of calls for business and management studies that help to expose the nature of power, politics and inequality in professional and organisational life have accelerated rapidly. Unfortunately, criticalist research is not well articulated in terms of process, partly because the field is relatively young and because some of the issues to be confronted are technically quite complex. On the other hand, the paradigm offers a first-time opportunity to generate knowledge and action in a poorly understood but very important arena. Understanding the criticalist paradigm is assisted by a comprehensive understanding of the elements of the positivist and interpretivist paradigms.

To help the researcher who is intent on a study of power and inequality in organisational life, there follows a guide for the successful completion of an informative and actionable criticalist study, but this should not be taken as an axiomatic prescription for all such studies. In order that a criticalist study is also rigorous, it is essential that the key assumptions and their contingent choices in methodology are explicit and clearly justified.

As indicated in Figure 8.1, key activities in criticalist studies generally do not proceed in a linear fashion, but rather occur in a reflexive and evolutionary way, and involve objective as well as subjective data. Notwithstanding this distinctive difference from the positivist and interpretivist approaches, the elements of criticalist studies typically include the following.

Investigative theory

Theoretical and empirically grounded concepts plus biographical sensitivity

Familiarisation with academic and other literature is used to broaden and stimulate theoretical imagination, broaden organisational awareness and reframe biographical experience. This helps us to stimulate and sharpen our topical interests, and question and reinterpret the ontological and epistemological lenses through which we view and interpret meanings.

Nominal and ordinal variables

Within this paradigm the use of the term variable may be used, not in the sense associated with positivist studies, but rather to identify an aspect of a concept or a relationship between concepts. The word *nominal* simply indicates that a variable can only be known through its description (that is, as a set of attributes) but not by further classifying (as a member of a category) or otherwise by some form of rank or even a numerical measure. Variables may be either discrete (such as units or categories) or continuous (such as height or income). In the case of continuous variables, we must distinguish clearly between the nature of the variable and the instrument and unit of measure.

To move from starting empirical and theoretical concepts the researcher selects variables (often nominal) as tentative representations of phenomena. This helps to delineate a clearer starting point, from the literature and/or exploratory research. Through this process of delineation and resulting focus, some starting concepts may lead to different representations of the phenomena being defined, for which data are generated and/or collected, while other starting concepts may lead to the construction of a tentative model.

To compare this paradigm with the positivist one, the cluster of concepts comprising the tentative model in the criticalist approach may be considered analogous to the independent variables in a positivist approach, and a criticalist description of the phenomena being studied may be considered analogous to the behaviour of the dependent variables in a positivist study. Of course, in a positivist study it is likely that both sets of variables will be numeric, whereas in a criticalist study variables will typically be descriptive and possibly complemented by some numerical data.

Question formation and evolution

Throughout the study, a prime task of the researcher is to ask and refine the best question to elicit the most valuable actionable knowledge which helps to reveal power and forms of inequality.

Considering confounding factors

In criticalist studies confounding factors will include the sort of issues listed in the introduction to this chapter. Two major types of confounding factors arise as a result of, first, the intrinsic complexity of the substantive paradigm and question, and second, the reactionary mediation of the substantive material by at least some participants, disadvantaged people or groups and/or power players in the background with interests they perceive may be challenged or enabled. Such confounding factors, whether present or not in the beginning, may be made manifest or change as the research proceeds.

Recognition of apparent confounding factors of itself may represent valuable knowledge rather than something to be controlled for or even excluded. So the crucial tasks for the researcher are to incorporate this awareness into the latest question and interpret the data astutely.

Population, sampling and data generation

A technically and purposively appropriate representative sample needs to be chosen to reflect the relevant population of the research and the intended use of the findings. In a criticalist study, a researcher's biographical and organisational experience is usually combined with their knowledge of the substantive field of inquiry. This helps the researcher to systematically and imaginatively develop theoretical and/or empirical perspectives on the topic. In this way concepts are rarely drawn directly from the literature alone, but rather reflect the researcher's creative interpretations as well.

Because the purpose of criticalist research is normally to interpret, explain and enable action on issues of power and inequalities, accessibility to informative participants and data can often be difficult. And depending on the nature and purpose of the research, a more than usual measure of ethical scepticism may be needed to ensure that candid and relevant data as well as safe participation are assured. So, it is likely that in criticalist studies, rigorous ethical as well as technical design issues will need particular attention.

As far as sample size is concerned, as the main aim of a criticalist research sample is to acquire rich and diverse data associated with power and inequalities, it is sample mix rather than sample size that is important. In addition, generalisability is sought, and in that case, as is normally the case in positivist studies, a suitably larger sample may be indicated.

Criticalist studies are usually guided by a core question and an emerging explanatory model. As a deeper and wider understanding of the phenomenon of interest emerges from tentative theorising about the accumulating data, such theorising may produce a progressively richer conceptual model, or occasionally an impasse that demands a new constructive approach.

Data generation spans various sources and various types, including theoretical concepts drawn from theoretical and/or empirical literature; successive refinement of questions that, in part, arise from tentative modelling; and discursive verbal and/or text and/or nominal or even ordinal categorical data (which may arise through data analysis as well as the successive refinement and testing of an increasingly plausible model). Typical forms of data generation span objective and subjective styles across at least primary and secondary sources. These typically include interviews, questionnaires, observations, focus groups, documents, organisation and industry statistics and reports.

Data distillation and analysis plus model development and confirmation

This step of criticalist research aims to distil all the data into a compact theoretical model which also provides comprehensive causal explanations of the phenomena of interest in the research question. In this process it is also necessary to confirm the pragmatic and legitimate value of the explanatory knowledge represented by the model. Ideally this includes internal verification with reference to the research question by a subsample of respondents, who are asked to comment on the model and its utility in their own domain, and external formal verification with reference to theoretical, empirical and methodological literature.

A central and controversial task in criticalist analysis concerns the creative combination and synthesis of objective structural data and subjective participant data to form a verified answer to the research question. This might even contain a range of differing typifications which affirm agreement to principles albeit with dissent about details.

Criticalist studies are exposed in so far as there is not a universally agreed technique for creative synthesis. Despite this there are important criteria that can be used to assess the product of creative effort and so establish the merits of the product of this part of the study. These include:

- Objective structural data should help to illuminate the subjective participant data (and vice versa). This is not the case with the other two paradigms, whose validity is only internally consistent because they each have only one form of data – either objective or (inter)subjective.
- Combinations are facilitated by recognition and/or explanation of the nature of power and/or inequality revealed to representative participants.

So objective and subjective data are not combined if they do not enable revelatory insight.

- Synthesis is the refinement of the emerging model to the extent that there is wider (dis)confirmation.
- Effective creative effort must reveal both doubts and assurances which comprise a critique of the research process by the researchers.

Reviewing aspects of data analysis in Chapter 6 and Chapter 7 may help the reader apprehend the comprehensive nature of data generation and data analysis that operates in criticalist research.

Investigative practice

Reporting the study's findings

This should be an interesting account which potentially enables and possibly even facilitates change. The report combines the researcher's language which subsumes findings from analysis of objective and subjective data, participants' accounts of issues of relevance in their worlds and the related explanatory value of the research model, and comparative highlights of the extant knowledge about the substantive phenomena, which demonstrates the advances in knowledge and its utility.

Critique of research

It is important to reflect on the study's conduct with particular reference to both the researcher's and participants' roles in data generation, data interpretation and validation of the eventual model and its utility for change. In particular, in criticalist studies, researchers combine objective dispassionate observation with collaboration, investigation and detection. Furthermore, as criticalist studies usually seek to explore, uncover and describe particular phenomena and refine an explanatory model, criticalist reflection must expose the dualistic nature of the study and the basis for verification.

While the philosophical foundations are long established, methodological guidelines are sparse. So it is important to highlight statements which arise from the conduct of a study and which help to clarify methodological challenges and their treatments.

The remainder of this chapter illustrates the approach and outcomes for Example 3 and Example 6, with a focus on the aspects shown in Tables 8.1 and 8.2. Table 8.1 notes typical features of investigative theory for a criticalist study about management of investments in business information systems and for a criticalist study of the politics of decision making for a firm's product portfolio. Table 8.2 notes typical features of investigative practice for these two criticalist examples. Aspects of investigative theory and practice for these two examples are then discussed.

Table 8.1 Highlights of investigative theory for two **criticalist** examples

Investigative theory		Example 3 Business information systems investments	Example 6 Politics of portfolio choices
Criticalist research			
Question or hypothesis		Do (and how do) political and technical considerations influence executives' go/no-go decisions about investments in strategic IT business information systems?	How are executives' preferences and choices for the firm's product portfolio mix informed and influenced by their organisation-political contexts?
Philosophy of science	**Ontology** How reality is viewed	**Realist and relativist** Dual reality: objective realities exist as institutional arrangements concurrent with local and individualistically relied-on subjective realities.	
	Epistemology How knowledge is generated	**Pragmatic constructionist** – a composite of objective and intersubjective data from which knowledge of reality is negotiated. An iterative process of pragmatic critical theorising generates a descriptive and explanatory model which is further used in a prescriptive or predictive way for the purpose of emancipation.	
Argument **structure**		**Iterative** and evolutionary development of plausibility that increases with more diverse evidence and the absence of contradiction.	
Inquiry's main **logic**		**Retroductive** reasoning iteratively refines an analogic model that is grounded in diverse objective and subjective data.	
Methodology	Purpose	**Nomothetic** – explain particular phenomena.	
	Tactic	Using empirical data, construct explanatory transformative theory.	
Researcher's **stance**		**Etic/emic.**	
Main **methods**		**Quantitative and qualitative** (e.g. statistical and language-based dialogic methods).	
Approach and outcomes		A typology of practice principles ... that results in ... a model of causal links and actions between funding decisions and funding outcomes for investment cases.	Classify and test elements of case-specific decision making ... to produce ... a model of causal links between characteristics of social context and new product choices.

Table 8.2 Highlights of investigative practice for two **criticalist** examples

Investigative practice		
Criticalist research	**Example 3** Business information systems investments	**Example 6** Politics of portfolio choices
Proposal focus to highlight ...	The importance of knowing more about decisions that enhance the life time value of a firm's portfolio of strategic IT-based business information systems.	The importance of knowing about, and being able to better mediate, the impact of organisational-political influences on decisions that affect the overall strengths of a firm's product portfolio.
Indicative **ethical** issues	Manipulation of data and find-ings to advantage or disadvan-tage executives as well as particular institutional views.	Discrimination and misuse of resources with differential advan-tage to different areas of the firm and its customers.
Likely **funding** sources	The potential value of the study implies that industry and government support should be sought plus support from firms.	Funding from individual firms see benefit in the types of results that may emerge from such a study.
Significant **scheduling** considerations	Obtaining comparable objective life time data for each business information system in the sample. Identify and access executives' and stakeholders' relevant first-hand experiences with sample cases.	Obtaining comparable product portfolio data. Identifying and accessing executives with first-hand experience of decisions, their contexts and their consequences.
Key **conduct** factors	Good technical supervision and strong samples with rich and comparable data. Wise political counsel about how to deal with political influence as well as ensure good participation and access to busy executives.	
Reporting	Industry and practice uses of the new model and accounts of, and reflections on, its explicit/implicit practice and ethical implications as well as advice about further research.	

EXAMPLE 3: INVESTMENTS IN BUSINESS INFORMATION SYSTEMS

Investigative theory

This comprises theoretical and empirically grounded concepts plus biographical sensitivity across the following elements.

Question

Do, and how do, political and technical considerations influence executives' go/no-go decisions about investments in strategic IT-based business information systems?

Philosophy

This type of study involves a dualist philosophy of science in which objective and subjective data are combined. In this type of research study one choice of *ontology* is realist. From this orientation underlying phenomena exist independently of the researcher and participants. Such objective phenomena may include, for instance, internal executive coalitions and the reported lifetime value to the firm of past and present strategic management information systems (MIS). From this perspective objective concepts about executives' decisions about the scope and progress of strategic MIS may be idiosyncratic and multilayered. One way to know these realities is through a pragmatic criticalist epistemology in which objective data are obtained using an observational language that emulates, as far as practicable, a theory-neutral stance.

In addition, a second type of ontology is relativist. From this orientation participants may offer concepts and meanings about, for instance, executives' likes and dislikes. In this orientation a constructionist epistemology is used to, first, generate executives' subjective concepts and meanings for technical and political considerations that they perceive as influencing go/no-go decisions; and second, negotiate intersubjective (shared) meanings between the researcher and executives, as well as between executives, about perceptions and meanings that play a part in the technical and political aspects of go/no-go decisions.

This dualistic methodology offers a way to augment and/or compare volunteered subjective and negotiated intersubjective meanings with independently acquired objective data. By doing this the researcher aims to acquire more broadly insightful understanding of otherwise more incomplete or inconsistent data.

Logic of inquiry

An overarching retroductive logic provides the reasoning basis for iteratively exploring, describing, analysing and testing an explanatory model for the phenomenon being studied. A retroductive logic serves the need to build insights about techno-political considerations and influences on executives' go/no-go decisions for strategic MIS.

Methodology

Objectively measured data will be needed recording the lifetime value of strategic MIS in a firm. In addition, and as a complement to this objective data, it will be necessary to explore and generate executives' accounts of political and technical issues and consequent considerations. Together with the objective data, these can be used by the researcher to tentatively explain the influence of political and technical considerations on executives' decisions about strategic IT-based business information systems. A mixed *nomothetic* and *idiographic* style of investigation through statistical data and case-study-based interview is indicated.

In a dialectical process, the researcher compares and contrasts objective and subjective data in order to progressively develop and refine an explanatory model of techno-political considerations and influences on executives' go/no-go decisions for strategic MIS. The research process stops when sufficiently widely affirmed theoretical understanding is reached about the nature of executives' sensitivities for techno-political contexts and their choices about approving, modifying or cancelling particular investments in the firm's portfolio of strategic IT-based business information systems.

Stance

The combined stance we choose is *etic*, in which the researcher uses externally acquired objective (for instance, statistical) data, and *emic*, in which the researcher as a collaborator with participants (the executives) works to access, co-generate and interpret executives' subjective and intersubjective accounts of decision-making processes and outcomes.

Methods

Both mathematical and language-based methods (typically appropriate to the study of verbal and written texts) are used to process the various forms of data. The resulting model which reflects assumed underlying mechanisms is likely to be described discursively, with the possible support of schematics and mathematical models to highlight relationships and rules about techno-political considerations and influences on executives' go/no-go decisions about investments in strategic MIS.

Investigative practice

Investigative practice for aspects of this criticalist study comprises the following elements.

Proposal

In this case specific proposal highlights can be expected to deal with motivation, importance and purpose. Characterising the study's *motivation* illuminates the nature of, and enables an informed and ethical dynamic between, executives' rational commercial and techno-political approaches involving their own and colleagues' interests in strategic IT-based business information systems.

The *importance* of such a study is reflected in the past 50 years' consistently poor track record of high-cost strategic MIS investments. This underpins strong political and economic pressures on executives to make decisions about the scope and future of investments in strategic MIS that are personally and organisationally beneficial. This setting creates opportunities for politically inspired competition between executives, and also sustains a disincentive to make bold and innovative decisions, and sustained executive action to implement the right investments in strategic MIS. Better understanding of intrinsic power arrangements and consequent imbalances help to better protect the firm's reputation for guiding long-run successful investments in strategic IT-based business information systems.

The study's *purpose* is about generating more useful and better theoretically grounded understanding of executives' political as well as commercial preferences for scoping and progressing MIS investments affecting their own business operations as well as the firm overall. It is also to show how the theoretical understanding of the substantive topic and research approach may be developed systematically and also enable change.

Ethics

Ethical risks include executives not being allowed, or prepared, to divulge techno-political perceptions and preferences that they rely on or ignore in their own practice; research findings being used to increase politicisation at the expense of optimal investment mix; organisation stakeholders being more or less preferred or ignored through poor research design and sampling; some executives' views being privileged or others excluded or downplayed; and the researcher being subject, by some participants or the organisation being studied, to (in)direct pressure (for instance through funding, facilities, reputation or such like) to modify the study's scope and/or its approach, or its findings.

Funding

This study has a prospect of providing valuable knowledge for industry, for boards of directors, for executives and for firm performance. It can be expected to provide useful material to be included in executive and business practice education about MIS governance. For this reason, in looking for funding sources the researcher should consider industry and government assistance as well as funding from specific firms interested in better executive practice.

Schedules

As this example is an exploratory and theoretical design, there are likely to be stage tasks whose scope are difficult to reliably estimate in advance. Major tasks in this study include:

- From the literature, tentative construction of a model for techno-political executive decision making when investing in strategic MIS.

- Choose one IT-intensive firm or a purposeful sample of suitable firms, each with appropriate cases to study, plus a sample of associated executives and others with a long-run stake in strategic IT-based business information systems.
- Construct interviewing schedules and select sources of primary and secondary data (such as case reports and reports of industry statistics).
- Carry out data reduction, coding and analysis.
- Refine and verify the tentative model of executives' techno-political decisions about strategic MIS.
- Report the theoretical and practice findings and their use.

As referred to in the investigative theory section, the data reduction, coding and analysis, and refinement and verification, steps are particularly complex and difficult to schedule or budget. Additionally, explanation of the process and research critique is especially important.

Because of the unpredictable nature of the dualistic character of criticalist research, process and timeframe are difficult to estimate. The research process stops when no new important insights emerge despite continuing efforts to discredit the explanatory model produced.

Conduct (execution of research)

In addition to the special role of literature in this study to develop the starting model, methods for eliciting and making sense of executives' subjective meanings at a micro level (such as through interviews) about techno-political considerations, consequent MIS investment decisions and their consequences must be combined with methods for obtaining, analysing and comparing objective macro data about outcomes of strategic MIS investments that are progressed as well as those that are suspended or terminated.

Because of the evolving link between data and the refined model, the different forms of data collection, condensation and analysis can be expected to proceed incrementally – in an interlocking manner – much like the teeth of a zip.

Reporting

Typical aspects include the formal account of the research study's aims, scope, conduct and limitations; a formal account of the study's findings and implications for practice and change as well as further research; the new model and a description of its meaning for executives' decisions and their techno-political considerations about strategic MIS; implications of the study's findings for techno-political considerations in executive's MIS-directed decisions and their subsequent use and value in executive and business education; and methodological insights for the paradigm which come from the conduct of a criticalist (pragmatic realist) study.

EXAMPLE 6: THE POLITICS OF PORTFOLIO CHOICES

Context

Senior executives in major firms with dominant investment products and/or services are often faced with the problem of choosing whether to favour new product or service releases or withdrawals at the expense of further supporting established and successful products or services in a particular portfolio. This raises interesting questions, including those related to the possible impact of executives' political aspirations and affiliations on their preferences and choices for product life cycle strategies, as well as their knowledge of, and preference for, particular markets and types of products.

In this setting an important issue relates to the organisational-political climate and market perceptions that mediate executives' strategic decisions about their own and their firm's product portfolios.

Investigative theory

This comprises theoretical and empirically grounded concepts plus biographical sensitivity across the following elements.

Question

The question relates to the extent to which executive choice may be informed by executives' organisational-political contexts. The precise question is, do (and how do) executive preferences and choices for the firm's product portfolio mix become informed and influenced by their organisational-political contexts?

Philosophy

This type of study involves a dualist philosophy of science in which objective and subjective data are combined. In this type of research study one choice of *ontology* is *realist*. From this orientation underlying phenomena exists independently of the researcher and participants. They include executives' likes, dislikes, internal executive coalitions, portfolios, products, investment levels and returns, and legal, technical and economic infrastructures.

In this perspective objective concepts and meanings about investment products and performances, executive remuneration, market share and strategy may be idiosyncratic and multilayered. One way to know these realities is through a pragmatic criticalist epistemology in which objective data are obtained using an observational language that emulates, as far as practicable, a theory-neutral stance.

In addition, the second type of ontology is *relativist*. From this orientation a constructionist epistemology is used to generate executives' subjective concepts and meanings. Doing this is likely to involve researcher and participants in negotiating intersubjective (shared) meanings.

This dualistic methodology offers a way to augment and/or compare volunteered subjective meanings with independently acquired objective data. By doing this the researcher seeks to acquire more broadly insightful understanding of incomplete or inconsistent data.

Logic of inquiry

An overarching retroductive logic is used to guide the way an explanatory model for this phenomenon is iteratively explored, described, analysed and tested. A retroductive logic serves the need to build insights about politically influenced executive action.

Methodology

The purpose here is to explore and generate a model that tentatively explains executives' politically influenced action. Objectively measured data recording a firm's investment performance, perceived prospects and forecast economic climate will also be required. A mixed nomothetic and idiographic style of investigation through statistical data and case study interview is indicated.

In a dialectical process, the researcher compares and contrasts objective and subjective data in order to progressively develop and refine an explanatory model of politically influenced executive action. This process stops when sufficiently widely affirmed theoretical understanding is reached about the nature of executives' sensitivities for organisational-political contexts and their resulting strategic choices in the firm's investment portfolio.

Stance

The combined stance that is chosen is *emic*, which positions the researcher as a collaborator with participants (the executives), as well as an *etic* stance, where the researcher uses externally acquired objective (for instance, statistical) data.

Methods

Both mathematical and language (typically spoken and written text) methods are used to process the varied forms of data. The resulting model which reflects assumed underlying mechanisms is likely to be described discursively, with the possible support of schematics to highlight rules, relationships and dynamics about politically influenced executive action.

Investigative practice

Investigative practice for aspects of this criticalist study comprises the following elements.

Proposal

In this case specific proposal highlights can be expected to include reference to motivation for the study, the study's importance and the study's specific purpose. Aspects of *motivation* to be noted are those aspects that illuminate the nature of, and enable an informed and ethical dynamic between, executives' rational and organisational-political approaches involving their own and colleagues' investment portfolio mixes.

Highlights about the *importance* of the study can be expected to refer to the significant economic weight and fast-moving nature of investment markets, and the related opportunities for politically inspired competition between executives. A better understanding of intrinsic power arrangements and consequent imbalances would help to better protect the firm's reputation and obligations to its shareholders.

The study's *purpose* can be expected to comment on the need to generate theoretical understanding of executives' (sometimes politicised) rational preferences for managing their own, and the firm's portfolio of, investment products. It may also aim to show how the theoretical understanding of the substantive topic and research approach may be systematically developed, and also enable change.

Ethics

Ethical risks include executives not being allowed, or prepared to, divulge organisational-political perceptions and preferences that they (sometimes unconsciously) account for in their practice; research findings being used to increase politicisation at the expense of optimal investment mix; shareholders and investors being disadvantaged through poor research design and sampling; some executives' views being privileged, or others excluded or downplayed; and the researcher being subject, by some participants or their organisations, to (in)direct pressure (through funding, facilities, reputation or such like) to modify the scope or approach to the study or its findings.

Funding

This study has a prospect of providing valuable knowledge for an industry and for executives. It can be expected to provide useful material to be included in executive and business practice education. For this reason, researchers looking for funding sources should consider industry and government assistance as well as funding from specific firms interested in better executive practice.

Schedules

As this example is an exploratory and theoretical design, there are likely to be stage tasks whose scope it is difficult to estimate reliably in advance. Major tasks in this study include:

- Use the literature to construct a tentative model for politically influenced executive action.
- Choose one or a few case study firm(s) and a sample of their executives.
- Construct interviewing schedules and select sources of primary and secondary data (such as reports of industry statistics).
- Carry out data reduction, coding and analysis.
- Refine and verify the tentative model of politically influenced executive action.
- Report on the theoretical and practice findings and their use.

As referred to in the investigative theory section, the data reduction, coding and analysis, and refinement and verification, steps are particularly complex, and both scheduling and budgeting are often likely to involve complex and frequently changing tradeoffs. Explanation of the process and research critique are also especially important as buy-in by participants with often competing interests and needs must usually be established and sustained in order that well-scoped, revealing and illuminating investigations can continue.

Because of the unpredictable and dualistic character of criticalist research, the investigative process and the nature of progress markers may remain challenging for most of the study's time frame. Ideally the research process ceases when no new important insights emerge despite continuing efforts to discredit the best emergent explanatory model.

Conduct (execution of research)

In addition to the special role of literature in this study to develop the starting model, methods for eliciting and making sense at a micro level (for instance, through interviews) of executives' subjective meanings about investments, portfolios, their firm's practice and organisational-political arrangements must be combined with methods for obtaining, analysing and comparing objective macro data about their industry, the economic climate and their investment performances and competitiveness. In particular, because of the evolving link between data and the emerging model, different forms of data collection, condensation and analysis can be expected to proceed in interlocking steps, much like the teeth of a zip.

Reporting

Typical aspects to be included in the research report are a formal account of the research study's aims, scope, conduct and limitations; a formal account of the study's findings and implications for practice and change as well as further research; the new model and a description of its meaning for executive practice and political influence in investment management; implications of the study's findings for politically influenced executive action in executive and business education; and methodological insights for the paradigm which come from the conduct of a criticalist (pragmatic realist) study.

ACTIVITIES AND RESOURCES

This section at the end of each chapter suggests further reading, and offers discussion and practice development activities.

1 Identify several key debates about the possibility of theory-neutral inquiry.
2 From the literature identify practical approaches that can help to develop self-conscious reflexivity in research participants and researchers.
3 From the literature identify contra-debates about the desirability and efficacy of self-conscious reflexivity in critical research.
    (a) Discuss the relevance of self-conscious reflexivity to situations where power and inequality mediate business and management practice.
4 Survey the literature in exemplary studies of critical business, organisation and management research.
    (a) Trace the prevalence and focus of studies of power, politics and inequality over recent decades.
    (b) What seems to be driving this?
5 The dual purposes of (i) interpretation that enables explanation. and (ii) understanding that enables action, may be criticised for embodying a self-serving interest.
    (a) Discuss the theoretical and practical challenges that this dual purpose raises.
    (b) Suggest ways to avoid compromising the integrity of either or both objectives in critical research.
6 Search for critical business and management research reports that describe challenges and approaches to interpreting (objective) structural data and subjective participant data.
    (a) How developed do these accounts appear to be, and why is this so?
    (b) What major theoretical and practical challenges do you see still needing to be accounted for?
7 Locate exemplary critical business or management studies that have generated independently validated revelatory insights from objective and subjective data.
    (a) What designs and methods resulted in this outcome?
    (b) Critique these designs and suggest improvements.

IN-DEPTH TOPICS

1 (a) Biography and biographical sensitivity are concepts that relate to self-awareness. Review the literature and develop an understanding of the importance and character of these concepts and their theoretical and practical relevance to criticalist research.

   (b) Similarly, culture, cultural heritage and related sensitivities have gathered an array of recent meanings. What are some of the main meanings and research implications of these concepts?

FURTHER READING

Agger, B. (1998) *Critical Social Theories: An Introduction*, Boulder, Colorado, Westview Press/HarperCollins.

Alvesson, M. and Deetz, S. (1996) 'Critical theory and postmodernism: approaches to organization studies' in S. R. Clegg, C. Hardy and W. R. Nord (eds), *Handbook of Organization Studies*, London, Sage.

Alvesson, M. and Deetz, S. (2000) *Doing Critical Management Research,* London, Sage.

Alvesson, M. and Willmott, H. (1988) *Critical Theory and the Sciences of Management. The Frankfurt School: How Relevant is it Today?* Rotterdam, Erasmus University.

Alvesson,M and Willmott, H. (1996) *Making Sense of Management: A Critical Introduction*, London, Sage.

Alvesson, M. and Willmott, H. (2003) *Studying Management Critically*, London, Sage.

Bauman, Z. (1978) *Hermeneutics and Social Science: Approaches to Understanding*, London, Hutchinson.

Bauman, Z. (1992) *Intimations of Postmodernity*, London, Routledge.

Beck, U. (2000) *The Brave New World of Work*, trans. P. Camiller, Cambridge, Polity Press.

Benton, T. (1984) *The Rise and Fall of Structural Marxism: Althusser and his Influence*, London and Basingstoke, Macmillan.

Bhaskar, R. (1975) *A Realist Theory of Science*, Brighton, Harvester Press.

Bhaskar, R. (1989) *The Possibility of Naturalism,* 2nd edn, Brighton, Harvester Press.

Birnbaum, N. (1971) *Toward a Critical Sociology*, New York, Oxford University Press.

Blackburn, R. (ed.) (1972) *Ideology in Social Science: Readings in Critical Social Theory,* Glasgow, Fontana/Collins.

Daniher, G., Schirato, T. and Webb, J. (2000) *Understanding Foucault*, St. Leonards, New South Wales, Australia, Allen & Unwin.

DeLauretis, T. (ed.) (1986) *Feminist Studies/Critical Studies*, Basingstoke and London, Macmillan Press.

Eichler, M. (1987) *Nonsexist Research Methods: A Practical Guide*, Boston, Mass., Allen & Unwin.

Evans, M. (1997) *Introducing Contemporary Feminist Thought*, Cambridge, Polity Press.

Giddens, A. (1971) *Capitalism and Modern Social Theory: An Analysis of the Writings of Marx, Durkheim and Max Weber,* Cambridge, Cambridge University Press.

Harré, R. (1961) *Theories and Things,* London, Heinemann Educational.

Hood, S., Mayall, B. and Oliver, S. (eds) (1999) *Critical Issues in Social Research: Power and Prejudice*, Ballmoor, Buckingham, Open University Press.

Johnson, P. and Duberley, J. (2000) *Understanding Management Research*, London, Sage.

Keat, R. and Urry, J. (1982) *Social Theory as Science,* London, Routledge and Kegan Paul.

Kincheloe, J. L. and McLaren, P. L. (1998) 'Rethinking critical theory and qualitative research', in N. K. Denzin and Y. S. Lincoln, *The Handbook of Qualitative Research*, Thousand Oaks, California, Sage, pp. 260–99.

Larrain, J. (1979) *The Concept of Ideology*, London, Hutchinson.

McLellan, D. (ed.) (1977) *Karl Marx: Selected Writings*, Oxford, Oxford University Press.

Morrow, R. and Brown, D. (1994) *Critical Theory and Methodology*, London, Sage.

Outhwaite, W. (1987) *New Philosophies of Social Science: Realism, Hermeneutics and Critical Theory*, London, Allen & Unwin.

Outhwaite, W. (1994) *Habermas: a Critical Introduction*, Oxford, Polity Press.

Pawson, R. (1989) *A Measure for Measures: A Manifesto for Empirical Sociology*, London, Routledge.

Pusey, M. (1987) *Jurgen Habermas, Key Sociologists,* Chichester, Ellis Horwood/ Tavistock.

Seidman, S. (ed.) (1994) *The Postmodern Turn: New Perspectives on Social Theory*, Cambridge, Cambridge University Press.

Sim, S. (ed.) (1998) *The Icon Critical Dictionary of Postmodern Thought,* Duxford, Cambridge, Icon Books/Penguin.

Willmott, H. (1992) 'Beyond paradigmatic closure in organisational enquiry', in J. Hassard and D. Pym, *The Theory and Philosophy of Organisations,* London, Routledge.

Willmott, H. C. (1995) 'What has been happening in organization theory and does it matter?, *Personnel Review*, 24 (9): 33–53.

Willmott, H. (1997) 'Rethinking management and managerial work: capitalism, control and subjectivity', *Human Relations*, 50 (11): 1329–59.

PART IV

SUMMARY

9

SUMMARY AND POINTERS FOR FURTHER UNDERSTANDING OF MAJOR PARADIGMS

This chapter is in two parts:

- **A summary** of the main messages in the book – especially the mental model about theoretical and practice aspects of doing business and management research, and the three indicative roadmaps for each of the positivist, interpretivist and criticalist paradigms.
- **Pointers for further understanding major paradigms**. This is for the reader who may wish to follow more conceptual depth within the three paradigms. To date, within the book, their character has been highlighted and juxtaposed using mental models of their styles, and illustrations of their use in the fields of MIS and strategic marketing.

PART 1: SUMMARY

Throughout this book we have variously referred to the mental model (or roadmap) depicted in Figure 9.1. Its importance rests in the way in which it integrates important theoretical and practical aspects of a programme of rigorous scientific inquiry.

A second important message about the nature of business and management research concerns the importance of selecting a paradigm of scientific inquiry and designing a research approach (for instance, specifying the purpose of the study and the nature of the research question, be it descriptive, exploratory or explanatory, for instance) as well as clearly specifying the gap in knowledge in the substantive area that is to be addressed. To help do this the reader has been introduced to three paradigms, each with two examples (one from MIS and one from strategic marketing), in order to illustrate the paradigms in use. Highlights of each the three paradigm-based approaches are captured in the thumbnail diagrams in Figure 9.2.

The examples used to illustrate each paradigm-based approach contrast differences in the application of each paradigm, and emphasise the link between the paradigm choice, research design and the type of knowledge that can be generated. From the examples it can also be seen that the same choice of paradigm generates similar forms of knowledge despite there being wide variety in the substantive topic and question.

Figure 9.1

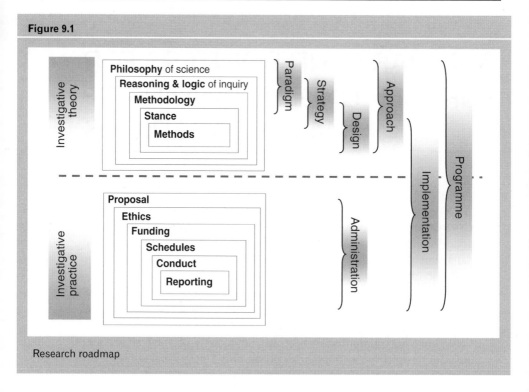

Research roadmap

Investigative theory

A counterpoint that also needs to be emphasised is that for the same substantive topic, and the same question, a different choice of paradigm and consequent design will generate different forms of knowledge and different insight and answers to the same question. This point is illustrated in the example below. This counterpoint example juxtaposes the positivist approach illustrated in Chapter 6's Example 4 (the substantive topic is about personal electronic goods and services, and the research question is, are the sales of products or services more affected by price, functionality or brand recognition?) with an interpretivist approach to investigating the same question.

The question 'Are the sales of products or services more affected by price, functionality or brand recognition?' is the same in both the positivist example (Chapter 6, Example 4) and the interpretivist example below. The subheadings in the example below parallel those used in Chapter 6 Example 4. This is done to simplify comparisons between the two examples while also clearly demonstrating differences between the two (paradigm) approaches to the same question.

The nature of reasoning

This question is addressed in two phases. The first is linear, and the major and subsequent phase is recursive. Sensitising concepts about factors associated

Figure 9.2

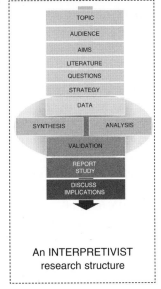

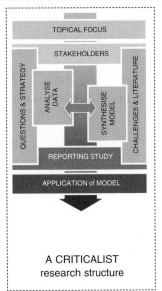

A POSITIVIST
research structure

An INTERPRETIVIST
research structure

A CRITICALIST
research structure

Positivist studies are characterised by their *linear* approach, and their early and detailed attention to constructing hypotheses and study conditions. After design and data collection, the remaining steps are completed comparatively quickly.

Interpretivist studies are characterised by an *iterative* exploratory phase integrated within a linear approach to establish and conclude the study. Most of the intellectual and physical effort in an Interpretivist study is taken up in the *iterative* phase. The early phase of familiarisation and design, as well as the final step to report the study, proceed in a broadly linear way, and are comparatively less onerous than the iterative middle.

Criticalist studies involve *cycles* of exploring, comparing, modelling and testing, which aim to develop robust explanatory models that incorporate inequalities and the role of power. They aim to report explanatory models that offer a validated probabilistic base for understanding and prediction. Criticalist studies work with objective data and subjective accounts and interpretations. Analyses of each class of data are used to direct exploration, propose and refine explanatory models, and develop hypotheses to test and qualify 'better-fit' models, and ultimately a 'best-fit' model.

Thumbnail outlines of three research paradigms

with the management of product or services marketing and sales, as well as consumer influences and buyer choices, are first developed from the literature. They may subsequently be modified according to the researcher's experience and as a consequence of the abductive logic used in which data are recursively generated, used and analysed.

Sensitising concepts and familiarisation

In addition to elaborating and refining the initially established sensitising concepts from the substantive literature, other sources of inspiration and clarification may arise from the stock of knowledge and the interpreted experience of seasoned marketers, retailers who are currently selling the product or service, and a range of present and prospective consumers. By doing this the researcher's interpretive framework may be modified and enlarged throughout the research process in order to better encapsulate participants' meanings while also facilitating use of the researcher's understandings. This produces the required rich and shared intersubjective meanings on which the interpretivist approach depends.

In this example there are four initial sensitising concepts: consumer, consumer choice, product or service, and the offer.

Nominal and ordinal variables

In this study, as a starting point and treating them as sensitising concepts, there are four nominal variables: the consumer, the consumer's choice, the product or service, and the offer (price, functionality and brand). As the purpose of the study is to explore the relative importance of offer factors, it is important to explore the nature and meanings of buyer intentions and buyer intentions in the field, and then to integrate these insights into a theoretical model of offer factors and the choices that buyers are expected to make.

The only obvious (continuous) ordinal variable is price, whereas the other (discrete) variables are, at first sight, multidimensional and incommensurate.

Choice of central concepts and their synthesis as variables

The central nominal variables are price, functionality and brand association. Price, which also incorporates a scalar value that reflects revenue and sales volume, can be thought of an ordinal variable. Functionality is a set of nominal categories that are prioritised by respondents; these categories describe the product's capabilities (including new or unique features) compared with other products for the same market. Brand association is a composite of nominal categories, familiarity with the brand or brand novelty, and attribution of trust in the brand compared with others.

In this example, confounding factors (such as peer sensitivity, economic climate, consumers' discretionary income levels, age and education) may influence consumer choices about new techno-gadgets and hence sales success. Awareness of these intervening variables may be accounted for through redefining the study's population and/or sample structure, as well as through collection of demographic data and the subsequent reduction and analysis of data and its reporting and interpretation.

Generation of data for the four concepts

In this example data instances about factors such as price, functionality, brand association and sales success are generated through focused interviews. These may be generated through a semi-structured survey of a sample of consumers which allows for the sample to be enlarged and possibly diversified as a result of the emerging analysis of data.

The emerging data are reduced (for instance, by open coding) into themes and categories according to each concept. Subsequent typifications are constructed from themes and sub-themes (for example, by axial and/or selective coding). When a comprehensive pattern of typifications and their relationships accounts for most, if not all, of the data, the research question has been addressed.

Considering confounding factors

Notions of competitive price, functionality, brand association and sales success may vary with different classes of personal electronic products or services. So a specific market may be regarded as a possible confounding factor. Similarly, the time of year may affect the perceived attractiveness of price, functionality and sales success. These complicating factors may affect the timing and location of the study, and also suggest that amplification and qualification of the questions is required. It may also be necessary to refine the population and/or sampling.

Population, sampling and data generation

This study aims to better inform product and marketing managers who are responsible for anticipating and delivering products that successfully capture and retain a significant and profitable share of particular markets or market segments.

This interpretivist study, in which exploration is key, requires a rich diversity of responses. Therefore a strata sample rather than a random sample is indicated. In this case it would be advantageous to include all relevant demographics of consumer types as suggested by sensitising literature and concepts. For instance it could use a strata sample of current and prospective consumers that reflects a wide variety of consumer types (varied in age, education, discretionary income levels, and peer sensitivity). It is important to be prepared to regard a strata sample as not fixed but amenable to expansion if emerging data indicates the need for altered directions and more in-depth inquiry.

Data distillation, concept confirmation and analysis

This step of interpretivist research distils all the data into compact theoretical notions which, together, interpret the phenomena that the data represents in a comprehensive and insightful way. It includes three important activities: reduction, condensation and integration.

Reduction of data involves creating themes according to the related attributes of different data. Some of the identified themes emerge as principal themes as they are more enlightening with regard to illuminating the research question. *Condensation* of the principal and related themes forms a few broad typifications (which sometimes resemble stereotypes but are entirely original – being grounded in the data, and being richer in subtle meaning), which reveal interrelationships between themes while also highlighting patterned differences between respondents' meanings. Typifications refer to combinations of qualities or characteristics of a set of themes, each of which shares a common thread within the theme while still preserving nuanced variety. *Integration* of most, if not all, typifications makes it possible to form a tentative theory which is a compact way of accounting for all the data and answering the research question in terms of a set of concepts and their interrelationships. The resulting interpretive framework and meanings help show how the concepts operate and are interrelated. When used together, the concepts and theory enable a comprehensive and insightful understanding of the phenomena studied.

In the current example, the first step of *reduction* starts with some form of coding to help locate a theme that is implied by many instances of participants' data which appear to refer to the same notion. In this example about price, functionality, brand association and sales success, we might expect that within the concept of functionality, the themes of fashion[fA], usability[fB], flexibility[fC] and value-option[fD] may be identified from participants' transcripts, and that these themes may themselves have associated sub-themes such as:

- fashion[fA] with sub-themes status[fA.1] (personal image) and being up-to-date[fA.2] (meaning perceived as the latest or leading edge)
- usability[fB] with sub-themes layout[fB.1] (which refers to screen and keyboard design), and ease-of-understanding[fB.2] (meaning clear supporting documentation and intuitive device operation)
- flexibility[fC] with sub-themes of connectivity[fC.1] (meaning the ability to attach the device seamlessly to other electronic goods and services), and contractual-freedom[fC.2] (meaning the ability of a consumer to vary contract terms more often and in more ways than offered by competitors)
- value-option[fD] with sub-themes of quality[fD.1] (meaning the replacement guarantee time), contract-terms[fD.2] (price points to pay for various levels of contractual flexibility) and service-level[fD.3] (meaning the volume of use that goes with the purchased price point).

While it appears that themes and sub-themes are developed from initial sensitising concepts, additional themes and sub-themes arising from the data may cut across some or all of these initial concepts and are likely to provide additional concepts. An example in this case could be the theme of environmental-portability[W] which comprises sub-themes about size[W.1] (practical miniaturisation), and composition[W.2] (for instance, a rubbery device rather than the common hard device, and/or with little or no environmentally dangerous materials such as mercury).

It is plausible that initial data from the strata sample will suggest that concern for environmental impact is strongly felt by a certain demographic but initially seems to be randomly distributed across the strata. So further exploration and even re-sampling may be needed to better qualify this tentative indication. (This may also arise in relation to the other emerging themes and typifications.)

In the next step of *condensation*, some sub-themes are combined from across the various identified themes to construct a comparatively small number of typifications of aspects of consumer factors connected with sales successes. Drawing on the illustrative themes above, one plausible typification is ENVIRONMENTAL-AWARENESS, which includes the sub-themes of composition[W.2] and connectivity[fC.1]. A second plausible typification could be STYLISHNESS, which comprises the sub-themes of status[fA.1], up-to-date[fA.2], ease-of-understanding[fB.2] and contractual-freedom[fC.2]. A third possible typification of consumers is VALUE-FOR-MONEY, including the sub-themes of quality[fD.1], contract-terms[fD.2], service-level[fD.3], connectivity[fC.1], contractual-freedom[fC.2], size[W.1] and up-to-date[fA.2].

These examples of condensation reinforce the point that *typifying* is a process in which the researcher creatively uses participants' meanings to look beyond surface themes in order to discern more fundamental patterns and differences across all the data. It is important to stress that typifications are constructed based on dominant (that is, strongly reinforced) patterns as they emerge from the data, and not from undisciplined preferences, or selective observations of the data.

As noted in this chapter's example, the step of *integration* systematically and imaginatively develops concepts and their mutual dependence from distillations of typifications and their interdependencies. Drawing on the three typifications exemplified in the condensation activity above, a plausible emerging theoretical construction that is consistent with the themes and typifications is:

Consumers' buying actions reflect a primary orientation to VALUE-FOR-MONEY which is mediated equally by consideration for ENVIRONMENTAL-AWARENESS and STYLISHNESS. Where the latter two compete for attention, then the choice reflects the consumer segment with affluent and younger consumers preferring ENVIRONMENTAL-AWARENESS over STYLISHNESS and other consumer segments preferring STYLISHNESS over ENVIRONMENTAL-AWARENESS.

It should also be noted the demographic of 'affluent and younger' requires closer examination, and may be confirmed or altered as a result of the unfolding research.

The logic of inquiry

The predominant logic of inquiry is *abduction*. It is also important to recognise that in this section we have highlighted what an interpretivist research approach must aim for. It remains for the researcher to select and use appropriate methods within this overall logic.

Reporting the study

The tentative theoretical assertions are expressed and illustrated in the language of the field, and then discussed with particular reference to application as well as to provide sensitising concepts for further research. Clearly identifying the time frames, locations and social context of the study will help to ensure that all uses of the findings are well-considered and ethical.

When discussing substantive and formal theoretical implications and limitations, further topical research and further development in the theory and practice of marketing personal electronic goods and services can be identified. It is also usually relevant to include thoughts about the philosophy and methodology of interpretivist study, and suggested improvements and extensions of a scientific and/or practical nature.

Critique of validity and reliability

As noted in this chapter's example, critical review includes the technical aspects and practical tradeoffs in relation to: research approach (including sampling and design), ethical questions, data generation methods, representativeness of data and data conversion, and validity.

Sampling frequently raises the need to balance representation, adequate variety and accessibility. *Design* involves choices between ideal and practicable strategies and logics of inquiry that fit with the sample and the paradigmatic assumptions. *Ethical challenges* arise in relation to disclosure, anonymity, the interpretation of data, and the implicit or explicit support or harm that may arise. *Data generation* methods may be compared with other methods for eliciting valid or valuable data. *Representativeness* of data is reviewed to ensure its diversity (for instance, richness and demographics). *Data conversion* is reviewed to check on the interpretation and inclusiveness of first and second-order constructs, and the accurate apprehension of the generated concepts from participants' meanings in order to meet requirements of rigour. *Validity* is reviewed by checking with a sub-sample of participants that essential meanings have been identified.

Investigative practice

Important elements of investigative practice that are likely to apply in this case are illustrated below.

Proposal

Likely requirements can be expected to include the commercial importance of the study for better informed marketing decisions; contributions to design and methods for researching the marketing of fast-moving personal electronic goods and services; and anticipated methodological highlights, and resource and facility requirements.

If the researchers' motivation includes, for instance, a strong desire to contribute knowledge about marketing research theory and practice for personal electronic goods and services (PEGS)-type offers and their market segments, then the proposal will include a succinct statement about the intended scope, practice supervision, and support requirements needed to support this objective.

Ethics

Different consumer segments (for instance teenagers, professional employees, retirees) may variously be more or less able to discern or critically assess, negotiate and buy specific offers within the PEGS market that best suit their needs and resources. A supplier's marketers may use such knowledge to package offers and to manipulate messages to segments that obscure data. This may exclude disadvantaged segments while emphasising desirability in other segments.

Knowledge workers, managers of knowledge workers, the study's researchers, and organisations providing funds and facilities as well as participant access are examples of stakeholders who may have competing interests.

This example raises the more general requirement to identify and respond to significant ethical risks that might arise within and between stakeholder groups (such as researchers, consumers, marketers, industry watchdogs, funds providers) who may be comparatively (dis)advantaged by the study's scope, conduct and findings in use. Responses may involve changes to the scope, disclosure, conduct, publication and follow-on audits of stakeholder behaviours that can reasonably be linked with the knowledge generated in the study.

For this study, two examples of specific risk are firms disadvantaging marketers who choose not to bias messages in favour of the firm but rather offer market segments messages that help segments reach well-informed buying decisions about the firm's PEGS offers, and researchers being denied resources in the event that the study's scope, conduct and reporting are perceived to disadvantage those who are asked to provide financial or in kind support for the study.

Funding

This type of study can be expected to generate findings that will benefit specific firms and possibly industry-level marketing practices, so direct funding and in-kind support by participating firms is to be expected. It is very unlikely that the study will offer findings that have broad industry and community benefit. Accordingly, researchers should not expect government funding, and industry-level funding is unlikely unless the study's scope and design are aimed at investigating specific industry questions.

Schedules

Data generation and interpretation in interpretivist studies evolve with ongoing work. This is as a result of emerging issues, leads, roadblocks and dead ends. For this reason it is difficult to conduct quality interpretivist studies according to a fixed-duration (or even fixed-budget) project schedule. Incorporating contingency elements into schedules and budgets is one practical approach. It may also be appropriate to structure the research so that interim findings and parallel or even largely independent streams of work can be undertaken. Then the effect of changes to time and money schedules as much as to the scope of the study can be accommodated with less wide-ranging impact.

Examples of nontrivial scheduling considerations in this example are negotiating and sustaining access to one or several firms and their associated target market prospects and existing customers. as well as product and marketing personnel in each firm; generating data using in-depth interviews and focus groups; iteratively interpreting emerging data in order to develop validated meanings and descriptive concepts about buyer preferences and buying decisions; and verifying the substantive theory that the study constructs from the data.

Conduct

This covers implementation of the research design up to and including the generation and verification of the study's findings. Constructing a sample that includes readily accessible consumers, prospects and marketers who voluntarily offer candid and rich accounts of their preferences, decisions and experiences is as much a matter of the way the study is presented and marketed as it is a matter of the way researchers connect with, and develop, an engaging stimulating and professional relationship with market participants through data generation, interpretation and validation.

The logistical and organisational challenges of handling large volumes of spoken and written language-based data, and the substantial workload needed to concurrently and iteratively (re)interpret the growing body of data, are also major practical considerations for interpretive studies. In this example this would involve reviews with cohorts of participant marketers, customers and prospective consumers in the first instance, and eventually a possible wider sample of marketers and consumers chosen from beyond the participating firms in order to strengthen the validation of the findings.

Reporting

Highlights can be expected to cover the aim of the study to help develop principles for ethical PEGS marketing, findings that can be used to help improve the development of relevant marketing practices within the participating firm(s), and contributions to methodology and substantive theory that may usefully inform further research.

PART 2: POINTERS FOR FURTHER UNDERSTANDING MAJOR PARADIGMS

There are informative texts about theoretical aspects of methodology (for example in the social sciences, Blaikie 2000, 2007) noting that research approaches (referred to as paradigms) are characterised and differentiated by the variability of epistemologies and accompanying ontologies. Similarly, in business and management research, authors (such as Johnson and Duberley 2000) describe approaches following from the variability in epistemology and then go on to add forms of ontology.

Rather than attempt to summarise the development of several centuries of philosophical thought about the principles of scientific enterprise, we offer a diagrammatic snapshot of highpoints in this evolution in order to demonstrate the continuing evolution of research methodology in which practice and philosophy are intertwined.

In the following pages simplified (visual) juxtapositions reinforce major philosophical influences on what constitutes scientific research in business and management studies, the importance to the researcher of fitting methodology to the character of the research problem, the growing repertoire of research approaches that are available for practice research problems, and the place of, and need for, recognising each paradigm's idiosyncrasies.

Figure 9.3 highlights some influences on the development of positivist epistemology in social and organisation research. For positivist business and management researchers, an important consequence of this evolving approach is the need to reflect on the experience, challenges and uses of research, and so contribute to the further development of epistemological theory and practice in positivist business and management research.

Challenges from the positivist legacy

The aim of a positivist epistemology is to produce and use knowledge that is patterned and has broad or general application. This serves the purpose of

Figure 9.3

> **Search for objectivity**
> e.g. Plato and Aristotle, the notion of
> establishing truth through objectivity.
> (Johnson and Duberley 2000: 2 and 70)

> **The Enlightenment**
> Systematic efforts to rid knowledge of
> superstition and ignorance (e.g. Kant).

> **Rationalists
> (knowledge from
> thinking)**
>
> (e.g. **Descartes 1637 and
> 1641**: the possibility of
> separating the knower
> from the known and the
> need for the development
> of a neutral observational
> language.)

> **Empiricists
> (knowledge from observation)**
>
> (e.g. **Locke 1690**: science should be of sense
> experience and not predicated in religious belief and
> experience.)
> (e.g. **Hume 1748**: causation is seen as the constant
> conjunction of one event with another even though the
> cause may not be observable.)
> (e.g. **Mill 1874**: the Vienna School of logical positivism
> that emphasised the key role of the senses in objective
> observation.)

> **Science**
> (e.g. **Kolakowski 1972**: an objective rational enquiry which aims at true explanatory
> and predictive knowledge of an external reality by reference to empirical evidence.)

> **Epistemology
> Systems of reasoning in order to know**

> **Positivism
> Knowledge is objectively reasoned**
>
> (e.g. **Comte 1853**: Positivist sociology.
> Methodology as an epistemic system
> which excludes metaphysical forms of
> knowledge and unobservable data.)

Features of the development of positivist epistemology in social and organisation research providing knowledge that is applicable to broad categories such as communities, industries and/or organisations. While is often useful to see the world through categorical lenses, there is also such variety within and between categories that precision and scholarly agreement may be problematic.

Consequently, to deal with this enigma, and also arising out of fundamental questions about it, foundational assumptions have been debated, and have included the following questions. While the positivist approach is a methodology well suited to natural science, should there also be separate methodologies for social and organisational inquiry? In order to exclude metaphysical influences on knowledge, positivists operate with assumptions of neutral observational language. However this position (that there can be a neutral observational language) is itself metaphysical. What is the role of human subjectivity in explaining human behaviour? Is the reality studied by a positivist epistemology which seeks explanation (or *Erklären* – see Dilthey in Weber 1949) capable of also illuminating and understanding the realities comprising human subjective experience (*Verstehen* – Weber 1949)? If language reflects reality and the (perceived) structure of reality provides the structure of language, is objective knowledge possible?

Developments in response to challenges about positivist epistemology

Non-positivist social inquiry is characterised by some important foundational assumptions including:

- Humans are active participants in the processes of perception (that is, human minds are not passive receivers of sense data but select, limit, organise and interpret experience of external reality).
- The so-called external world is a construction of human cognitive structures working on sensory inputs from an external world.
- Language – which is socially constructed – shapes and constructs reality, and so knowledge is also socially constructed and authenticated.
- Humans endow the world with meaning and this is constantly being reconstructed.

A group of approaches, which have been termed both elsewhere and in this book interpretivist, have been developed to address these types of alternative foundational assumption. Figure 9.4 highlights some milestones.

The critique of the evolution of positivist science as an ontological and epistemological system of assumptions and practices has been increasingly informed by the application of positivist science to an ever wider array of human problems – well beyond the inquiries of natural history and physical phenomena which have underpinned its historical performance. Accompanying the wider application of positivist science (for instance, in social and organisation research)

Figure 9.4

Positivist epistemology assumes that:
- the knower is separate from the known
- an external reality that can be objectively observed
- a neutral language can describe external reality.

Conventionalism challenges positivist positions:
- How can scientists operate from a 'value-free' stance?
- How can scientists operate from a 'theory neutral' stance?
- Does scientific knowledge influence reported experience?

Nominalism raises an alternative position:
- Reality is a product of human thought with no independent reality.
- Language reflects a cultural heritage that colours new knowledge.
- Science is time and space contingent.

Neo-positivism: refining positivism
- Neo-positivism attempts to acknowledge some of the criticisms while still serving the fundamental premises of objective observable realities that can be directly known.
- Neo-positivism relies on objective realities.

Alternative scientific assumptions
- External reality exists whether it is observed and observable or not.
- Internal and public realities are socially (re)constructed.
- Knowledge is culturally relative and local and truth cannot be absolute.

Interpretivism
- Reality is socially constructed and so it may or may not be known and knowable to 'outsiders'.
- In the process of constructing and using meaning, truth and validity are negotiated relative to participants.
- Knowledge is culturally relative and 'momentary', so reality is the knowledge that is privileged.
- The truth value of knowledge is reflected in its cultural authority.

Critical theory and critical realism
- External reality exists, observed or not.
- Reality is known by its patterned characteristics together with participants' differing accounts.
- Reality can be modelled and so its behaviour can be anticipated, and thus reality is known.
- The truth value of such knowledge about reality increases as the comprehensive and predictive value of the model increases.

Sciences emerge in response to empirical and philosophical limitations and opportunities

have been increasingly self-conscious challenges to the assumptions of the possibility of theory-neutral, value-free, objective and independent human inquiry and participation. Figure 9.4 highlights some of the dominant assumptions and emerging challenges associated with the evolution of science beyond positivism.

Integrating approaches to scientific inquiry

Milestones in the development of different paradigms for inquiry reflect two common themes:

- the dual conversation between the development of practice experience and modes of inquiry in which developments in the assumptions and consequent structure and rules of inquiry are stimulated by the experience of practice variety, and ways of perceiving and making sense of practice are shaped and extended by innovations in approaches to inquiry
- the importance of characterising and fitting research challenges with appropriate modes of inquiry, so that chosen assumptions and perceptions of experience and consequent sense making (for instance, description, interpretation, explanation, prediction) are illuminating, and rigour and dependable insight are products of inquiry.

Figure 9.5 depicts the evolution of three paradigms of inquiry and these common themes.

For researchers and reflexive practitioners in business and management, the challenge is to be aware of the evolving nature of knowledge about the process of inquiry and the nature of practice. Active awareness and professional sensitivity to the nature of scientific inquiry and professional practice may typically involve practitioners and research methodologists working more closely to increase perceptions and understanding of what is a dialectical activity.

Different ontologies can be linked variously with different epistemologies (see Figure 9.6), and where the combination is plausible, it is a fundamental guide for research design as well as guiding implementation of the research design and the role of the researcher.

In conclusion, different combinations of ontology and epistemology lead to different paradigms, and the paradigm choice that is made will underpin the research design, which then generates different knowledge about the substantive topic.

We have also highlighted the notion that key concepts about various sciences continue to evolve as a result of empirical experience and philosophical reflection, and researchers who aim to develop their methodological repertoire and expertise are encouraged to pursue the deeper philosophical premises and arguments on which all sciences must be based.

Figure 9.5

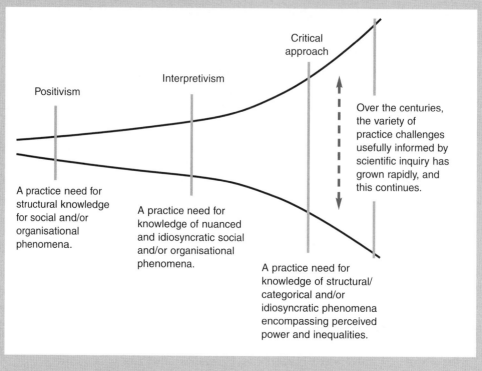

Paradigms of inquiry have developed to inform widening practice challenges

CONCLUSION

Business and management research must be rigorous. Rigour touches both the theoretical and practical aspects of the research. It is the quality that is constructed through attention to design and research work that is consistent, comprehensive and convincing.

In business and management research, theoretical and practical aspects of the research are mutually dependent and theoretical choices are shaped by problematic practical aspects of the research and vice versa. For instance, small budgets, limited staff and the need for findings in a short timeframe will challenge the best theoretical design that requires international travel to gather comparable data through long-term case studies.

Indicators of good research include a lucid and insightful description of the research problem and its context, a clear focus and salient detail, evidence of rigorous design and conduct, and balanced and mutually consistent theoretical and practical dimensions. Good research is an interesting, carefully

Figure 9.6

Ontologies	Epistemologies
Positivist ontology Access via objective sense observation and theory-neutral language. **Realist** ontology Objective whether viewed by the observer/researcher or not.	Realist epistemology
Conventionalist ontology Objectivity from acceptability of conformance to scientific standards. **Nominalist** ontology Reality is a product of our (own) cognition; no independent reality.	Constructionist/ idealist epistemology

Linking ontologies and epistemologies

constructed and professionally executed investigation, and delivers a report that makes a significant and compelling contribution to knowledge.

ACTIVITIES AND RESOURCES

This section at the end of each chapter suggests further reading, and offers discussion and practice development activities.

EXERCISES AND QUESTIONS

1   Johnson and Duberley (2000) and Blaikie (2000 and 2007) are strongly recommended for the purpose of starting to read about aspects of methodology and their relevance to business and management research.

IN-DEPTH TOPICS

1   The mental model or roadmap for research that we have presented in this book is not exhaustive, but serves as a useful heuristic device for pedagogical and practice purposes.

2   Remember that for the same substantive topic, and the same question, a different choice of paradigm and consequent design will generate different forms of knowledge, and different insight and answers to the same question.

3   The superscripts help to identify sub-themes and the themes to which they apply.

    (a) It is instructive to use a matrix arrangement to highlight the relationships between the two types of themes and their sub-themes. This emphasises the within and between nature of themes and emerging abstractions and typifications.

    (b) Discuss challenges for investigative theory that are raised by the illustrated process of coding, direct thematising, imaginative abstraction and typification.

    (c) Discuss practical and competency challenges that are raised by the illustrated process of coding, direct-thematising, imaginative abstraction and typification.

FURTHER READING

Blaikie, N. (2000) *Designing Social Research: The Logic of Anticipation*, Cambridge, Polity Press.

Blaikie, N. (2007) *Approaches to Social Enquiry*, 2nd edn, Cambridge, Polity Press.

Comte, A. (1853) *The Positivist Theory of Auguste Comte*, London, Chapman.

Descartes, R. (1637/1968) *Discourse on Method*, Harmondsworth, Penguin.

Descartes, R. (1641/1968) *Meditations on Philosophy*, Harmondsworth, Penguin.

Dilthey, W. in Weber, M. (1949) *The Methodology of the Social Sciences*, New York, Free Press.

Hume, D. (1748/1975) *An Enquiry Concerning Human Understanding*, Oxford, Clarendon Press.

Johnson, P. and Duberley, J. (2000) *Understanding Management Research*, London, Sage.

Kant, I. (1787/1959) *Critique of Pure Reason*, Letchworth, Adeline Press.

Keat, R. and Urry, J. (1982) *Social Theory as Science*, London, Routledge & Kegan Paul.

Kolakowski, L. (1972) *Positivist Philosophy*, London, Heinemann.

Locke, J. (1690/1988) *Essay Concerning Human Understanding*, Oxford, Clarendon Press.

Mill, J. S. (1874) *A System of Logic*, London, Longman Green.

KEY TERMS IN THIS BOOK

Absolutism

Ever since ancient Greek philosophy the nature of absolute truth has worried philosophical thinkers. For example, there is the question of whether knowledge can ever be absolutely true, even in the present time and space, let alone prospectively. More recently, for example, John Dewey, the 20th-century American pragmatic philosopher, believed that the idea that knowledge could be absolutely true was a fictitious product of humanity's quest for certainty. This idea of achieving absolute truth, whether substantiated by empirical claim or religious fervour, is counterpoised with the idea/possibility of being true within certain conditions and levels of probability (e.g. Johnson and Duberley 2000: 159).

Argument

A research-informed argument is a logical contention together with an explicit logical structure that is built on evidence and theory with appropriate references. A sound argument will also explicitly justify the selection or omission of noteworthy sources as well as the chosen premises, the logical form of the argument and the selected references.

Concepts

Intellectually, business and management research belongs in the social sciences. In these sciences, concepts come from ideas in research questions or hypotheses and need to be developed carefully in research projects. Categories of concepts can refer to different kinds of phenomena: events, people or objects.

Concepts as variables can be measured at four different levels from lowest to highest: these are nominal, ordinal, interval and ratio. The first two produce categorical variables because objects, events or people are placed into one of a set of mutually exclusive categories. In nominal level measurement, categories are homogeneous, mutually exclusive and exhaustive. All objects, events or people allocated to a particular category share the same characteristics, each instance can only be allocated to one category, and all of them can be allocated to some category in the set. There is no intrinsic order to the categories (Blaikie 2003: 23). An example of nominal level variables which can be differentiated descriptively from each other arises when classifying customers as rural or urban, yet these are not ranked (nor able to be ranked) in relation to each other.

By contrast, ordinal variables can be ranked (such as lower, middle and high income earners). The second two produce metric variables, as objects, events or people are mapped on to an established measuring scale (Blaikie 2003: 35).

Constructionism

Constructionism or social constructionism refers to meanings that are intersubjectively negotiated and socially recognised. When the development of data is intersubjective – that is, when humans explore and negotiate (in a culturally relative way) what aspects of some phenomenon are to be considered and how those aspects constitute data about the phenomenon – then the process of establishing the data and its meaning may be considered to be constructionist.

To some degree meanings are collectively generated and transmitted. Meaning is not discovered but constructed, with the researcher or observer playing some part in the construction with the participants, as well as, of course, the nature of the things themselves and understandings that already exist (Crotty 1998: 8–9).

Constructivism

Constructivism means the cognitive meaning-giving activities of the individual human mind. Some texts conflate constructivism with social constructionism, the latter being more precisely centred on a shared intersubjectively constructed meaning.

Content analysis

Content analysis is an iterative process in which themes and resultant typifications are distilled from systematic and imaginative macro reviews of all the data and micro-level reviews of subsets of the data that express or refer to some distinctively common qualities or phenomena.

When eliciting and interpreting participants' data and subsequently reducing and analysing it, it is imperative for the researcher and the participant to know and be able to describe the context from which the data is drawn, because the meaning of data is influenced by its context.

Conventionalism

Social and natural realities are not things outside the discourse of science. They are, to various degrees, constructed not only by human subjects/actors but also by scientists and their traditions. Conventionalists dismiss the idea of sets of standards that can specify objectivity as obsessive and futile (Johnson and Duberley 2000: 64).

Criticalist (management or business) research

This is our shorthand term for research that takes account of how the practices and institutions of business and management are developed and legitimised within relations of power as in capitalism (Habermas 1972). It is aimed towards enabling change, or more generally taking a synthetic approach to research, via pragmatism and realism, by combining a constructionist epistemology with ontological realism.

Critical realism

The philosophical territory of critical realism rejects both positivism and relativism, and provides another realm of consideration of whether knowledge (only) consists of what is immediately and empirically knowable. A distinction is made between the domains of the empirical, the actual and the real. Social reality is viewed as a socially constructed world in which either social episodes are the products of the cognitive resources that social actors bring to them (Harré 1961) or social arrangements are the products of material but unobservable structures of relations (Bhaskar 1978, Blaikie 2007: 181).

Key aspects of Bhaskar's critical realism are summarized by Johnson and Duberley (2000: 154) into six commitments:

1. A metaphysical ontology is emphasised which assumes that social and natural realities consist of intransitive entities which exist independently of our human knowledge.
2. The entities may not be observable, and different people may apprehend different (that is, transitive) realities according to the varying paradigmatic, metaphorical or discursive conventions deployed through their human agency.
3. The perceived epistemic role of human agency means that critical realism rejects the possibility of a theory-neutral observational language and a correspondence theory of truth.
4. Critical realists do not see science as being merely a prestigious artefact of conventionally derived self-directed and self-deferential paradigms, or discourses, or language games and so on. Instead, and despite the pivotal role of its collective unconscious, science is construed as being about something other than science itself.
5. The model of science propagated by positivism has little bearing upon actual scientific practice save for the manner in which scientists often explain themselves and their activities to each other.
6. Critical realism entails an epistemological defence of causal explanation – causation is not solely expressed through a constant conjunction of events as in positivism.

Critical realists identify causation by also exploring the mechanisms of cause and effect which underlie regular events; mechanisms which Hume (1748/1975) claimed were unobservable but which critical realists claim can be shown to be real through their deployment of what Bhaskar calls retroductive argument.

See also Forms of reasoning/Logics of inquiry.

Data

All major research traditions regard data as a basis for information about some kind of phenomenon, and an individual datum as relating to some aspects of that phenomenon. However, the relationship between data and phenomena depends on assumptions made about the nature of reality and how that data can be known (Blaikie 2003: 16).

Blaikie noted that the concept of data, on the surface, appears to be a simple and unproblematic idea. But lurking behind it are complex and controversial philosophical and methodological issues that need to be considered (Blaikie 2003: 10).

Data reduction and analysis

These involve transforming the data into forms through which they can be analysed. This transformation typically occurs as simplification through coding (meaning classifying, associating or separating, comparing or linking categories implied or displayed in the data), in either quantitative numerical forms or qualitative descriptive themes and typifications. Coding is not only used to reduce data but also, through linking concepts, can be used to find opportunities for new concepts, ideas and theories.

Deconstruction

Essentially deriving from literary criticism and a tool of postmodernist research, the researcher dismantles the socially constructed meanings (linguistic constructions) of the subjects and their texts to show, for instance, their assumptions, emphases, inconsistencies, contradictions and surprising omissions based on their subjective relativism. However, as Johnson and Duberley (2000: 100) point out, a relativistic position for deconstruction does not get the deconstructor closer to a fixed or privileged truth, but offers alternative social constructions of reality within a text, which are then themselves available for deconstruction. No finalised truth is then allowed, and in this respect, postmodernism is parasitic in that it can only feed off existing texts.

Design

The mental map for doing research: being a way of apprehending major considerations and their relationships in a way that helps the researcher to systematically and thoroughly assemble and integrate detail, and so meet a challenge in a manner that others are likely to consider *prima facie* as deserving of careful criticism and reflection.

Epistemology

In management and business research this term is the key to how the knowledge that is acquired through the research process is made intelligible. The variability and diversity of epistemologies are closely connected with different ways of researching any substantive area or field of work.

The roots of the word epistemology come from the Greek *episteme*, meaning knowledge or science, and *logos*, being knowledge or account. That is, epistemology is knowledge about knowledge.

In effect, epistemology is the study of the criteria by which we can know what does and does not constitute warranted or scientific knowledge; that is, consideration of the criteria used, and by which justified knowledge is possible (see Johnson and Duberley 2000: 3). Crucial to this is recognition that there are no secure or incontestable foundations from which we can begin any consideration of our knowledge of knowledge (Johnson and Duberley 2000: 4). However, there are recognised starting points in acquiring research knowledge which largely can be separated into direct or empiricist knowing or indirect (relativist constructionist) knowing.

Epistemology essentially is knowledge as beliefs about whose validity we are reasonably confident. Epistemology is philosophical grounding for establishing what kinds of knowledge are possible, as in what can be known, and criteria for deciding how knowledge can be judged as being both adequate and legitimate (Crotty 1998: 8). It is a set of axiomatic assumptions (within a philosophy of science) that defines the way knowledge about a particular view of reality (that is, an ontologically well-defined reality) is to be generated, represented, understood and used.

A positivist epistemology will typically seek to establish descriptive and predictive principles and rules for a reality that exists independently of an observer or participant. Knowledge is commonly generated by operationalising concepts and variables in order to test hypotheses using, for instance, quantitative data and analytic methods. This empiricist epistemology assumes that by observing the world around us, knowledge can be produced by the human senses.

Interpretivist epistemologies commonly seek to describe and understand socially constructed realities. They commonly aim to generate socially relative knowledge about some social phenomenon, and often proceed by interpreting individuals' accounts of their experiences and observations using language-based methods. A resultant production of theoretical constructs offers a comprehensive description and insightful understanding of the phenomenon.

A realist or neo-realist epistemology is likely to be involved in both describing and explaining. A realist approach to creating knowledge about some phenomenon will often involve empirical observation of its manifestations, symptoms and consequences, and empirically validated theoretical constructions of its underlying mechanisms. Affirmation of real underlying mechanisms increases with the confirmation of counterintuitive predictions and the failure of assiduously sought-after disconfirming evidence, as well as the descriptive adequacy of broader and more varied patterns of regularities in observable phenomena.

See also Critical realism.

Erklären

Erklären is the explanation of behaviour (Dilthey in Weber 1949) by providing a deterministic account of the external causal variables that brought about the behaviour and antecedent conditions of that behaviour (Johnson and Duberley 2000: 34).

Fact: scientific facts

Truth or fact is observed and recorded by neutral observational language and/or at least partially as the outcome of the scientist's thinking and style of thought.

First-order and second-order constructs

Schütz (1963a, 1963b, 1970, 1976) constructed the ideas of first-order constructs being the meanings of the social actors in their own language and from their own points of view, and second-order constructs as the technical derivations of the researcher, based on these first-order constructs. The technical derivations are understood to require the applications of rules of systematic classification – much as a taxonomist would develop and apply them – together with a theoretical imagination that is on the one hand, creative in an inventive and biographical sense, and on the other hand, informed by a wide appreciation of extant theory likely to induce plausible new associations and categorical possibilities affirmed, or discarded, through evidence-based tests.

First and second-order constructs are essential terms in the reduction and coding of qualitative data (respondents' own words, for example, in an interview-based research): they are basic to presenting results in a descriptive, discursive form.

Forms of reasoning/logics of enquiry

A study's reasoning and logic of inquiry argue for, and explain, the major form of reasoning to be used in answering the research question with the use of empirical data, and the particular logic(s) on which such reasoning is to be based. Particular types of logic that are illustrated in this book include deduction, induction, abduction and retroduction. (For extensive consideration and discussion of these forms of reasoning see Blaikie 2000, 2003, 2007.)

In assessing empirical evidence from research to address a research question, forms of logic are used for argument. Blaikie (1993: 8) pointed out that these research strategies specify a starting point, a series of steps and an end point, and are based on particular (distinctive) styles of reasoning (Blaikie 2007: 3).

An important aspect of research is the justified choice of a principal logic on which the research argument is to be based. An assessment of the clarity and merit of a research argument is based on making clear what sort of data is needed, how it is to be interpreted and what forms of conclusion may flow from these data. This assessment reflects the justification for, and implementation of, a mutually consistent form of science and logic.

Four common forms of logic are discussed below.

Induction. This logic of enquiry is essentially a movement from observing specific statements or instances of a phenomenon and then, from their similarities or differences, adducing general statements.

Deduction. As a logic of enquiry, this involves moving from general statements to specific instances, or testing ideas against particular cases/instances. Popperian science (Popper 1959) proposed the maxim of falsificationism. A scientific theory must be capable of empirical testing that involves vigorous attempts at falsifying a theory (Johnson and Duberley 2000: 29). Instead of using an inductive approach of generating theory out of specific instances of observations and experience, Popper asserted that it should be a process of deducing testable hypotheses from theoretical ideas/concepts/conjectures and then confronting them with a cognitively accessible world. For him, science was a sequence of conjectures and refutations which deductively proceed from the universal to the particular through the elaboration of predictive hypotheses (Popper 1959, quoted in Johnson and Duberley 2000: 29).

Abduction. Abductive logic is a creative process in which concepts and theories are derived from social actors' everyday conceptualizations and understandings. It is derived especially from the work of Schütz (1963a, 1963b). This reasoning involves making an hypothesis which appears to explain what has been observed (Blaikie 1993: 164), but is used in different ways from hypotheses in the deductive strategy. Such hypotheses are possible answers to questions that emerge as the research proceeds, and are used to direct further stages of the research (Blaikie 2000: 10). Abductive research strategy is based on the hermeneutic tradition and is used in interpretivism.

The abductive research strategy has a very different logic from the other three. It is sometimes described as involving induction, but this grossly underestimates the complexity of the task involved. The starting point is the social worlds of the social actors being investigated: their construction of reality, their way of conceptualising and giving meaning to their social world, their tacit knowledge. This can only be discovered from the accounts that social actors provide. Their reality, the way they have constructed and interpreted their activities together, is embedded in their language. Hence, the researcher has to enter their world in order to discover the motives and reasons that accompany social activities. The task is then to redescribe these motives and actions, and the situations in which they occur, in the technical language of social-scientific discourse. Individual motives and actions have to be abstracted into typical motives for typical actions in typical situations. These social-scientific typifications provide an understanding of the activities, and may then become the ingredients in more systematic explanatory accounts (Blaikie 2000: 25).

Retroduction. Blaikie (2007: 3) used Bhaskar's (1975) usage of retroduction to refer to the use of reason and imagination to create a picture or model of the structures or mechanism responsible for producing observed phenomena. The task is then to try to establish their existence. (*See also* Critical realism).

Following Bhaskar (1975: 15), Blaikie (2007: 83) saw the logic of retroduction referring to a process of building hypothetical models of structures and mechanisms that are assumed to produce empirical phenomena. This process requires a disciplined scientific imagination. Also, following Harré (1961) and Keat and Urry (1975), Blaikie summarised the steps in a retroductive strategy. These are:

a. In order to explain observable phenomena, and the regularities that obtain between them, scientists must attempt to discover appropriate structures and mechanisms.

b. Since these structures and mechanisms will typically be unavailable to observation, we first construct a model of them.

c. The model is such that, were it to represent correctly these structures and mechanisms, the phenomena would then be causally explained.

d. We then proceed to test the model as a hypothetical description of actually existing entities and their relations. To do so, we work out further consequences of the model (that is, additional to the phenomena we are trying to explain), that can be stated in a manner open to empirical testing.

e. If these tests are successful, this gives good reason to believe in the existence of these structures and mechanisms.

f. It may be possible to obtain more direct confirmation of these existential claims, by the development and use of suitable instruments.

g. The whole process of model building is then repeated, in order to explain the structures and mechanisms already discovered (Blaikie 2007: 83).

See also Logic of inquiry.

Generalisability

This is about the extent to which findings of a study may be applied to other settings. Important considerations typically reflect the evidence for claims to wider applicability, limitations or constraints on wider applicability, and the confidence that may be associated with wider applicability.

Generalisation

A generalisation is a widely applicable proposition or propositions based on deductions from specific instances of a phenomenon's occurrence/s.

Grounded theory

This practice involves the use of inductive logic through which theory as general statements or hypotheses is developed through the generation of data from observations or interviews. Theory generation emerges as a research phase (Glaser and Strauss 1967).

The generation of a grounded theory about some phenomenon involves a recursive cycle in which data are developed and analysed in order to construct a tentative descriptive or explanatory theory, which is then tested by further deliberate generation of data and more analysis. What emerges is a cycle of proposing, empirically testing, then affirming, refining or rejecting propositional theory. The outcome is tentative theory which is bounded in time and space but is not exclusively based on research participants' meanings.

Hermeneutics

Classical hermeneutics arose in 17th-century Europe in order to understand mainly biblical texts or cultures through an interpretive process, using text-based accounts (typically oral and/or written) of psychological, sociocultural or biographical lived experiences.

Hermeneutic circle

Our meanings can only be described and explained in the social world through social constructs. This is termed a trap because the knowledge that is generated is self-referential – with no start or end point. The notion of a trap refers to not being able to objectively or neutrally step out of this world.

The metaknowledge generated in a hermeneutic circle is both self-awareness and the ability to know about self. As such it is not possible for outsiders to validate or negate it because they have no shared cultural experience on which the construction of the metaknowledge depends.

Heuristic

Used as a demonstration for learning purposes, heuristic or a heuristic refers to a dependable rule of thumb or dependable practice procedure.

Hypothesis

A hypothesis is a tentative (theoretical) answer to a research question leading to, or requiring, empirical or rational testing. Hypotheses may posit or assert objective or subjective statements, and the process for testing them may typically be correspondingly objective and theory-based, or intersubjective and based on socially relative interpretation.

Interpretivism

Used as a research paradigm, interpretivist epistemology is anti-positivist, with the pivotal assumption being that there is a fundamental difference between its research methods and those of the natural sciences. It especially involves an insider perspective on social phenomena and how individuals construct meanings, interpret and reinterpret their worlds and make their meanings intersubjectively intelligible to others. It is derived from the hermeneutic tradition and social phenomenology.

Essentially, research content concepts have their origin in the language used by the social actors (as research participants) to describe their worlds. Using an insider view, this paradigm is used to generate mutual knowledge within individuals' social or organisational contexts even though this knowledge may be semi opaque to the social actors until they can make it mutually intelligible to the researcher. The paradigm also carries an assumption of multiple realities existing amongst human beings in cultural contexts.

Literature

In this context, literature refers to scholarly publications about concepts and thoughts (critical reflections, arguments, informed creations and discourse or debates and the like) based on theory, empirical evidence, critical analysis and new theorising.

Logic of inquiry

A study's reasoning and logic of inquiry reflect the deliberate choice of reasoning paths and associated forms of reasoning (such as deduction, induction, abduction or retroduction) that constitute an argument structure. A study's logic of inquiry should be consistent with its ontological and epistemological assumptions and choices, and may even require justification if rigour and validity are likely to be contested.

Justification is more important with a study that aims to challenge conventional wisdom or apply an unusual approach to a traditional problem. When fully developed, a study's reasoning and logic reflect and tie together the choices and consequences that arise from the researcher's motives and background, the study's aims and constraints, the knowledge sought and identified in the literature, the study's overall approach and detailed procedures, the administrative aspects of the study, the study's execution, and the research report's structure and its emerging content.

Principles of reasoning such as deduction, induction, abduction or retro-duction that are used in a study provide the logical basis for making claims about, and testing the integrity of, knowledge generated through the research's design and empirical work. The dominant logic of inquiry shapes the process of research, just as foundations and a framework shape a building. The logic of inquiry should be a bridge between the chosen philosophy of science, and the situation-specific methodology and methods that characterise the theoretical approach to the investigation that will address the research questions.

It is not unusual for several forms of reasoning to be applied in one piece of research, although there is often an overriding logic that carries the dominant argument structure. Specific tasks within the argument structure must be addressed with the most appropriate logic for the task. This multi-phase character of logic is illustrated in our example cases throughout the book.

See also Forms of reasoning/Logics of inquiry.

Methodology

A methodology of inquiry is a set of tactics and supporting steps that opera-tionalise the chosen science and logic of inquiry. As a research process blue-print, it highlights situation-specific arguments and choices for sampling, assembly of data, data analysis, production and validation of findings, and eventually reporting of the study. It can be thought of as a map that describes the major phases, their primary tasks and the key steps within those tasks which together constitute the way the research questions are to be answered. A common methodological framework is the exploratory type (such as a theory-forming study), and another is the experimental type (a theory-testing study). A study's methodology operationalises the particular form of science that has been selected for the study.

Methods

Methods refer to the procedures, tools, techniques and associated skills (such as sampling and interviewing) that are needed to perform the specific tasks required by the methodology. Some procedures, tools, techniques and skills may be predefined and well known, while some may be specifically devised and verified for the study. Procedures and tools tend to appear as objective artefacts (such as questionnaire construction and implementation), whereas techniques and skills tend to appear as empirically and experientially grounded recitals (such as coding and reduction of qualitative data) which can be developed into repeatedly consistent performances.

To maintain a study's integrity and rigour, the choice and application of methods should be clearly described and justified, and must remain consistent with the chosen philosophy of science, the logic of inquiry and the methodology. Typical tasks for which specific methods are used include sampling, data generation (through for example observation coding, item measurement, interviewing), statistical or text-based analysis, and presentation of findings. Choosing methods involves close attention to practical as well as theoretical (that is, investigative and substantive) requirements and constraints that must be addressed in order to maintain methodological consistency.

Particular methods and techniques are usually carefully chosen to implement particular tasks or even steps within tasks. The array of available methods and techniques is extremely large, with combinations of methods and techniques possibly being counted in the hundreds.

Examples of the wide range of methods and techniques are:

- literature reviews (such as taxonomic analyses, citation networks, bibliometric analyses)
- sampling (such as purposeful sampling, random sampling, simulation)
- data generation (such as from forms of open interviewing and of embedded observation, event observation and measurement)
- data reduction and analysis (such as discourse analysis, statistical analysis, focus group transcripts, analysis of narrative text)
- validation (such as participant co-validation, peer reviews, replication)
- presentation of findings (such as grounded concepts, structural equations)
- reports (such as impersonal reports of findings as objective facts, relativist and personal accounts of the research).

The ubiquitous nature of many methods, the apparently well-defined procedures that accompany them and the familiarity and certainty of the symbols and language that help convey their message, can be appealing to the unsuspecting researcher. For the unwary researcher, the reassurance of familiar territory or common practice can encourage unjustifiable confidence and premature commitment to a method and its execution as the way to answer a research question.

As noted at the beginning of this section, the mental model in Figure 3.1 helps to avoid the pitfall of premature and inappropriate choice of method as the starting point rather than the end point of good science in research.

Normative

In a research setting, normative relates to what is typically expected (or even tacitly or explicitly prescribed) within some social context or contexts, such as specific and distinctive cultural or disciplinary traditions and their associated perspectives.

Objectivism

This is the contrasting ontology to subjectivism. It posits that phenomena and social entities exist within a reality external to and independent of the specific social participants.

Observable

This refers to phenomena knowable directly and neutrally through the human senses.

Ontology

The term ontology is derived from the Greek words for being (*ontos*) and theory of knowledge (*logos*). Ontology must always be considered in connection with a study's epistemology. It concerns the nature of what exists and the existential reality of the phenomena being researched. In some contexts, consideration of the reality of the subject matter of research has been seen as independently real or subjectively idea-based, but more precisely it relates to whether that reality can be conceived of as objective, and therefore potentially comprehensible and even objectively measurable by scientific means, or whether it depends on understanding the subjective cognitions, relevant meanings and precise language of the producers of that reality. The latter ontological form has been defined as *idealist*, assuming that the external world has no independent existence beyond our ideas of it.

A *realist* ontology presumes that social and natural reality exist independently of human cognitive structures. That is, an extra-mental reality exists whether or not human beings can actually gain cognitive access to it. An idealist ontology presumes that what is taken to be external social and natural reality is a creation of our consciousness and thinking; it being a projection of specific human cognitive structures with no independent status (Johnson and Duberley 2000: 67). Johnson and Duberley noted that a realist ontology assumes that Kant's noumenal world (things in themselves directly knowable) is apprehensible, but an idealist ontology assumes that all that exists is the phenomenal world, in accordance with Kant's own metaphysical beliefs (Johnson and Duberley 2000: 65–7).

Margolis (1986: 283) noted the connection between metaphysical (that is, ontological) realism (in which the structures of the world do not depend upon cognitive structures of human investigators) and what he called empirical realism, which reflects the view that such structures are cognitively accessible to those investigators. Blaikie (2007) identified six subtleties in alternative realities. We are assuming that three suffice within the process of designing and conducting research. They are forms of objective reality that are (1) knowable through human senses, or (2) real but directly unknowable or inaccessible to human subjects, or (3) constructionist/idealist, the last of these being *intersubjectivist reality*. (Too many described subtleties may force the researcher into ultra-fine distinctions and justifications being made in choosing the research design.)

Two of the three paradigms of doing business and management research described in this book match ontology and epistemology. That is, positivism combines an objectivist/absolutist ontology with an objectivist epistemology. Interpretivism combines an idealist/relativist ontology with a relativist/constructionist epistemology. On the other hand pragmatic critical realism (Johnson and Duberley 2000) (which we term criticalist research) rejects any attempt at collapsing ontology and epistemology into one another. Also, more than one reality may be engaged in one research study.

It is important to note that whatever approaches researchers decide to take in a particular research project, while epistemology and ontology must be made explicit, they may not necessarily axiomatically reflect the researcher's own underlying (metaphysical) world views. What is important however is a cogent argument for a particular choice, and then a rigorous and explicit commitment to its implementation through research design, conduct and reporting.

So an ontology is the set of explicitly stated axiomatic assumptions (within a philosophy of science) that define the way a reality is conceived and perceived. A realist ontology employs the objectivist assumptions and perspectives of an independent reality that exists, and is characteristic of the traditional natural sciences. Methods employed in this setting commonly involve the operationalisation of concepts as variables that can typically be quantified and measured, so that relationships between the variables can be measured and compared.

From this premise, the observable empirical domain of interest is considered to arise from underlying, albeit largely unobservable, cause–effect mechanisms whose operation may be modified depending on attempts to access them. This reality may be partially obscured, and only empirical tests can reinforce plausible theoretical knowledge of the reality.

An idealist ontology employs the intersubjective assumptions and relativist perspectives of reality that are so distinctive in the social sciences. In an idealist ontology, reality is socially constructed from individual cognitive processes informed by experience and language. Methods employed in interpreting this reality commonly reflect linguistically negotiated constructions that evolve into concepts that are ideal typical abstractions of instances of research participants' perceptions or manifold behavioural or observational experience.

Paradigm

Although it has been considered a controversial term ever since it was introduced in Kuhn's views on scientific developments (Kuhn 1970), a paradigm is taken to mean a philosophy of science and its specified ontology and epistemology which serve as foundations for a research procedural framework. A paradigm comprises a set of traditions associated with forms of research that share a specific combination of ontological and epistemological premises and their consequent perspectives, ways of knowing and relied-on forms of knowledge.

A paradigm is a commitment to a culture of practices and beliefs about reality and knowing, with many assumptions, conventions and practices being tacitly assumed as obvious to others within the culture or tradition, although they are unknown or even unintelligible to those from outside the tradition.

A paradigm embodies a combination of philosophy of science and logic of inquiry. This particularises the normal use of paradigm as philosophy of science alone. We use this definition because the specification of a logic of inquiry in the context of a philosophy of science is the most compact choice that determines highly distinctive and widespread, yet largely implicit, consequences for all remaining theoretical and practical aspects of a study.

Phenomenology

Stimulated by the philosophical ideas of Husserl in the early 20th century and the earlier hermeneutic tradition, phenomenology emerged as strong reactions and important alternatives to the use of natural scientific methods in the social sciences when it is necessary to study how phenomena appear in human consciousness. Transcendental and existential phenomenology can be distinguished from each other, the former being more ontologically idealist and the latter realist. (See discussion in Johnson and Duberley 2000: 68–76.)

Philosophy of science

A philosophy of science refers to a set of explicit fundamental assumptions and frames of reference that underpin a way to conceive of, and know about, a particular reality being studied in a research frame of reference. These foundational assumptions are known technically as ontological and epistemological assumptions. It is good practice to state explicitly these assumptions and their rationale. Variations in epistemology and ontology combinations constitute what are now usually referred to as research paradigms.

Population

The complete set of instances or members of a group of relevance to a research study. Defining the characteristics of a population serves to constrain the application of research findings to those instances or members for which findings can be justifiably considered to be relevant. A clear definition of a population's membership also serves to help specify a sample (that is, a subset of population members or instances) that a research study will actually consider as far as selecting and examining data is concerned.

Positivism

This is exemplified as a research paradigm which epistemologically accesses an external, observable social reality via the human senses. Its scientific method is structured, enabling replication, with aims of producing generalisations – as in the natural sciences. Language used to describe knowledge observed by the human senses is neutral and can correspond directly to the concepts described. A central tenet of positivism is that there is no causation in nature, only regularities or constant conjunctions between events, such that events of one kind are always followed by events of another kind (Blaikie 2007: 111).

In forms of positivism, truth and merit refer not only to general requirements of rigour and insight or utility, but also to representativeness (also referred to as validity) and reliability (also referred to a repeatability).

Halfpenny (1982) identified 12 varieties of positivism, and Outhwaite (1987) reduced these to three (Blaikie 2007: 111). For a detailed discussion of positivism see Blaikie (2007: 110–13).

Post-modern epistemology

The post-modern idea of epistemology departs from the Enlightenment philosophy in its ultrasubjective relativism, and is sometimes connected with an epoch-based view of society or social realities as post-modernity. It implies a break with the idea of a rational and unified subject postulated by much modern theory in favour of a socially and linguistically decentred and fragmented subject (Best and Kellner 1991: 4). It also implies a conflation of Bhaskar's transitive and intransitive realities, entailing both epistemic and judgemental relativism, so that reality becomes an outcome of our variable epistemological engagements (Johnson and Duberley 2000: 152).

Proof

A notion of proof commonly takes two forms: as verification of a theoretically founded proposition, and as a demonstration or construction of a theoretical position. A propositional proof typically involves a logical argument together with supportive evidence which together are used to accept or reject an assertion with a level of confidence that is traditionally framed within traditionally acceptable parameters of statistical probability. A truth value between 0 and 1 may also be associated with a proof based on the presence of strong arguments (using several logics, such as inductive and deductive, and a variety of alternative and widely accepted theories) and strong data (widely representative of a large population as opposed to weakly representative of a narrower population). In this way a proof may be considered to have more or less merit.

A theoretical concept or position may be claimed as a direct result of logical argument and supportive evidence when no evidence to the contrary is yet available to reject the tentative theory. The merit or truth value of a constructed theory increases as further diverse evidence fails to negate or constrain the theory. In this case we can speak of a proof of concept or proof of construct, together with its truth value. Furthermore, as with the case of a propositional proof, we can also speak of its truth value being a value from 0 up to 1 (the ideal), as more diverse justification becomes available and limiting evidence fails to arise.

Quantitative data

Data of a quantifiable nature are based on operationalised concepts: this means that terms or variables are based on numerically and statistically measurable entities with either interval-based properties or ratio-based properties. When members of a set share interval-based properties, then gaps of the same size between pairs of the set have the same meaning, regardless of which members are selected. When members of a set share ratio-based properties, not only is it the case that gaps of the same size between pairs of the set have the same meaning, regardless of which members are selected, it is also the case that the ratio between intervals has a uniform meaning throughout the set.

Qualitative data

Qualitative data are discursive, word-based descriptions which may also be treated nominally (that is, as members of categories which are not necessarily able to be ranked) or even ordinally (for example, as members of sets that may themselves be arranged in rank order).

Instances of a set of data may be regarded as nominal when each member of the set may clearly be seen as a member of a category – even if different categories bear no apparent relationship to each other or any common characteristics. Instances of a set of data may be regarded as ordinal when each member of the set may clearly be seen as a member of a category, and when the categories and even (but not necessarily) members within categories can be ranked according to some agreed common characteristic(s).

Realism

Realism has a variety of meanings, especially based on a rejection of subjectivist ontologies (or rejection of the acceptance of the world being created by human observers: see Johnson and Duberley 2000: 149) and epistemologies. Some writers have confused the ontologies of realism and positivism. These are not the same: the latter relies on observable reality, while in the former, reality exists objectively as external to individuals' meaning constructions, but is not necessarily directly observable by human observers. Rather, it is detected according to its manifest symptoms: that is, the observable effects it is held to cause.

See also Critical realism.

Reductionism

This assumes that explanations can be achieved by reducing and describing elements of a system into a set of elements and rules without recognising the entire character of the phenomenon.

Reflective

A reflective view involves a considered mirroring in which some thing of interest (some phenomenon, object, behaviour, theory or data) is self-consciously reviewed with the intention of illuminating aspects of the thing of interest, together with concurrently and self-consciously illuminating one's frames of reference (assumptions, habits, prejudices, preferences, values and so forth) through which the attributes and meanings of the thing of interest are perceived. A reflective view differs from a passive or unconscious view, in as much as the latter is not self-consciously aware.

Reflexive

This involves recognising the need for researchers to be aware of their own values, thinking and presuppositions, especially within a criticalist research paradigm. Reflexivity refers to the construction of reflective views that in turn lead to actions that recreate an actor's or researcher's frames of reference, and/or create new meanings for things of interest, or even change the nature of the thing of interest. In this recursive or dialectic process the actor or researcher may become part of the domain of action rather than being divorced and distant from it.

Relativism

Relativism is a reaction against claims of objectivism/objectivity being achievable in the human/social sciences. As a concept it is connected with the denial of the right of members of one culture to make judgements about the values or practices of another culture, on the grounds that there is no culturally neutral position from which humans can make objective judgements about anything, let alone another culture (Blaikie, 2007: 50).

Bhaskar (1978) made a distinction between epistemic relativism of knowledge as a social construction, but not necessarily entailing judgemental relativism in which there would be no grounds for preferring one knowledge claim over another.

Reliability

Reliability in research usually refers to other researchers using the same methods of assembling and analysing data to produce consistent findings; in this sense reliability is synonymous with reproducibility. Reliability may also refer to a comprehensive and precise description of how a researcher has constructed meanings from data reduction and synthesis; in this sense reliability is synonymous with rigour. Finally, reliability may refer to the reproduction and affirmation of findings by alternative means; in this sense reliability is synonymous with comparative verification.

Research approach

A research approach comprises a philosophy of science, a study's reasoning and logic, a methodology, stance and methods. Collectively these represent a study's investigative theory as shown in Figure 3.1 (Chapter 3).

Research design

Design is the term we use when referring to the combination of methodology, researcher's stance and methods. It is this theoretical set that provides all detailed operational guidance in a study's empirical work. Design is what is often referred to when talking about a study's detailed theoretical blueprint. Design failures typically arise as failures of integrity or consistency within and between theory and practice; that is, the way in which research is designed and carried out.

Research ethics

Research ethics involves concerns for rights and avoidance of harm. In business and management studies ethics is primarily focused on the rights of, and avoidance of harm to, the subjects of research or members of other populations who may be directly affected by the research or the product of the research. It is the part of investigative theory and investigative practice that involves a stakeholder orientation to identifying and dealing with moral dilemmas that the research's design, process, reporting and use may trigger or involve.

In more detail, research ethics is about identifying stakeholders and any corresponding ethical issues, risks, potential harm and consequent mitigation and/or response arrangements. Typically these can be expected to include policies and required procedures about empirical practices, administrative disciplines and oversight and accountability. Identifying and agreeing with the way ethical issues are to be handled can often be expected to involve negotiation whilst effectively accounting for policy requirements.

Administration and management of agreed ethical issues and treatments commences with a systematic and sensitive examination, assessment and negotiation of arrangements. It is also necessary to set out agreed practice principles and methods for auditing and reporting implementation of agreements covering compliance and breaches. If failures in agreed ethical arrangements have serious adverse consequences for stakeholders and/or public policy interests, then principles of arrangements for treating breaches, and possible remedies, may also need to be outlined.

Research proposal

A research proposal is the document that communicates the administrative aspects of a research programme, such as the main purpose and outcomes sought from the research, the expected benefits and the nature and levels of support needed to properly undertake the research. A full proposal will set out the main requirements and approach to be taken to administer and manage resources and facilities, compliance, quality, progress and stakeholder reporting. An effective research proposal clearly documents and persuades stakeholders to approve the programme's purpose, scope, approach, ethics and funding requirements. It will also alert research management to specific challenges and suggested approaches that may reasonably be expected to arise through the course of the research.

Research questions

Blaikie (2007: 2) noted that a research project builds on the foundations of its research questions. These are formal expressions of intellectual puzzles and vehicles through which a research problem is framed and made researchable. They give focus and direction, and delimit the research's boundaries, make the project manageable, and anticipate an informative outcome.

There are three main types of research questions: what, why and how. *What* questions seek descriptions, *why* questions seek understanding or explanation, and *how* questions are concerned with intervention and problem solving.

Rigour

Rigour in research is essentially based on having a transparent process and content as well as self-reflexive critique. Important specific characteristics include internal consistency, clear justification for starting assumptions, methodological as well as substantive critique, and elaboration of meta theory and meta practice that reveals and/or develops strengths and limitations of the study's science, its research design and methods, and its research practice.

Sample

A sub-group or part of a larger population. Across all studies it is important to recognise that a sample's characteristics and membership must be a deliberate choice that is consistent with the study's aims and constraints, the research question(s), the specific form of science that is chosen for the study and the intended uses of the study's findings.

Sensitising concepts

Sensitising concepts arise within the conceptualising tradition as against the operationalising tradition, and can be used instead of, or as complementary to it. As well as elaborating and refining initially established sensitising concepts from the substantive literature, other sources of inspiration and clarification may arise from participants' own stock of knowledge and interpreted experience. In this way the researcher's interpretive framework is adjusted and expanded throughout the research process in order to better encapsulate participants' meanings whilst also facilitating use of the researcher's understandings. This leads to the necessary rich and shared intersubjective meanings on which the paradigm depends.

Sensitising concepts are usually developed from theoretical and/or empirical ideas in the substantive (that is, the topical) literature as well as the researcher's ideas and other sources. A third recognisable tradition in the construction of concepts in research is the hermeneutic tradition, in which the researcher constructs technical concepts (to reduce or distil, for example, Schütz's second-order constructs from the first-order constructs/meanings and concepts referred to by research respondents in their response to interview questions or in the course of their observed activities/behaviour) (Blumer 1969; Denzin 1970).

Science

The definition of science depends on the research paradigm in use.

Scientific method

Scientific method may include or exclude taking account of human subjectivity/ies. Both positivism and realism (following Keat and Urry 1982: 44) define scientific method as objective, rational inquiry which aims at discovering true, explanatory and predictive knowledge of an external reality, using empirical evidence. This method is subject to verification.

Interpretivism considers scientific method to be about the social construction and validation of meaning and descriptive or explanatory theory about social phenomena from intersubjectively generated exchanges of data; being accounts of participants' experience.

Social construction of reality

Essentially, this phrase means culturally based knowing or epistemic processes.

Social sciences

These sciences concern human behaviour and the various meanings attached to it. Historically, there has been much contention over whether or not physical scientific methods can be applied to the social sciences.

Stance

A researcher's stance is an essential but too often ignored part of comprehensively rigorous research. A description of a researcher's stance must express, with supporting reasons, the relationship that the researcher will have with the process and substance of: generating, assembling and analysing data; determining and validating the study's findings; and reporting the study's conduct and results. The stance must also be mutually consistent with the resulting paradigm. Deciding the researcher's stance is about acknowledging and articulating the researcher's attitude to their own knowledge and to the way they should operate in relation to the field of inquiry and in relation to the research process overall.

For example, an *etic* (objective outsider) stance is one common position. With this stance a researcher (or research team) operates as an objective and dispassionate observer and analyst; collecting and analysing data using a theory-neutral observational and analytic language. In this orientation the researcher remains subjectively disengaged from influence on the selection of data; the eventual meaning that is placed on the data; and from its representative significance. From this perspective validity is about the extent to which phenomena of interest are represented, utility or value is about the extent to which the findings are held to apply more generally, and reliability is about the extent to which successive replication of results is maintained across related population samples.

Alternatively, an *emic* (subjective insider) stance is another common position. From this orientation a researcher (or research team) operates as an engaged co-participant who deliberately and self-consciously works in the field with others in a process that continually generates and makes sense of aggregate data. This sense-making evolves as reflexive field work. Such reflexivity is influenced by the collective meaning frames, biographical experience and world knowledge of the participants. It is also influenced by the researcher's curiosity about what the data discloses as well as new questions it raises. From this position, validity of the findings is based on what the participants and the academy acknowledge are valuable specific and idiosyncratic descriptions, explanations and operational insights.

Standpoint critique (relates to criticalist theorists)

How can critical realists reject the claim that objectivity results from scientific detachment yet still aspire to express more than a speculative opinion? They do so by claiming that more self-conscious forms of objectivity are achieved by working to explain how values and interests affect the research process and looking at the strengths and limitations of various standpoints (Jermier 1998: 239).

Strategy

In research, strategy involves the use of a transparent process and explicit content. It may be considered as the combination of a study's overarching reasoning structure, its primary logic and its related methodology. Strategy refers to the distinctive combination of a logic of inquiry, methodology and stance. Because some methodologies can separately but consistently be implemented using different logics of inquiry, and because stance can vary within a combined logic of inquiry and methodology, all three must be specified and operate together before the criteria for rigour of a particular implementation can be determined. While a well-defined strategy implies only one philosophy of science, it is still appropriate to specify explicitly the chosen philosophy of science to ensure clarity and consistency in the research.

Subjectivism

This is an ontological position, assuming that phenomena or entities are created/constructed from, and internal to the perceptions and meanings of social actors.

Survey

A survey involves the collection of data in response to a research question via questionnaires, structured observations or structured interviews, usually including a large sample of a population.

Theory

A theory is a statement (which may or may not have been tested) that concerns ideas or concepts and their relationship(s) as well as tentative conjectures about the world, about human behaviour or knowledge, about an organisation or about some aspect of such entities. A theory typically includes some form of cause and effect relationship(s) between ideas or concepts which may themselves be expressed as variables.

Theory-neutral observational language

Despite their recognition of various internal disagreements in forms of positivism, Johnson and Duberley (2000: 23–7) distilled four interrelated webs of epistemological commitments that are present in all forms of positivism. One is that observation of the empirical world through human senses provides the only foundation for knowledge, and that such observation can be neutral, value-free and objective. Second, as this observable reality is paramount, there is no place for unobservable phenomena such as subjective realities or unconscious realities, since these are metaphysical and therefore beyond the realm of science to know. (Consequently, the key to scientific research is that all theoretical statements must be capable of empirical testing and empirical verification.) Third, the natural sciences, especially physics, provide the model for all the sciences including the social sciences. Their fourth point is that the task of science within positivism is to enable prediction and control of social and natural events and produce instrumentally useful knowledge (Johnson and Duberley 2000: 23–7).

These four interrelated epistemological commitments necessitate a theory-neutral observational language. However, as Hindess (1977: 135) pointed out, positivism contradicts itself as it excludes from its conceptualisation of warranted knowledge its own grounds for warranted knowledge. Owing to the circularity that is evident in any epistemology, it appears that positivism cannot account for itself on its own terms and is in danger of slipping into the a dogmatism that its epistemology was aimed at destroying. While dismissing metaphysical phenomena as not being accessible to research, it relies on metaphysics to establish a neutral observational language (Johnson and Duberley 2000: 33). This has led to great debates about the important role of human subjectivity in explaining human behaviour, and also in the actual languages and meanings used to describe the world, as well as the languages and meanings so generated.

Thesis

A thesis is a research project with an argument and evidence, written for an academic setting (for example, for a Doctor of Business Administration, a Doctor of Philosophy or a Research Masters degree).

'Thin' or 'thick' descriptions of behaviour/meanings

In research data reduction, coding and analysis, Geertz (1973) used the term thin descriptions to describe facts, while thick descriptions include rich descriptions of the contexts in which the facts about observations, participants (including the researchers), human behaviours, interactions and socially constructed meanings take place.

Uncertainty principle

Heisenberg (1958), in the physical sciences, noted that it is not possible to observe something without influencing what is seen. This point has been reiterated in the social sciences.

Validity

This is the extent to which data-generation methods and the findings they elicit reflect and measure what they set out to describe and/or measure.

Variable

An idea or concept expressed in a form (even as a proxy) which can be described or measured and then systematically processed for the purpose of reduction and analysis. *Independent variables* are those whose values can deliberately be set, or that can be considered as inputs to a process or phenomenon. *Dependent* variables are those that can be considered as outcomes of some process that operates on or between independent variables. *Intervening variables*, known or unknown (and later sometimes also referred to as confounding factors) may change the relationship between the independent and dependent variables. They may include 'controls' or parameters that can be set while collecting a set of related data (which records descriptions or values of dependent variables for corresponding values of independent variables). *See also* Concepts.

Verification

Verification is bound up in the testing the genuineness of a proposition. Positivists are interested to know conditions under which a proposition can be seen as true or false, whereas interpretivists for instance are interested in authenticity and in revealing or illuminating meanings that participants in the domain of study consider to be dependable or even insightful.

Verstehen

Human action has logic and multiple logics of its own. Weber (1864–1920) used the German term *Verstehen* (and there are no precise one-word English translations) in his attempts to establish sociology as an objective science of human subject matter. *Verstehen* is the interpretive understanding of human actions from social actors' points of view (Johnson and Duberley 2000: 34).

BIBLIOGRAPHY

Alvesson, M. and Deetz, S. (1996) 'Critical theory and postmodernism: approaches to organization studies' in S. R. Clegg, C. Hardy and W. R. Nord (eds), *Handbook of Organization Studies*, London, Sage.

Alvesson and Deetz, S. (2000) *Doing Critical Management* Research, London, Sage.

Alvesson, M. and Willmott, H. (1988) *Critical Theory and the Sciences of Management. The Frankfurt School. How Relevant is it Today?* Rotterdam, Erasmus University.

Alvesson, M. and Willmott, H. (1996) *Making Sense of Management: A Critical Introduction*, London, Sage.

Alvesson, M. and Willmott, H. (2003) *Studying Management Critically,* London, Sage.

Anderson, R. J., Hughes, J. A. and Sharrock, W. W. (1987) *Classic Disputes in Sociology,* London, Allen & Unwin.

Arksey, H. and Knight, P. (1999) *Interviewing for Social Scientists: An Introductory Resource with Examples*, London, Sage.

Babbie, E. (2008) *The Basics of Social Research: issues, methods and process,* 2nd edn, Ballmoor/Buckingham, Open University Press.

Bauman, Z. (1978) *Hermeneutics and Social Science: Approaches to Understanding,* London, Hutchinson.

Bauman, Z. (1992) *Intimations of Postmodernity*, London, Routledge.

Beck, U. (2000) *The Brave New World of Work,* trans. P. Camiller, Cambridge, Polity Press.

Benton, T. (1984) *The Rise and Fall of Structural Marxism: Althusser and his Influence,* London and Basingstoke, Macmillan.

Best, S. and Kellner, H. (1973) *Postmodern Theory: Critical Interrogation*, London, Macmillan.

Bhaskar, R. (1978) *A Realist Theory of Science*, Brighton, Harvester Press.

Bhaskar, R. (1989) *The Possibility of Naturalism*, 2nd edn, Brighton, Harvester Press.

Birnbaum, N. (1971) *Toward a Critical Sociology*, New York, Oxford University Press.

Blackburn, R. (ed.) (1972) *Ideology in Social Science: Readings in Critical Social Theory,* Glasgow, Fontana/Collins.

Blaikie, N. (1993) *Approaches to Social Enquiry*, Cambridge, Polity Press.

Blaikie, N. (2000) *Designing Social Research: The Logic of Anticipation*, Cambridge, Polity Press.

Blaikie, N. (2003) *Analyzing Quantitative Data: From Description to Explanation*, London, Sage.

Blaikie, N. (2007) *Approaches to Social Enquiry,* 2nd edn, Cambridge, Polity Press.

Blumer, H. (1969) *Symbolic Interactionism: Perspective and Method,* Englewood Cliffs, New Jersey, Prentice Hall.

Bryman, A. (1988) *Quantity and Quality in Social Research,* London, Unwin Hyman.

Bryman, A. (1992) *Research Methods and Organisational Studies,* London, Routledge.

Bullock, A., Stallybras, O. and Trombley, S. (1998) *The Fontana Dictionary of Modern Thought,* London, Fontana.

Bulmer, M. (1982) *The Uses of Social Research: Social Investigation in Public Policy-Making,* London, George Allen & Unwin.

Bulmer, M. (ed.) (1982) *Social Research Ethics: An Examination of the Merits of Covert Participant Observation,* London, Macmillan.

Burrell, G. and Morgan, G. (1979) *Sociological Paradigms and Organizational Analysis,* London, Heinemann.

Chalmers, A. E. (1976) *What is this Thing called Science?* St. Lucia, University of Queensland Press.

Clarke, T. and Clegg, S. (2000) *Changing Paradigms: The Transformation of Management Knowledge for the 21st Century,* London, HarperCollins.

Collier, A. (1994) *Critical Realism: An Introduction to Roy Bhaskar's Philosophy,* London, Sage.

Collis, J. and Hussey, R. (2003) *Business Research Methods: A Practical Guide for Undergraduates and Postgraduates,* 2nd edn, Basingstoke, Palgrave Macmillan.

Comte, A. (1853) *The Positivist Theory of Auguste Comte,* London, Chapman.

Craib, I. (1992) *Anthony Giddens,* London, Routledge.

Crotty, M. (1998) *The Foundations of Social Research: Meaning and Perspective in the Research Process*, Sydney, Allen & Unwin.

Cuff, E. C., Sharrock, W. W. and Francis, D. W. (1998) *Perspectives in Sociology,* 4th edn, London, Routledge.

Daniher, G., Schirato, T. and Webb, J. (2000) *Understanding Foucault,* St Leonards, New South Wales, Australia, Allen & Unwin.

De Lauretis, T. (ed.) (1986) *Feminist Studies/Critical Studies*, Basingstoke and London, Macmillan.

De Vaus, D. A. (1995) *Surveys in Social Research,* 4th edn, St Leonards, New South Wales, Australia, Allen & Unwin.Denzin, N. K. and Lincoln, Y. S. (eds.) (2000) *Handbook of Qualitative Research,* 2nd edn, Thousand Oaks, California, Sage.

Denzin, N. (1970) *The Research Act in Sociology*, London, Butterworth.

Descartes, R. (1637/1968) *Discourse on Method,* Harmondsworth, Penguin.

Descartes, R. (1641/1968) *Meditations on Philosophy,* Harmondsworth, Penguin.

Dewey, J. (1929) *The Quest for Certainty*, New York, Milton Bach.

Easterby-Smith, M., Thorpe, R. and Lowe, A. (2002) *Management Research: An Introduction,* 2nd edn, London, Sage.

Eichler, M. (1987) *Nonsexist Research Methods: A Practical Guide,* Boston, Mass., Allen & Unwin.

Evans, D. (1995) *How to Write a Better Thesis or Report*, Melbourne, Melbourne University Press.

Evans, M. (1997) *Introducing Contemporary Feminist Thought*, Cambridge, Polity Press.

Flick, U. (2002) *An Introduction to Qualitative Research*, 2nd edn, London, Sage.

Frankfurt-Nachmias, C. (1997) *Social Statistics for a Diverse Society*, Thousand Oaks, California, Pine Forge Press.

Geertz, C. (1973) *The Interpretation of Cultures*, New York, Basic Books.

Germov, J. and Williams, L. (1999) *Get Great Information Fast*, St Leonards, Australia, Allen & Unwin.

Giddens, A. (1971) *Capitalism and Modern Social Theory: An Analysis of the Writings of Marx, Durkheim and Max Weber*, Cambridge, Cambridge University Press.

Giddens, A. (1976) *New Rules of Sociologtical Method*, London, Hutchinson.

Giddens, A. (1979) *Central Problems in Social Theory: Action, Structure and Contradiction in Social Analysis*, London, Macmillan.

Giddens, A. (1984) *The Constitution of Society: Outline of the Theory of Structuration*, Cambridge, Polity Press.

Glaser, B. G. and Strauss, A. L. (1967) *The Discovery of Grounded Theory*, Chicago, Illinois, Aldine.

Gubrium, J. F. and Holstein, J. A. (1997) *The New Language of Qwualitative Method*, New York, Oxford University Press.

Gummerson, E. (2000) *Qualitative Methods in Management Research*, 2nd edn, Thousand Oaks, California, Sage.

Habermas, J. (1972) *Knowledge and Human Interests*, London, Heinemann Educational.

Halfpenny, P. (1982) *Positivism and Sociology: Explaining Social Life*, London, Allen & Unwin.

Hallebone, E. L. (2001) 'Phenomenological constructions of pyschosocial identities', in R. Barnacle (ed.), *Phenomenology: Qualitative Research Methods*, Melbourne, RMIT University Press.

Hammersley, M. (1972) *What's Wrong with Ethnography?* London, Routledge.

Hammersley, M. and Atkinson, P. (1983) *Ethnography Principles in Practice*, London, Tavistock.

Harré, R. (1961) *Theories and Things*, London, Heinemann Educational.

Harré, R. (1972) *The Philosophy of Science: An Introductory Survey*, London, Oxford University Press.

Hassard, J. (1991) 'Multiple paradigms and organizational analysis: a case study', *Organization Studies*, 12 (2): 275–99.

Hassard, J. and Pym, D. (1993) *The Theory and Philosophy of Organizations*, London, Routledge.

Heisenberg, W. (1958) *Physics and Philosophy*, New York, Harpers Brothers.

Hindess, B. (1977) *Philosophy and Methodology in Social Science*, Hassocks, Harvester.

Hood, S., Mayall, B. and Oliver, S. (eds) (1999) *Critical Issues in Social Research: Power and Prejudice*, Ballmoor, Buckingham, Open University Press.

Hughes, J. (1976) *Sociological Analysis: Methods of Discovery,* Walton-on-Thames, Nelson.

Hughes, J. (1980) *The Philosophy of Social Research, New York,* Longman.

Hume, D. (1748/1975) *An Enquiry Concerning Human Understanding,* Oxford, Clarendon Press.

Jermier, J. M. (1998) 'Introduction: critical perspectives on organisational control', *Administrative Science Quarterly,* 43 (2): 235–50.

Johnson, P. and Duberley, J. (2000) *Understanding Management Research,* London, Sage.

Kant, I. (1787/1959) *Critique of Pure Reason,* Letchworth, Adeline Press.

Keat, R. and Urry, J. (1975) *Social Theory as Science,* London, Routledge & Kegan Paul.

Keat, R. and Urry, J. (1982) *Social Theory as Science,* 2nd edn, London, Routledge & Kegan Paul.

Kellner, D. (1988) 'Postmodernism as social theory: some challenges and problems', *Theory, Culture and Society,* 5: 239–69.

Kent, R. (2001) *Data Construction and Data Analysis for Survey Research,* Basingstoke, Palgrave.

Kincheloe, J. L. and McLaren, P. L. (1998) 'Rethinking critical theory and qualitative research', in N. K. Denzin and Y. S. Lincoln, *The Handbook of Qualitative Research,* Thousand Oaks, California, Sage, pp. 260–99.

Kolakowski, L. (1972) *Positivist Philosophy,* London, Heinemann.

Kranzler, G. and Moursund, J. (1999) *Statistics for the Terrified,* 2nd edn, Upper Saddle River, New Jersey, Prentice-Hall.

Kuhn, T. (1970) *The Structure of Scientific Revolutions,* 2nd edn, Chicago, Chicago University Press.

Kvale, S. (1996) *InterViews: An Introduction to Qualitative Research Interviewing,* Thousand Oaks, California, Sage.

Laing, R. D. (1967) *The Politics of Experience and the Bird of Paradise,* Harmondsworth, Penguin.

Larrain, J. (1979) *The Concept of Ideology,* London, Hutchinson.

Lewins, F. (1992) *Social Science Methodology: A Brief but Critical Introduction,* South Melbourne, Macmillan Education Australia.

Locke, J. (1690/1988) *Essay Concerning Human Understanding,* Oxford, Clarendon Press.

Margolis, J. (1986) *Pragmatism without Foundations,* Oxford, Blackwell.

Mason, J. (1996) *Qualitative Researching,* London, Sage.

May, T. (1997) *Social Research: Issues, Methods and Process,* 2nd edn, Thousand Oaks, California, Sage.

McLellan, D. (ed.) (1977) *Karl Marx: Selected Writings,* Oxford, Oxford University Press.

Mill, J. S. (1874) *A System of Logic,* London, Longman Green.

Morris, T. (2006) *Social Work Research Methods: Four Alternative Paradigms,* London, Sage.

Morrow, R. and Brown, D., (1994) *Critical Theory and Methodology,* London, Sage.

Morse, J. M. and Richards. L. (2002) *Readme First for a User's Guide to Qualitative Methods,* Thousand Oaks, California, Sage.

Neuman, W. (1997) *Social Research Methods: Quantitative and Qualitative Approaches,* 3rd edn, Boston, Allyn & Bacon.

O'Leary, Z. (2005) *Researching Real-World Problems: A Guide to Methods of Inquiry,* London, Sage.

Outhwaite, W. (1987) *New Philosophies of Social Science: Realism, Hermeneutics and Critical Theory,* London, Allen & Unwin.

Outhwaite, W. (1994) *Habermas: A Critical Introduction,* Cambridge, Polity Press.

Pawson, R. (1989) *A Measure for Measures: A Manifesto for Empirical Sociology,* London, Routledge.

Polonsky, M. J. and Waller, D. S. (2005) *Designing and Managing a Research Project: A Business Student's Guide,* Thousand Oaks, California, Sage.

Popper, K. (1959) *The Logic of Scientific Discovery,* London, Hutchinson.

Priest, J. G. (2000) *Managing Investments in Information Systems: Exploring Effective Practice,* Doctor of Business Administration thesis, Melbourne, RMIT University.

Priest, J. G. (2001) *Publications* [online] www.InfoServ.com.au.

Punch, K. F. (1998) *Introduction to Social Research: Quantitative and Qualitative Approaches,* London, Sage.

Punch, K. (2000) *Developing Effective Research Proposals,* London, Sage.

Pusey, M. (1987) *Jurgen Habermas,* Key Sociologists series, London, Ellis Horwood/Tavistock.

Ronan, C. A. (1983) *The Cambridge Illustrated History of the World's Science,* Cambridge, Syndicate of the University of Cambridge.

Rose, D. and Sullivan, O. (1996) *Introducing Data Analysis for Social Scientists,* 2nd edn, Buckingham/Philadelphia, Open University Press.

Rubin, H. J. and Rubin, I. (1995) *Qualitative Interviewing: The Art of Hearing Data,* London, Sage.

Sarantakos, S. (1998) *Social Research,* 2nd edn, Melbourne, Macmillan.

Saunders, M., Lewis, P. and Thornhill, A. (2007) *Research Methods for Business Students,* 4th edn, Harlow, Essex, FT Prentice-Hall/Pearson Education.

Sayer, A. (1984) *Method in Social Science: A Realist Approach,* London, Hutchinson.

Schütz, A. (1963a) 'Concept and theory formation in the social sciences', in M. A. Natanson (ed.), *Philosophy of the Social Sciences,* New York, Random House, pp. 231–49.

Schütz. A. (1963b) 'Common-sense and scientific interpretation of human action', in M. A. Natanson (ed.), *Philosophy of the Social Sciences,* New York, Random House, pp. 302–49.

Schütz, A. (1970) 'Interpretive sociology', in H. R. Wagner (ed.), *Alfred Schutz on Phenomenology and Social Relations,* Chicago, University of Chicago Press, pp. 265–93.

Schütz, A. (1976) *The Phenomenology of the Social World,* London, Heinemann.

Schütz, A. and Luckmann, T. (1973) *The Structures of the Life World*, trans. R. M. Zaner and H. T. Engelhardt, Chicago, Northwestern University Press.

Seale, C. (1999) *The Quality of Qualitative Research*, London, Sage.

Seidman, S. (ed.) (1994) *The Postmodern Turn: New Perspectives on Social Theory*, Cambridge, Cambridge University Press.

Shaw, I. (1999) *Qualitative Evaluation: Introducing Qualitative Methods,* London, Sage.

Silverman, D. (1970) *The Theory of Organizations,* London, Heinemann Educational.

Silverman, D. (1993) *Interpreting Qualitative Data*, London, Sage.

Sim, S. (ed.) (1998) *The Icon Critical Dictionary of Postmodern Thought,* Duxford, Cambridge, Icon Books/Penguin.

Somekh, B. and Lewin, C. (eds.) (2005) *Research Methods in the Social Sciences*, London, Sage.

Stacey, M. (1969) *Methods of Social Research,* Oxford, Pergamon Press.

Trigg, R. (1985) *Understanding Social Science*, London, Blackwell.

Wagner, H. R. (ed.) (1970) *Alfred Schutz: On Phenomenology and Social Relations: Selected Writings*, Chicago, University of Chicago Press.

Weber, M. (1949) *The Methodology of the Social Sciences*, New York, Free Press.

Willmott, H. (1992) 'Beyond paradigmatic closure in organisational enquiry', in J. Hassard and D. Pym, *The Theory and Philosophy of Organisations,* London, Routledge.

Willmott, H. C. (1995) 'What has been happening in organization theory and does it matter?' *Personnel Review,* 24 (9): 33–53.

Willmott, H. (1997) 'Rethinking management and managerial work: capitalism, control and subjectivity', *Human Relations,* 50 (11): 1329–59.

INDEX